Tarot Well Done

ELENA OLYMPIA COLLINS

DEDICATION

To Pamela Coleman Smith, whose voice lives forever in the cards.

CONTENTS

CHAPTER 1

GETTING THE BEST FROM THIS BOOK

Firstly, thank you for buying my book. It has been a labor of love to write. My genuine desire is for you, the reader, to feel as though this book has achieved what I intended it to, and that is to demystify the topic of tarot cards, using the world's most recognized tarot deck, Rider-Waite, as an example.

The imagery contained within the Rider-Waite tarot deck is easy to understand, once you have deciphered the codes provided in the brilliant imagery of Pamela Coleman Smith. The use of color, proportions, positioning, and gender, along with numbers, ancient symbols, and biblical references, come together to provide a language that anyone can learn to speak. As with any new language, there is a need for commitment to learn, and the willingness to practice, and practice, and practice.

This book proposes to teach you to read tarot in the same way that I learned to read tarot. The only difference is that I did not learn from a book, because no book of this kind was available to me at the time that I was learning. Yes, there are plenty of "learn to read tarot" books and online resources. Just as there are plenty of tarot card teachers. And yet, so many people continue to find learning to read tarot cards, a near impossibility.

Most learning resources provide basic card definitions, and include explanatory dialogue laced with words like "perhaps." The reason for this is to encourage the learner to reach their own conclusion about what the card may be referring to, and to "follow their intuition." The problem with this suggestion is that a new or inexperienced tarot card reader is also likely to be struggling to differentiate between intuitive insight born from prior earthly experiences, and intuitive insight gained from having connected to an otherworldly messenger. What happens as a result is that the learner develops into a tarot card reader who is using guesswork and calling it intuition. Alternatively, they may spend their time focusing on a hunch while simultaneously missing a message from an external source.

To excel at tarot card reading, you need to connect to a realm that sits outside of yourself, and you need to be able to communicate in a common language. However, this is not a book that will help you to become psychic. It is a book that will help you to know when you are receiving a message. You will never need to be psychic to know, but after time, you will gain an increased sense of awareness, which may in fact be a manifestation of the intuitive faculties you have always had inside you. As you continue to become more proficient you will recognize the difference between a message received, and a form of psychic ability.

You will find your own way to get the best from this book. However, I have structured the book in a way that I hope proves helpful. My suggestion is that you initially read the book's chapters consecutively to absorb the foundational learning before you attempt to memorize the card definitions. Many of the cards' symbols and definitions are obvious, once you know what prompted their design.

I have separated chapters so that you can use the book as a reference for individual cards. You can also check the relevance of colors, numbers, and symbols. Towards the end of the book, I also include examples of the spreads I frequently use, some of which I designed myself.

CHAPTER 2

THE PROFICIENT TAROT CARD READER

Tarot cards are easily available and can be bought inexpensively and with minimal effort. The Rider-Waite deck of tarot cards is widely regarded as the most popular in the world and is often portrayed as the standard-bearer for all other tarot card decks. There are countless forums in which the basic definitions of each of the Rider-Waite tarot cards can be learned and memorized, and many people who are willing to teach tarot to others. Some print versions of the deck even include keyword definitions on the surface of each card. For those who simply wish to play a game of tarot, or to use the cards as a prompt for whatever they intuitively feel is a message coming from a spiritual source, this may be sufficient.

However, when such a basic method of reading tarot cards is used, there is no way of knowing whether the interpretation of the cards is anything more than guesswork. It is a similar principle to buying a lottery ticket or wagering on the stock market. You win some, you lose some.

The clever artistry of Pamela Coleman Smith transforms the Rider-Waite tarot deck into a simple yet strikingly sophisticated language. Not only can the tarot card reader receive guidance or validation from the cards, but their confidence in the message is also supported by being able to prove how the message was received. When a person invests their time in learning to understand the language available to them in the cards, the door towards a new world (and beyond) of possibilities begins to open.

I am yet to find another set of tarot cards that provide a language as consistent as that of the Rider-Waite deck. And so, to favor the Rider-Waite deck is to gain an advantage, in my view. However, there is also a need for the tarot card reader to accept the challenge of working with a set of cards that can expose fraud. Once commitment has been made to a set of language principles, it becomes obvious to observers, when the language principles are being ignored, in favor of confirming a hunch.

Let us begin with setting the stage of what a tarot card reader needs to know before he or she embarks on understanding how to interpret the cards. It is important to understand where the tarot card reader fits into the relationship, what they bring to the table, and how maintaining the right mindset will enhance the tarot card reader's ability to understand and converse with the cards.

Intuition versus instinct

Often the words instinct and intuition are confused with each other. To understand the foundational principles of this book, it is important to know the difference between the two terms.

Instinct is a biological impulse, earthly in nature, evolved over time, and designed to help living entities survive. It is a bodily function like breathing that responds to a trigger. Examples of instinctive behaviors include flinching at an unexpected loud noise, fight or flight responses to perceived danger, and instantaneous, reactive feelings of emotion. An instinctive action is a person's primal response that promotes their continued survival.

Intuition is the feeling of knowing something to be true, as though it is already familiar and has been experienced before. Earthly science describes intuition as a subconscious thought that occurs too quickly to appear as a conscious thought process; a skill or ability that is born from earlier experience. Spiritual intuition is the connection to "higher self" and the quiet inner voice that helps us to navigate an earthly existence with the use of a higher level of perspective. An intuitive person senses things directly, relying on feelings or insights rather than conscious reasoning. Intuition is available to everyone, naturally or as a learned skill. The keys to developing intuition are quietening the mind and increasing awareness of the body and surrounding elements.

From my perspective, a tarot card reader is a specific breed of intuitive, that may or may not be combined with other breeds of intuitive. A person may also be psychic, clairvoyant, or empathic. However, it is not necessary for a person to be any of those things, to be a tarot card reader. To understand the foundational principles of a highly proficient tarot card reader, it is important to first recognize the difference between the various forms of spiritualism that exist, and how the tarot card reader fits into the mix.

Types of intuition and how they differ from each other.

There are a variety of different titles given to people who communicate with the spiritual realm on an intuitive level. Whilst a person may have more than one intuitive attribute, the attributes themselves are not entirely interchangeable. It is easy to confuse the labels and to assume that a tarot card reader is psychic, or that a clairvoyant communicates with the use of tarot cards. There are instances in which this may be the case, but not always. Below is a description of commonly referred to intuitive titles, and the unique qualities that each have.

The term *clairvoyant* originated in 13th century France. It combines the words "clair" (meaning "clear"), and the derivative of the Latin term "videre" (meaning "sight"). A clairvoyant is a person who claims to have a supernatural ability to see an object, event, location or individual with the use of extrasensory perception. Relevant images or sounds, including voices, may appear in their mind's eye. Clairvoyants see things that are relevant to the present moment. In theory, a clairvoyant is a person to go to if you have a present-day dilemma that you would like to help to resolve.

The term *empath* derives from the ancient Greek word "empátheia" (meaning "in feeling"). This later evolved to become "pathos" (meaning "passion"), and then was translated into German as "Einfühlung" (meaning "feeling within"). The German-to-English translation appeared for the first time in 1908. An empath is a person who tends to have a greater than average sense of empathy towards others. The sensation felt by the empath is like an emotional form of telepathy. An empath has a heightened understanding of how other individuals may be feeling, and their emotional state. An empath may be able to ascertain an individual's emotions by looking at their face, hearing their voice, seeing their photo, or by forming a picture of them in their mind. In theory, an empath may claim to recognize how a person is feeling before that person exhibits any physical sign of their emotion.

The term *medium* is Latin and dates to the 16th century. It means "in the middle." A medium is a person who claims to provide an intermediary connection for communication between the earthly and spiritual realms. Sometimes, a medium may offer comfort to those who have experienced the loss of a loved one, by channeling messages from the spirit of the person who has passed and sharing those messages with the person who remains in this earthly life. A medium may also theoretically be a person to assist you in connecting with your own spirit guide, or spiritual guides.

There is evidence to suggest that the term mystic originated from the ancient Greek word "muo" (meaning "to conceal"). Until around the mid-19th century, mysticism carried Christian overtones. It later appeared in England as a reference to anything occult, supernatural, nebulous, or esoteric ("connected to mystery"). A mystic is a person who pursues, or claims to have achieved, a direct connection to a higher spiritual realm. Mystics are referred to in religious literature as having connection with God, but mysticism is not limited to religious faith and can pertain to any belief centered around a single creator or source of creation, and connecting to, or become one with, that source. A mystic may, in theory, be someone you wish to consult with if you are seeking a spiritual awakening or a greater sense of your life's purpose.

The term *prophet* originates in ancient Greece and means to "tell in advance." The earliest reference to a prophet appears in the Bible's Old Testament (Genesis 20:6-7) and was depicted as an individual on Earth who was chosen by God to speak for God. A prophet claims to be speaking on behalf of God and acts as an intermediary so that humanity can learn from God's wisdom. Theoretically, a prophet is someone that may provide insight into how humanity should adopt a closer relationship to God so that it may follow His intentions as set out in scripture.

The term *oracle* derives from the Latin verb "ōrāre" (meaning "to speak"). An oracle is a person who claims to be an authority on matters requiring wisdom, and an infallible source of knowledge. The implied perfection of an oracle is derived from its earliest roots. In ancient Rome, Oracle was a title given to a priest or priestess who proclaimed to have received direct advice or prophecy from the gods. Oracles are unlikely to appear in modern day, due to the inference that they have absolute, unquestionable, wisdom. This is not in keeping with the principle of free will. However, theoretically speaking, the purpose to consult with an oracle would be to learn of the divine wisdom that exists on any issue.

The word *psychic* originates from the Greek word "psychikos" (meaning "of the soul"). In Greek mythology, the maiden Psyche personified the ascension of the human soul. Her mythological beloved was Eros (also known as Cupid), the god of physical love and desire. A psychic is a person who claims to have telepathic knowledge or physical abilities that are inexplicable. Extrasensory perception may be how a psychic obtains information, and teleportation may produce physical outcomes which sit outside the societal consensus of what constitutes the natural laws of earth and humanity. You may wish to consult a psychic if you wish to understand the wisdom associated with a particular situation, and the karmic outcomes likely to arise from a range of available choices.

Spiritualist is a term that originates in North America. It means "to communicate with spirit." A spiritualist is a person who believes that communication between earthly and spiritual realms is possible, either naturally, or with practiced effort. A spiritualist may seek or provide insight into issues of morality, ethics, or the intentions of the source of creation, and the afterlife. Some spiritualists claim to rely on spiritual guides who communicate answers, guidance, or other messages from the afterlife. The differential that resulted in spiritualism, and set it apart from religious faith, was a belief that evolved beyond that of Old and New Testaments, in which God was often depicted to be harsh or punishing towards people. Spiritualists believe that spiritual entities possess a higher sense of knowledge and awareness, in which tolerance, kindness and forgiveness are fundamentally crucial. You may wish to consult with a spiritualist if you are looking to understand the moral, ethical, or karmic implications of choices which may be available.

The concept of reading tarot cards originated in Northern Italy in around the 15th century. The word *tarot* derives from the Italian word "tarocchi," which is likely to have relevance to the Taro River, situated in Northern area of the country. The earliest known reference to tarot, however, appears in Ancient Egyptian writings. A *tarot card reader* claims to interpret messages depicted in the deck of tarot cards, of which there are many types. The unique symbols and imagery in a tarot card deck form a language that the tarot card reader uses to communicate with the spiritual realm. It is not necessary for a tarot card reader to have supernatural or extrasensory abilities, although having such skills does not negatively affect the tarot card reader and may be considered helpful in understanding the context of any messages that appear in the tarot cards. A tarot card reader may be a suitable person to consult on matters of past, present and future, along with issues of morality, ethics, and the afterlife.

Reading tarot cards is a balancing act.

It is possible for a person to consider themselves to be a proficient tarot card reader, whilst also having one or more of the other skills or abilities described in this chapter.

I do not dwell on whether I am anything other than proficient at reading tarot cards, but if I were expected to choose from any of the above, I would also consider that I have empathic tendencies, because I often feel a type of awareness of other people's emotions. I wholeheartedly believe that communication between the physical and spiritual realms is possible. I have also experienced encounters and phenomena in my life that reinforce this viewpoint and have been able to communicate with a spiritual element through either dreams or the use of tarot cards. It seems, therefore, that I fit the definition of a spiritualist. Finally, I sometimes wonder if I might be a little psychic. Although, I do leave the door open that I may merely be highly perceptive, and that whatever 'hunches' I get are generated from an acute sense of intuitive awareness. I also suspect that some proclaimed "psychics" are in fact highly perceptive, and that they manifest an awareness, incorrectly interpreted as psychic ability.

I must confess that I try not to think about it too much. What I have discovered over the many years that I have taken an interest in and developed a proficient understanding of tarot is that I am human, and therefore I am flawed. I consider the key to becoming the best tarot card reader that I can be, is to forego the earthly desire to appear exceptional by adopting a title such as psychic, medium, or clairvoyant. I passionately believe that all of humanity has an opportunity to develop skills and abilities that are otherwise considered contrary to natural laws. There can be no exceptional people, or exceptional skills if we are all one, a single creation from a sole source creator. Exception is therefore an illusion, and to consider oneself the exception is to fall into the trap of taking advice from a human flaw.

My belief, and the central principle guiding this book, is that a humble openness to receive is the way to universal truth.

It is on this principle that I endeavor to read the tarot cards to the best of my knowledge and abilities, and on this principle that I author this book and offer its contents to everyone who reads it.

Reading tarot cards well is not just about having intuitive abilities. There is much more to this balancing act, and at first it may seem overwhelming. However, it really is not as complicated as it seems. In fact, the skill is based on the concept of simplification.

This is where the Rider-Waite tarot deck is often seen to be the supporting cast for the tarot card reader, who often takes center stage as the assumed star of the show. In fact, the opposite is true. Once the language of the Rider-Waite deck is learned to a proficient level, the cards do all the work. All the tarot card reader must then do is read what he or she sees. It is very much like reading a book, or more accurately, reading the ancient hieroglyphics on the walls of a cave somewhere in Egypt.

After all, the supporting cast of any film is the lifeblood that makes the star look good.

Left brain, right brain.

The most challenging aspect of learning to read tarot well is likely to be the task of fully embracing both sides of the brain, without letting either side dominate. This is a skill that may take years to fine-tune, particularly for people who have a fixed mindset about who they are, and how they respond to external stimuli.

The phrase "left-right brain" relates to the left and right hemispheres of the brain and how each is believed to influence a person's natural inclinations.

The left hemisphere is where the cognitive functions associated with speech and language reside. It is also associated with logic, analytical thinking, and processing information. People who are skilled at reading, writing, mathematics, or sciences, particularly involving complex computations, are often described as "left brain." They excel at logical reasoning, analytics, and linear thinking.

The right hemisphere is where brain functions linked to creativity, intuition and holistic thinking are found. People with strong spatial awareness, artistic flare, vivid imagination, and who are good at noticing the non-verbal cues of others, are often described as "right brain." They excel in creative environments and may make decisions that are based on how they feel.

People often consider themselves to be either "left" or "right" brain, but very rarely both. However, relying too much on one side, and not enough on the other, places undue pressure on the ego to pick up the slack.

Have you ever heard someone proclaim themselves to be psychic, and then later it transpired that they were wrong about a confident prediction? It is likely that the person has relied too heavily on the pride they have in their left-brain intuition, or their right-brain logic, and has then relied on their ego to fill in the gaps.

The ego will always take a person into self-protection mode. Examples of ego-based gap fillers include jumping to conclusions, conflating unrelated matters, or presenting their own opinion as though it is a spiritual message from a higher source.

To avoid this far too common ego trap, practice shifting your mindset from left to right, or from right to left, depending on the circumstances. For example, pick a topic you have a fixed viewpoint on. How do you feel about the matter (right brain)? Do you have evidence to prove that your feelings are validated (left brain)? What is the evidence in your possession, and how does it prove the specific truth (left brain)? How would you feel if someone you trusted told you that you were wrong (right brain)?

When I was younger, I did not do particularly well at school. Mostly, it was lack of interest, and a tendency to search outside of the traditional structure of schooling (right brain). I did however enjoy my art classes (right brain), and home economics, which primarily involved activities such as cooking or sewing (right brain). I was not particularly sporty, but I did excel at sports that required good spatial awareness, including volleyball, shotput, and discus (right brain). I could barely sit still during history (left brain), geography (left brain), and science studies (left brain). My math teacher may as well have been speaking Swahili, I had no idea what he was talking about, even after my parents engaged a private tutor to help me (left brain). However, I did develop a deep crush on my tutor (right brain). It is now easy to see that I had a natural tendency to be a right brain thinker.

Without having finished high school, I had limited employment options. I worked in bars, tried sales jobs, delivery jobs, and then ended up where most undereducated women of my generation landed, in general office work, supporting somebody else's ambitions. I did temporary office work for almost 10 years and found it incredibly boring. Of course, I developed a skill for it after a decade of practice, so my practical office skills became strong (left brain). I then decided to go to university overseas, which is expensive. After my own funds were depleted, my parents paid for my tuition, books, and foreign student insurance. However, I paid for my housing, food, clothing, vehicle costs, travel, and entertainment. It was this experience of having to survive and thrive in a foreign country as a student, which brought my left brain to life.

Suddenly, I wanted my "money's worth" when it came to university. I paid close attention to classes and lectures, took copious notes, studied hard and graduated with just under a 4.0 grade point average (left brain). I could not reach 4.0 because when my Anatomy professor threatened to fail me unless I participated in the dissection of a cat, I stopped going to that class altogether (right brain). Consequently, I still have no idea what any of the body parts are called (right brain).

Following university, my career transitioned into policy analysis (left brain). My roles consisted of research, analysis, complex writing, and negotiation in a highly political, central government law enforcement environment (seriously left brain). I was born with a natural inclination towards right brain thinking but spent most of my life practicing my left brain thinking. The result is a tarot card reader who is highly adept at switching between the left and right hemispheres of the brain as needed. There is evidence of this adeptness scattered all over my daily life, in many different ways.

I wanted to share my own experience with you so that you can see how our lives give us examples of both left and right brain thinking opportunities from which we can draw. It may take practice, but one of the best advantages you can give yourself as you progress through this book, is to find ways to recognize your left and right brain strengths and weaknesses, and to consider how to strengthen potential gap areas, so that the ego doesn't end up muscling in.

Modesty is your greatest superpower.

I cannot overstate the importance of putting aside the desire to become a world-renowned psychic medium, or other equally ego-based ambition of grandeur. It will not in the slightest, help you to learn to read tarot well. On the contrary, it is likely to make it far more difficult, depending on how big an ego you have.

This book is designed to help you to develop your language skills, so that you will begin to understand the message when the point in time arrives that a message is being sent to you.

Imagine if you were tasked to listen into the night's sky for a sign of alien life. The entire fate of humanity needs to know at that moment that aliens exist, because we desperately need their help. Your job is to wait, listen, and watch for recognizable signs of life, and the moment a sight or a sound appears, you must hear it, see it, understand it, and harness it for the benefit of all humankind. Our survival depends on it.

But instead of doing your job, you are on the phone, chatting about how big a deal you are with your new fancy job. The message comes, and goes, and you have missed it.

Do not worry. When you get it right, you will know. When you get it right repeatedly, you will discover that others know too.

CHAPTER 3

KEY INFLUENCES FOR THE RIDER-WAITE DECK

The creation of the Rider-Waite tarot deck consists of multiple influencing components, which would require an entirely separate book to adequately explain in detail. However, to aid you in being able to learn to interpret the cards well, this chapter provides a basic understanding of where the cards' imagery derives.

Context

The cards were first published by the Rider Company in London England in 1909. During this time, London was a diverse city with people of different religious beliefs. The majority population was Christian, with the Church of England being the largest denomination. Other Christian denominations, such as Roman Catholicism, Methodism, and Baptism, were also present at the time. London also had significant Jewish and Muslim communities.

The study of the occult was also popular in the early 1900s, leading to various London-based occultist societies having been founded during the period. The earliest of these was the Freemasonry (founded in 1691). Freemasonry continues to influence esoteric societies around the world today.

Many of the world's prominent occultists from this period resided in London when interest in occultism was at its peak. One example is Madame Blavatsky, who went on to co-find the Theosophical Society in the United States.

Hermeticism

Hermeticism is a religious philosophy, based on the combined teachings of the ancient Greek god, Hermes, and the ancient Egyptian god, Thoth. The teachings are referred to as "Hermetica" and relate (on the technical side) to astrology, medicine, pharmacology, alchemy, and magic, plus, (on the religious side) to the relationship between human beings, the cosmos, and God.

Developing in around the first century AD, Hermeticism loosely resembles a form of esoteric Christianity, or Gnosticism, in which a mystical sense of personal spiritual existence is emphasized above that taught within the world's organized religious institutions.

The Hermetic Order of the Golden Dawn was founded in London on 12 February 1888 by Samuel Liddel MacGregor Mathers, William Wynn Westcott, and William Robert Woodman. The founders were all Freemasons and members of Societas Rosicruciana.

Arthur Edward Waite joined Golden Dawn in 1891. His involvement in the Order was sporadic, and primarily focused on Christian mysticism. In around 1903 he became head of the Order's Isis-Urania Temple, relating to ritual practices.

Pamela Colman Smith, the artist who provided the illustrations for the Rider Waite tarot deck, joined Golden Dawn in 1901. She was commissioned to create the deck by Arthur Edward Waite, shortly after the two met and shared their common interest in the study of the occult and mysticism.

Golden Dawn was a presumed magical order. Its members devoted themselves to the study and practice of the supernatural, and the evocation of a divine presence or deity, using magic and other occult rituals.

Hermetica informed the Golden Dawn's teachings, with regards to the four classic elements (air, fire, water, earth), and then later, the fifth element (ether). Rider-Waite's Minor Arcana suite is based on the first four elements, while the fifth element embeds itself within the Major Arcana suite.

Astrology

Astrology and the alignment of the cosmos influenced the order of both the Major and Minor Arcana suites.

Each of the twelve zodiac signs depicted in astrology fall within one of the four classic elements. There are also three different qualities of sign, which relate to the influence of energy and how Humanity responds to the environment. The three qualities include cardinal, fixed or mutable. Qualities are also divided into positive or negative. Each of the Minor Arcana cards has a cross-referenced association with one of the elements, one of the qualities, and its directional energy.

The twenty-two cards of the Major Arcana suite are matched with corresponding zodiac signs. When reading a spread, the relationships between the card and its corresponding element, zodiac sign and quality attributes can help with context, such as time, place, or individuals relevant to the reading. Far more important, however, is to recognize that astrology influenced the development of the Rider-Waite tarot deck. For the purposes of this book, it is not necessary to fully understand the complexities of this influence. After lengthy consideration, I therefore decided not to add superficial cross-referencing. I would rather, when the time comes, write a follow-up book that serves the subject well.

Kabbalah

Kabbalah is a complex mystical branch of Judaism. Most kabbalistic scholars date the faith's origins back to the "Garden of Eden," described in Genesis and Ezekiel of the Christian Bible.

Kabbalah's primary written wisdom is the Book of Zohar, a complex written account of the creation, purpose and evolution of life, the world, and the cosmos, which is notoriously difficult to understand from an analytical, scientific, or philosophical standpoint. The mystical nature of the text requires a student of Kabbalah to feel its messaging, to appreciate and gain a sense of immersion or spiritual alignment to the faith.

A visual representation of the ancient wisdom of Kabbalah appears in the Tree of Life, which consists of ten spheres and twenty-two pathways, eternally connected to one another, and which collectively represent the journey of spiritual enlightenment that occurs with each human life. Each of the spheres corresponds to one of the numbered Minor Arcana cards in each elemental suite, and each of the pathways corresponds to one of the Major Arcana cards.

The Tree of Life demonstrates how the earthly and spiritual senses of an individual are developed through lessons of learning, the attainment of essential virtues, and how a person chooses, or is chosen to repeat a particular life lesson again and again, either for the duration of their physical life, or until the lesson has finally been learned.

As with astrology, a detailed understanding of the relationship between Kabbalah and the creation of the Rider-Waite deck is not necessary to learn to read tarot proficiently. Images can be located online showing the relationship between the Major and Minor Arcana, and the spheres and pathways of the Tree of Life. Additionally, this book provides a detailed account of The Fool's journey of spiritual enlightenment, which is a key example of the Kabbalistic influence as depicted by the Tree of Life.

The Four Essential Virtues

Classical and Christian theology discusses four essential virtues of mind and character (strength, prudence, temperance, and justice). These virtues appear in the Major Arcana suite and relate to the acquisition of positive construct as symbolized in the Wheel of Fortune, the card which immediately precedes Justice.

Each essential virtue relates to a conscious and deliberate decision of the mind to be virtuous, rather than rely upon involuntary or instinctive emotion. The four essential virtues correspond with the cards Strength, The Hierophant, Justice, and Temperance.

Other influences

Alchemy is a natural tradition with broad geographic and cultural origins. It covers influences from China and India, and the cultural practices of the Muslim and early European worlds. An example of alchemic influence includes the use of discrete color variations between cards, relating to metal components, such as crowns, body armor or other adornments, plus solid or stone structures.

The Rider-Waite tarot deck also contains unexplained supernatural references that do not clearly link to known esoteric teachings or appear to retranslate traditional teachings. For example, the four-winged angels that appear in Wheel of Fortune and The World are attributed to the Four Evangelists of the New Testament, despite there being no direct link between those specific evangelists and their corresponding animals. Some theologians are open to an inference of extraterrestrial life in these and other similar instances. Whilst no officially recognized biblical text provides direct evidence to support the claim of extraterrestrial life, subsequent text of similar origin does allude to 'watchers' refenced in text originating from around the same period as the Old Testament. In particular, 'The Book of Giants' related to "The Book of Enoch' which was first located in 1947, and expands upon the writing of Genesis, the first book of the Old Testament. It refers to fallen angels that inhabited the earth from the sky, and whose existence entirely recalibrates the ancestry of the Bible's Noah, and the officially reported reason for God's great flood. When considering the significance of either competing theory, note that The Book of Giants precedes the New Testament by at least seven hundred years. Neither theory is proven nor disproven, and therefore each remains possible. The concept of supernatural, spiritual, and divine, extends beyond that of practicing religion and faith, or other official attributions. In other words, the entire concept behind tarot's acceptance of the supernatural leaves it open to any number of possibilities, limited only by the individual's interpretation of its messaging.

As you progress through this book, it will become easy to see examples of how each of the abovementioned influences have come together to provide a visually astute, complex description of the practical, philosophical, and spiritual components that make up Humanity's cycle of existence. The way Pamela Coleman Smith was able to communicate the complexities of life with such streamlined visual precision, makes the Rider-Waite deck a uniquely enduring vessel for communication that I believe will never become obsolete.

CHAPTER 4

ARCANA BASICS

Arcana refers to secrets or mysteries. The word traces its roots to the Latin term *arcanus*, meaning "secret" or "hidden." The Rider-Waite tarot deck is divided into two types of arcana suite which are referred to as the Minor Arcana and the Major Arcana.

Minor Arcana
The Minor Arcana includes fifty-six cards which are divided into four elemental suites which are based on the four classic earth elements of fire, air, earth, and water. Each suite comprises ten numbered cards and four court (or royalty) cards. In no particular order, the four elemental suites are summarized herein.

Wands Suite
The Wands Suite is ruled by the classic element, Fire, which is a masculine element relevant to willpower and male energy. The Wands Suite refers to instinct, energy, creativity, and action. The activating source of wands and fire is the soul. There are three fire signs in astrology (Leo, Sagittarius, Aries) and a reading that contains court cards from the Wands Suite may relate to individuals from these signs.

Swords Suite
The Swords Suite is ruled by the classic element, Air, which is a masculine element relevant to overt and covert power. The Swords Suite relates to intellect, communication, and decision-making. The activating source of swords and air is the mind. There are three air signs in astrology (Gemini, Libra, Aquarius) and a reading that contains court cards from the Swords Suite may relate to individuals from these signs.

Pentacles Suite

The Pentacles Suite is ruled by the element, Earth, which is a feminine element relevant to nutrition, material things, and stability. The Sword Suite relates to prosperity, money, ownership, and well-being. The activating source of pentacles and earth is the body. There are three earth signs in astrology (Taurus, Virgo, Capricorn) and a reading that contains court cards from the Pentacles Suite may relate to individuals from these signs.

Cups Suite

The Cups Suite is ruled by the element, Water, which is a feminine element relevant to feelings, the unconscious, and intuition. The Cups Suite relates to emotions, relationships, and sense of self. The activating source of cups and water is the heart. There are three water signs in astrology (Cancer, Scorpio, Pisces) and a reading that contains court cards from the Cups Suite may relate to individuals from these signs.

Major Arcana

Just as each of the Minor Arcana suites relates to one of the four classic earthly elements, the Major Arcana suite relates to the fifth element, which is ether, also known as spirit. The relevance of this point is often underappreciated by tarot enthusiasts and is key to gaining a solid understanding of how the Major Arcana is relevant to tarot card reading.

So, let us consider this point in greater detail. There are an estimated eight billion people living in the world today, each of whom are uniquely different to one another. The average lifespan of a person is 80 years, which translates into around 2.5 billion seconds. Each second is a moment in life, which makes up the potential of just how different one person's life journey can be, compared to another person's life journey. This is the case for people who are related, or who live together. It is even true for 'identical' twins. No single human being is precisely the same as another. And so is the case for the physical and spiritual path of life that each person uniquely follows.

There is, however, one thing about each of us that is the same. Somehow, despite our infinite differences, each of us is born for the purposes of travelling through human experience. The human experience is universal, and every person on earth, regardless of age, gender, culture, geographic location, appearance, degree of prosperity, or other exceptional characteristic, must constantly navigate the human experience during every second of their life, from the moment of their birth, until the moment of their passing. Each moment of experience feeds into the spirit of the individual, in the form of memories, learning points, and habits. Each memory, learning point and habit continuously feeds into the individual's spirit, transforming it into something which is utterly unique, that can only ever be possessed by that single person, and will define them as an individual.

The spirit is often confused with the soul; however, the two differ from each other. There is only one soul, which is universal and relates to the source of creation of all things. The spirit belongs to the person and is always with them for as long as they travel through life. The spirit is the collection of everything that person has become because of their life journey. Upon death, the spirit reincarnates and begins a new life journey.

The twenty-two cards of the Major Arcana suite collectively paint a picture of the life journey that each person travels, which makes up the human experience and either feeds or starves the soul. Individually, each Major Arcana card presents us with a profound aspect of our existence and teaches us the most fundamental of life's lessons.

The way we travel through the universal human experience, and what we learn (or do not learn) and adopt (or do not adopt) from it, shapes us into the person we become. What we become is the spirit that we uniquely possess, and which defines us as the unique earth being that we are.

The Major Arcana suite is sometimes thought to be more profound than the Minor Arcana. A tarot card reading that produces a sizeable percentage of Major Arcana cards is considered to be an intense reading, in which the Querent or subject of the reading is undergoing simultaneous major life challenges, such as serious health conditions, or huge ethical dilemmas. This is neither true nor untrue, but an assumption about the gravity particular cards in isolation of the entire context of the reading, may skew the interpretation of the reading.

For this reason, I tend to stay away from making assumptions when I see a lot of Major Arcana appear in a tarot card reading. I learned to see the Major Arcana cards as a collection of essentials to bring with you when you travel through life. If you happen to forget one of those essentials, then a relevant Major Arcana card may pop up in a reading, to remind you. This is a far less threatening way of exploring the Major Arcana and can help stabilize the reading and avoid unnecessary anxiety.

For example, what is a Querent likely to feel if the Death card appears in the middle of a reading about his or her upcoming surgery? If the Major Arcana are purely seen as major life challenges, then the Querent is likely to become anxious about the possibility of dying under the knife, when in fact, the appearance of the Death card, in the context of the overall reading, may pertain to the positive, transformative impact that the surgery will have on the Querent's life. Death relates to the end of a cycle and may be expressing an end to the Querent's history of living with pain.

There are instances in which a tarot card reading that evokes a larger percentage of Major Arcana cards is likely to reflect circumstances involving simultaneous life lessons. However, the more experienced you become, the more you will be able to see that context is key, and understanding context requires thoughtful consideration of the entire reading, and how each card placement interacts with the other cards in the reading.

The key distinction between Major and Minor Arcana

Whereas the Major Arcana demonstrates life's lessons or crucial points of passage that must be navigated on the path towards spiritual enlightenment, the Minor Arcana depicts the day-to-day elements of existence. Individual events, routine experiences, habits, and people of consequence in varying degrees may be expressed in a tarot card reading with Minor Arcana cards.

22

CHAPTER 5

THE SIGNIFICANCE OF NUMBERS

Each elemental suite of the Minor Arcana consists of fourteen cards. The first ten cards are Ace, followed by numbers 2-10. The remaining four cards (Page, Knight, Queen, and King) are called Court or Royalty cards and are not numbered.

Each of the numbered cards in the Minor Arcana has an association with its corresponding numbered card in the Major Arcana suite. This association demonstrates the interdependence between our uneventful moments in life, and the bigger picture relating to life's lessons. The lessons of life are not always obvious at the time, but each moment of life contributes to the person each of us becomes, and the interdependence between our experiences, our actions and thoughts is continuous throughout our material existence.

Numbers are an essential part of the Minor Arcana. It is not, however, simply a matter of looking out for a prominence of a certain number in a reading. The sophistication of the Rider-Waite tarot deck seems almost mathematical once you begin to fully appreciate the clarity with which numbers, along with colors and other symbols collectively bring a tarot reading to life.

Numbered cards provide depth to tarot messages and give the tarot card reader the opportunity to stretch the interpretation of a reading, so that its messages begin to unfold in a story-like manner.

As with other aspects of the Rider-Waite deck, its numbering never occurs by chance. Everything you see in a card is there to serve a purpose, and combines as a glorious tapestry of messaging, derived from multiple theological or doctrinal sources.

The following is a summary of what each of the numbers 1-10 represent in tarot, and how the number system within the Rider Waite deck coincides with recognized ancient numerological systems, whilst also marrying together the Minor and Major Arcana suites.

One

In Western and Chinese Numerology, the number one represents independence and new beginnings, plus the wholeness of a single thing. It can also relate to business and intellectual pursuits, assertiveness, determination, and leadership.

In the Minor Arcana suite, the number one is represented as an Ace. Each of the Ace cards denotes a presentation of a single, independent, and new example of the suite's significance. As with everything new, one signifies the momentum and potential made available by a brand-new beginning.

In the Major Arcana suite, the number one is associated with The Magician. The Magician stands alone, confidently asserting his determination to manifest, and needs no more than he is, which suggests that he is whole.

Two

In tarot, as in Chinese Numerology, two represents balance of two or more elements, harmony, pairings, and partnership. There is a world of possibilities, but each possibility has a knock-on effect, and a potential legacy that it leaves behind once activated.

All two cards in the Minor Arcana carry two (or more) opposite or competing considerations that should be balanced. Duality or choices may be present, and harmony may need to be achieved through decision making.

In the Major Arcana, two is associated with The High Priestess. She is the complementary opposite of The Magician, and together they form a balanced union.

Three

In Chinese numerology, the number three represents separating from the past and living life and all its experience. Following your inspiration, embarking on something new, creation, connection and embracing change are all common themes of life denoted by the number three.

In the Minor Arcana suite, the number three often relates to an endeavor or creation of an event. Collaborations and celebrations with others, along with the effects of interconnectedness, may be relevant.

In the Major Arcana, the number three is associated with The Empress. The Empress denotes motherhood, growth, and the creation of abundance.

Four

In tarot, the number four relates to stability, structure, and the creation of an anchor point. The prospect of growth, endurance, and evolution made possible by the existence of something foundational, or tangible.

In Chinese numerology, the number four is unlucky in an equivalent way that the number thirteen is unlucky in Western interpretations. The Chinese relate the number four to death, which is the only moment in life during which a person surrenders all sense of security and safety so that they may experience their fate. The shedding of one's earthly body, which occurs in the process of death, is an experience that releases a person from earthly anchorage. In this respect, the number four is a reminder to appreciate the concept of stability and structure, while on this earthly plane.

In the Minor Arcana suite, four can depict a focus on matters that serve as a foundation, as relevant to the suite. For example, Pentacles may relate to financial security, Cups to emotional security, Wands to secure relationships, and Swords to mental stability.

In the Major Arcana suite, the number four is associated with The Emperor, a card focused on matters of materialism, resilience, and tangible security.

Five

Number five represents instability, fluctuations, and the conflict that arises from a lack of cohesion. In Chinese Numerology, five relates to 'me' or the focus on one's own ego and singularity. An inflated self-focus can sometimes apply, which further amplifies the sense of crisis.

In the Minor Arcana suite, five can appear as instability, lack of cohesion, sadness and other issues that often arise when support of others is not present, or when an unresolved issue is in play.

In the Major Arcana, the number five is associated with The Hierophant. As God's representative on Earth, the Hierophant acts like a silver thread, which sews together on a single set of beliefs, traditions or principles, an otherwise disparate humanity.

Six

The number six relates to communication, harmony, and cooperation. In Chinese Numerology, six represents good fortune and happiness, and is particularly positive when related to business ventures.

In the Minor Arcana suite, the number six represents a coming together of the collective. It may appear as a group win, an act of kindness, or other success in which a group effort or partnership was a key component of the outcome.

In the Major Arcana, the number six is associated with The Lovers. By its definition, The Lovers unite and share the impact of that union.

Seven

The number seven refers to the determination for something that may or may not be achieved. In Chinese Numerology, seven is a mixture of lucky and unlucky (hit and miss), and ranges in meaning from 'rising up' to 'deception and lies.' In tarot, seven involves contemplation and introspection, relating to what caused us to appear as we have in the context of events.

In the Minor Arcana Suite, the number seven relates to what appears within us that will activate in accordance with the relevant suite. For example, are we willing to accept a challenge (Wands), do we trust our own instincts (Cups), would we defy expectations (Swords) or, will we persist beyond life's disappointments (Pentacles)?

In the Major Arcana, seven is associated with The Chariot. The Chariot persists beyond any perceived limitations, to achieve an agreed way forward.

Eight

Eight relates to inner strength and the resources you have inside you to draw from, so that you may action a response and succeed at whatever you have aimed to achieve. The number eight is also the luckiest number in Chinese Numerology and signifies wealth and prosperity. In fact, the more eights that appear in something, the luckier it is. To demonstrate this, the "888" license plate is the most coveted in the world.

In the Minor Arcana suite, the number eight speaks of motivation to act in ways that achieve a positively perceived outcome.

In the Major Arcana suite, the number eight is associated with Strength, and the humble but continuous act of positive self-development.

Nine

Number nine is a configuration of three times three and relates to the mind, body, and spirit, multiplied unto itself to produce a wisdom from previous multiplied experiences. In Chinese Numerology, nine represents matters which are long-lasting. Nine relates to the need for personal fulfilment to progress to satisfactory completion.

In the Minor Arcana, nine often represents attainment, achievement, the niggle of a final loose end, a last-minute intensity, or a long and winding journey that has very nearly reached its destination.

In the Major Arcana, nine is associated with The Hermit. The Hermit appears as the last step in the journey of earthly wisdom. He reflects on all his prior experiences and readies himself to transition from the material to spiritual plane.

Ten

The number ten represents the culmination of everything that preceded the moment, and the end of a cycle. Ten can also be the point of renewal and return to a starting point, so that the cycle may begin again. This is demonstrated by adding one and zero together. The result is number one, representing another new beginning.

Ten does not appear specifically in Chinese Numerology, but as it is comprised of One and Zero, there is relevance to its meaning. One can relate to being alone or single. Zero appears just prior to a beginning.

In the Minor Arcana suite, the number ten relates to a kind of revelation. This may appear as an outcome or ending, or a realization of wasted effort.

In the Major Arcana, ten is associated with Wheel of Fortune. All our earthly choices, decisions, thoughts, and actions are compiled and used as fuel for the directional force that propels us into a new beginning.

CHAPTER 6

SYMBOLS AND COLORS

The Rider Waite tarot deck uses a variety of imagery that combines to provide the tarot card reader with a wide range of spiritual messages. The best-known of these are the four Minor Arcana elements represented by Wands, Cups, Swords, and Pentacles.

The remaining symbolism of the Major Arcana, including colors and types of imagery set the tone for all seventy-eight cards in the deck.

It is important to consider symbols and other imagery in the context of the card in question, and relative to how the card presents in a reading and for what purpose.

The sky

The sky has two distinct aspects to consider. Firstly, color is important as it provides an indication of the mood reflected in the card. Proportion of sky is equally important. More sky depicts greater freedom, light, or a higher degree of consciousness or spirituality. Less sky denotes secrets, mystery, lack of clarity, or even a reduced access to spirituality or consciousness.

Clouds

Clouds carry a variety of meanings. Common examples include an association with air, higher consciousness, abstract ideas, and intellectualism.

Clouds can sometimes depict movement, or mystery and camouflage. Cloud imagery will also combine color, proportion, and proximity to illustrate relevant weather conditions.

Solid structures

Solid, manufactured structures such as pillars, thrones, platforms, and dwellings connect to materialism and the earthly plane. They also reflect safety, security, and having a solid foundation from which to progress. If no solid structures exist in a card, then the card may reflect a greater closeness to the spiritual realm. Alternatively, it may represent less foundational support, greater risk, or the whimsical and unpredictable aspects of life.

Nature

Natural landscapes and images of nature represent harmony, abundance, and fertility. There may be a maternal relevance to the card, related to nurturing or growth. Specific natural images may also carry specific meanings. For example, water relates to emotions, but also may present opportunities for growth. Mountains represent turbulence, or a reach towards the heavens, depending on color, height, and other factors. Trees may reflect an aspect of abundance, or carry other symbols, such as air or animal life.

Flowers

Flowers form part of nature, and they may appear as an enhancement of the natural environment and landscape. However, flowers can also have specific meanings, depending on the species of flower, its color and how it appears in a certain card.

Certain species of flower may cross-reference to religious scripture or philosophical principles. Reflection, nostalgia, opportunity, happiness and joy, celebration and renewal are all potentially symbolized by types of flowers.

Proportions and central figures

When a person or thing is disproportionately larger or smaller in a card, this tends to reflect its message significance. A large central human form may reflect their power or perceived hierarchy, a large angelic form may relate to an abundance of spiritual wisdom. The preponderance of a color may emphasize the relevance of the mood related to that color. Smaller figures may be subtle reminders of a bigger picture, or a risk to be mindful of.

Cards with humans
Most cards in the Rider Waite tarot deck include images of people. Whether one, two or even groups of people appear in a card relates to an aspect of the human experience.

Cards without humans
There are few cards in the Rider Waite tarot deck that do not include images of people. Each of the Ace cards in the Minor Arcana suite includes only a hand, and in each instance the hand presents the suite's element for the first time. This relates to a new beginning, and the unlimited potential of the experience before the limitations of the human experience sets in.

Eight of Wands and Three of Swords are also cards without human figures. In both instances, the purpose is to reinforce a message central to the card's meaning.

Landscapes
The Rider-Waite tarot deck uses landscapes to richly describe the motivation and wider context of the central message. For example, an entirely natural landscape can denote harmony between man and earth. A cultivated landscape may relate to the effort required to achieve goals, or the consideration of a wider community. When a body of water appears in a card, it often depicts our need to navigate emotional situations. Mountains may appear as aspirations or obstacles. Dwellings may reflect security or material aspirations.

Posture
The human figures that appear in the Rider Waite tarot deck may take on an active (alert) or passive (relaxed) posture. The relevance of the posture within a particular card may be specific to the card's unique

messaging. However, tarot does separate the Minor Arcana into distinctly active or passive categories. The Swords and Wands suites are active, while the Cups and Pentacles suites are passive. Whether a suite is active or passive, relates to the elemental qualities of the Minor Arcana Suite.

Direction of card

When a card is upright, the symbolic messaging tends to be intricately linked to proportions. Often, the correlation between proportion and symbols inverts when the card appears reversed. This is due to the risk factors, and the increase probability of risk becoming reality when the card is reversed. For example, if a card contains solid structures, concepts of security and safety apply when upright. When reversed, the weight of such structures may be interpreted as a dominating feature that may be imposing or difficult to navigate.

Left and right.

The positioning of any imagery in the Rider Waite deck is not by accident, and this includes whether it appears as a left or right directional image. For example, the left hand represents the subconscious and receiving something, and the right represents the conscious and giving something.

Each of the Ace cards of the Minor Arcana suite includes a hand, which is a dominant feature of the cards. The hand protruding from the parameters of the card in Ace of Wands (fire, and of inspiration) is the right hand. This is also true for Ace of Pentacles (earth, and of materialism) and Ace of Swords (air, and of intellect). The explanation for this is that inspiration, materialism, and intellect are all derived from the conscious mind. So, which hand appears in Ace of Cups (water, and of the heart)?

The imagery is deliberately unclear in its interpretation of the hand to demonstrate the conflicting or dual aspects of emotion, love, and spirituality and from where it derives.

Use of Gender

The imagery and character assignments within the Rider Waite tarot deck are not gender specific. Male or female characters illustrate the archetypal aspects of the human experience.

The inclusion of a female character may allude to a gentler or more passive approach to an issue, or a closeness to the spiritual realm.

Comparatively, a male character may indicate a direct action or material goal. Men and women are equal in the Rider-Waite deck, but with opposite and complementary features.

Female

The Rider Waite tarot deck uses female characters in its imagery to represent distinctive features of archetypal femininity. This is particularly the case in the Major Arcana Suite. For example, The Empress is portrayed as nurturing and maternal. The High Priestess is depicted as intuitive. Strength represents inner strength and participative leadership. Justice relates to equality and fairness, and Temperance refers to moderation.

Male

Male characters tend to represent distinctive features of archetypal masculinity. For example, in the Major Arcana, the Magician represents creativity and confidence. The Emperor relates to structure and stability. The Hierophant provides guidance and a sense of tradition. The Chariot refers to having determination to do what it takes to overcome obstacles, and The Hermit relates to wisdom and reflection.

Youth

Each Page card in the Minor Arcana Suite depicts a youthful character, for the purpose of illustrating the vitality and learning aspects of the human experience. The Pages are each a messenger of information, and include element of query or fascination with life, typical of someone who may still be in the early years life, with much of life's experiences yet to be encountered. In other cards, the inclusion of a younger character may relate to innocence, purity, or lack of experience.

Couples

The most recognizable card depicting a couple is The Lovers, in the Major Arcana Suite. In this instance, depiction of a couple includes a range of meanings, including partnership, soulfulness, and unity. However, other couples, both human and non-human, appear in the Rider Waite tarot deck.

The inclusion of a couple, whether opposite or the same in appearance, gender, or other qualities, is never by chance. It will relate to the consideration of opposing sides, the need for harmony and balance, shared responsibility, or something else. The meaning may be specific to the relevant suite, whether the couple comprises two identical or opposing sides, and the considerations that may become relevant whenever there is more than one.

Groups

Imagery that includes a group of people tends to relate to shared effort and the benefits, successes (or failures) of that group. Three of Cups is a card that often comes to mind when considering groups. It shows women coming together to celebrate friendship and the support they give each other. Similarly, Ten of Pentacles depicts a multi-generational group of people who collectively contribute and benefit from a prosperous representation. When a group appears in a card, there is likely to be an element of group involvement included in the card's messaging.

Angels

The four most prominently depicted angels in the Rider Waite tarot deck are those of The Lovers, Temperance, The Devil and Judgement in the Major Arcana deck. These angels are modelled after the human form, are disproportionately large, and are typically associated with spiritual guidance and divine intervention. These angels are also sometimes related to specific archangels of biblical origin and comprise Raphael (angel of air, The Lovers card), Michael (angel of fire, Temperance card), Uriel (angel of earth, The Devil card), and Gabriel (angel of water, Judgement card). Other angels within the deck are modelled on the human form. They appear in the Wheel of Fortune and The World and demonstrate different forms of angel presence.

Animals

The inclusion of animal species in the Rider-Waite deck is subtle yet purposeful. An animal may appear with a human to provide comparison between base instinct and conscious deliberation (e.g., Strength). Animals may also express human characteristics ordinarily attributed to that animal. For example, cats (independence), dogs (loyalty), and horses (energy or progress).

Clothing

The symbolism of clothing comprises of two key factors. The first is the type of clothing and the purpose it would ordinarily serve. For example, simple unadorned clothing may represent an unassuming or humble attitude. Armor is likely to serve as protection or a sign of strength. The patterns in an elaborate style of dress are likely to contain relevant symbols.

The second factor relates to the color of the clothing, which carries its own symbolism. A lack of clothing will also be relevant to the card's messaging.

Adornment

Jewelry, belts, crowns, and other types of adornment will never be by chance. For example, a wrist bracelet may relate to vanity, or broken restraints. Crowns are symbols of material wealth but may also relate to reverence and wisdom. Belts, shoes, flower adornments, everything in the card will carry a message which will fit within the overall concept of the card.

Colors

The colors that appear in the Rider Waite tarot deck provide richness and subtle layers to the symbolism of each card. As with the figurative depictions within each card, the colors never appear by chance. When reading a tarot card spread, color proportions of each card should be considered. A preponderance of one color across the spread may set the mood for the reading and carry contextual significance.

The table below includes basic descriptions for frequently applied colors.

White	Purity, innocence, new beginnings, and lack of judgement.	*Green*	Freshness, immaturity or inexperience, growth, abundance, good favor, and nature.
Black	Mystery, danger, the unknown, emotional darkness, oppression, and suppression.	*Violet*	Spirituality, wisdom, and a higher level of consciousness.
Blue	Intuition, spirituality, indifference, openness, clarity, and truth.	*Orange*	Warnings, warmth, vitality, and creativity.
Red	Passion, energy, desire, love, wrath, strength, power, and materialism	*Brown*	Stability, foundational, natural, and of original intent.
Yellow	The conscious state, dissonance, envy, sun energy, caution, success, joy, and illumination.	*Grey*	The unconscious state, indifference, disinterest, impartiality, shadow considerations, and unknown outcomes.

Combinations, patterns, and shading

There are only five colors that appear independently within the cards. These include the three primary colors (blue, red, and yellow), plus black and white. All other colors derive from two or more of the independent colors. For example, orange is a combination of red and yellow, grey combines black and white. Often, a color is achieved through the combination of other colors and will relate to mixed concepts. This also applies to patterns and shading, although patterns may appear with smaller symbols that have minor or often neglected relevance.

The fifth element

In addition to the four elements represented by the four Minor Arcana suites, a fifth element is represented by the entire Major Arcana Suite. This is the element ether, which in literal translation refers to the atmosphere, the sky, the heavens, or space. Ether also relates to interdependence between Humanity, other species, the material world, spirituality, and the cosmos. Cards in the Rider-Waite deck that combine multiple features not traditionally expected to co-exist, may be referring to aspects of interdependence, spirit, or the wider Collective.

CHAPTER 7

THE FOOL'S JOURNEY

Any person wishing to gain a meaningful understanding of how to read tarot proficiently will need to become well acquainted with the natural progression of life. The Fool's Journey is a metaphor for exactly that. It begins with The Fool, ends with The World, and demonstrates how each of the Major Arcana cards represents a stage in the accumulation of knowledge and experience, plus the development of one's character.

The Fool begins his journey with no prior sense of existence. He travels through each of the Major Arcana cards, every card representing a different stage of life and the various joys and challenges that form part of his personal development.

The Fool's Journey is one of self-discovery, growth, and spiritual transformation. By the end of his journey, the Fool is anything but a fool. He has learned from life's adversities, has accumulated essential character virtues, and has reached full maturity.

As you delve into the concepts described by The Fool's Journey, consider your own life path and the joys or challenges experienced; the choices and decisions made, and each moment of your life that turned you into the person you are today.

The following is a progression through The Fool's Journey, summarizing the learning points associated with each of the consecutively numbered Major Arcana cards.

0 - The Fool

The Fool card, which is numbered Zero, reflects the absence of prior existence and the starting point for the journey. At this stage, The Fool has no perceptions of life. He is infant-like, impressionable. He is like a sponge, soaking up everything to which he is exposed. Nothing good or bad has happened to him so far, and therefore, no learning points or emotional baggage influences his decision-making. The Fool is spontaneous and fearlessly unaware of anything other than his own existence. There will be joys and heartaches, challenging situations to navigate, but this is all in The Fool's future. For now, he is eager to embark on his journey, and so he does so by absentmindedly stepping off the edge of a cliff into the unknown.

I - The Magician

As The Fool sets forth on his journey, he immediately meets The Magician. The Magician represents the potential arising from a new beginning, and the primal energy of the individual. The Magician is active, like the positive end of a magnet. He is masculine, creative, and has a heightened sense of his conscious awareness. The Magician is capable of manifesting material desires, and he teaches The Fool that he has the power to get things done.

II - The High Priestess

The Fool's next encounter is with The High Priestess. She is the complementary partner to the Magician. In contrast to her partner, The High Priestess is passive, like the negative side of a magnet, and has a heightened sense of the unconscious mind. She teaches The Fool that there is more than that which the eyes can see. The High Priestess is The Magician's equal, and together they represent a duality that creates balance.

III - The Empress

As The Fool continues his journey, he meets The Empress. The Empress embodies motherhood, nurturing, and growth, and she provides The Fool with an awareness of his surroundings. The Empress teaches him that not only can a person draw from the world's natural abundance, but they can also impact the world with an idea or sense of purpose. The Fool begins to develop his earthly senses, which aids him in the continuation of his journey.

IV - The Emperor

The Fool's next encounter is with The Emperor. The Emperor embodies fatherhood and material mastery. He is the complementary partner to The Empress and shows The Fool how the world's resources can be cultivated. The Emperor is powerful, but also represents The Fool's first interaction with the concept of limitation. He teaches The Fool that rules and discipline create a sound basis from which power can thrive. The Fool becomes aware of the importance of self-regulation, and the risks associated with excess.

V - The Hierophant

As he continues his journey, The Fool meets The Hierophant. The Hierophant introduces The Fool to a defined body of beliefs, traditions, and continuities. He teaches The Fool to accept regulation as a means of providing stability and structure. The establishment of doctrines, moralities and other principles gives recognition, replication, and reassurance to The Fool, and to others he may encounter in his journey. The Fool departs his encounter with The Hierophant having begun a process of maturity beyond that of a child. He now understands that being among others is a concept that can exist in parallel with his own sense of identity and that rules and structure provide safety.

VI - The Lovers

With the development of The Fool's early maturity and a growing awareness of his earthly senses, the desire to connect with others begins to emerge. He has seen from The Magician and The High Priestess, plus The Empress and The Emperor, that partnership with others can create a harmony of co-existence. The Fool learns at his stop at The Lovers that relationships and intimacy create a blended impact on each participant.

He learns that practical considerations are important, and when a person ceases to travel alone, they take on the joys and burdens that their companion brings to the relationship. The Fool's lesson at The Lovers is to consider all that he is so far, and to choose his partnerships with consideration of the consequences to follow.

VII - The Chariot

The Fool has almost reached adulthood when his journey takes him to The Chariot. What remains of his youthfulness is an arrogant unawareness of just how different his journey may have been so far, when compared to the journey of others. By respecting diversity and seeking compromise solutions, The Fool learns that he can gain agreement on how to move forward in a way that will benefit everyone's journey. So far, The Fool's life path has been smooth. Should he encounter challenges later in his journey, his ability to gain the trust of others and to negotiate positive outcomes will aid in his safe passage.

VIII - Strength

The Fool has discovered that there is comfort in traveling with others. However, at times he will also need to travel alone. Self-reliance and personal fortitude are virtues that cannot be borrowed from others, and it is necessary to draw courage and resilience from within.

As The Fool advances forward, the journey will become littered with obstacles and complications. These are tests of Strength. To continue beyond each obstacle, he must learn to take note of his anguish but find ways to press on regardless. The lessons of Strength include self-adjustment, tolerance, and perseverance. By learning to overcome setbacks and challenges, The Fool emerges from his encounter with Strength, an adult.

IX - The Hermit

The Fool continues his journey as an adult who has developed a mature view of the material world. There is much to reflect upon, and the questions about life that begin to emerge are proof of a developing mind. The Fool pauses at The Hermit to consider all that he has encountered so far, and how the experiences have given him knowledge, but also leave him with a complexity of unanswered questions. He asks himself, "what is the purpose of this journey, what is the purpose of this life?"

The Hermit teaches lessons of solitude and reflection. As The Fool reflects on what he knows, and questions what he is yet to learn, he discovers that to continue forward he must recognize and adopt the virtue of prudent deliberation of that which exists so that he may gather wisdom from his experiences.

X - Wheel of Fortune

At this point in his journey, The Fool has focused on the outer, material domain, where the manifestation of earthly desires, and influence over the world around him are dominant aspects of life. Now The Fool must enter Wheel of Fortune, the constantly revolving propellant of his fate, which takes in all that he has encountered, all that he has learned, and combines it into a directional force that will determine how next to proceed in his journey. Wheel of Fortune teaches The Fool that his destiny is comprised of one part circumstance, and one part free will. How The Fool has journeyed so far will determine his direction moving forward.

XI - Justice

The Fool's journey so far has given him the adult perspective that is born from living through experiences, good and bad, that shape who he has become in the material or earthly sense. Now it is time for him to appear before Justice, so that he can gain a clear insight into the path he has travelled so far. The Fool must face the consequences of all that he has left in his wake. Has he caused others to suffer? Has he absorbed the two essential virtues presented by Strength and The Hermit? Will The Fool absorb the virtue of clear-eyed and fair evaluation of himself before he departs the material world and embarks on the spiritual leg of his journey?

XII - *The Hanged Man*

The Fool's encounter with Justice has put his journey into full perspective and turned his material existence upside down. He hangs in suspension as he awaits the next leg of his journey. All that he has become has been handed over for clear-eyed evaluation. The Fool's only possession that remains is his free will, and there is only one decision left to make before he can move forward. The decision to surrender to his fate. The lesson that takes The Fool forward from materialism and into a spiritual realm, is to know that by being fair, and contributing himself supportively to those around him, he opens the door for the world to reciprocate in kind. This awareness gives The Fool a sense of serenity, and a willingness to let go and accept whatever may come next.

XIII - *Death*

So far in his journey, The Fool has been able to indulge his desire for material comforts. His departure from the material realm now requires that he relinquish the unnecessary load of an earthly existence. Material burdens, longings and possessions are forgotten, they are no longer of value. Aspects of The Fool's past are left behind, so that he may continue forward with abundant intention. All that was once a familiar comfort, foregone in The Fool's quest for a new beginning, and transition towards spiritual fulfilment.

XIV - *Temperance*

The Fool began with his free will, which at first was unconstrained. As his journey progressed, he began to encounter deliberation turnpikes, obstacles and challenges that taught him to consider his virtues. The fourth and final lesson of virtue is that of Temperance. The highs and lows that The Fool has encountered teaches him that moderation, balance and the considered restraint of primal impulses will enable him to get the remainder of his journey right. The biggest and most challenging tests are yet to come. Learning to acknowledge his heart but lead with his conscious mind will give The Fool the tools needed to navigate the remainder of his journey.

XV - The Devil

The Fool has come a long way in his journey. He has discovered his conscious and unconscious powers to manifest desires and impact the world around him. He has learned to co-exist with others, recognize their sameness, and respect diversity. He has learned courage, self-reflection, fairness, and moderation. The Fool must now encounter The Devil, an imposing force that feeds on complacency and bad habits. The moment The Fool lets his guard down, The Devil unexpectedly confronts him. The Devil evokes negative forces such as hopelessness and temptation, which reside within every person. It takes constant vigilance to keep the forces dormant. The Fool's sense of serenity becomes one of complacency, which now provides an opportunity for The Devil's negative forces to rise within him. The result is an obstruction of the light that illuminates The Fool's way forward. The Devil feeds on toxic people, materialistic excesses, and the enslavement to habits that may take The Fool off his path towards spiritual fulfilment. The only way for The Fool to pass beyond The Devil is to deny him, and instead focus on each of the lessons that he has already learned from his journey. Without sustenance, The Devil begins to wither, exposing a splinter of light in the distance, into which The Fool may pass.

XVI - The Tower

The Fool's encounter with The Devil came, as it always does, as a surprise. It caused him to lose his footing, and in doing so, his journey takes him to The Tower. The encounter is one of intense turmoil, threatening to become a catastrophe. The Fool is powerless to prevent the chaos of this moment. There is nothing that he can do, and so, he does nothing. Instead, The Fool allows himself to let go completely and become wholeheartedly committed to his fate. By releasing himself from the egotistical pursuit of believing that he has the power to control everything, The Fool experiences a revelation and realizes that there is more to the existence of life than that which any person may know.

XVII - *The Star*

The Fool's release of egoism brings him to The Star. Despite his vivid memory of all he has encountered, The Fool emerges from troubling times and can see the positivity that awaits him, beyond any challenges he could face. The Fool is hopeful and believes that every experience of his journey, even the encounters that presented obstacles to overcome, were merely the prelude to another chance to complete his journey. The Star teaches The Fool that peace and optimism are always within reach.

XVIII – *The Moon*

The Fool sees his destination, The Sun, up ahead. His encounters so far have taught him to believe in the direction of his path, and his ability to reach his destination. However, as he approaches, The Moon also appears in the sky and begins to eclipse The Sun. For a moment, The Fool becomes disoriented. He can no longer see his destination; the sky is dark without The Sun's illumination. The Fool acknowledges this moment of uncertainty, along with the anxiety it may bring. Nonetheless, The Fool presses on, because although he can no longer see proof of his knowledge, he still knows.

The Moon teaches The Fool that unlike The Tower, which is a single calamity that comes and then goes, his journey through life will also present a series of ongoing deceptions, illusions, and attempted exploitations. He is The Fool, and to protect himself from vulnerability, he must remember and practice each of the lessons he has learned from his journey, in the way that may appear throughout his life.

IXX - *The Sun*

The Fool has succeeded in reaching his destination. The Sun greets him with a smiling face. The long and winding path it took to arrive at his destination seems an effortless instant. The Fool is revitalized, content, and blessed.

XX - *Judgement*

The Fool has completed his journey and takes measurement of all he has become in the process. The good and the bad have revealed a method of discovery, of the material world in which he lives, the spiritual world that makes it possible, and of The Fool himself. Ego dissolves and forgiveness takes over. The Fool is reborn.

XXI - *The World*

The Fool has journeyed through his existence and come to realize that he is no fool at all. And so, it becomes clear that the end of every journey is merely the beginning of another.

CHAPTER 8

THE FOOL

If you have been patient enough to begin to read this book from the beginning, you will already understand the importance of considering individual cards as sitting within the context of a journey

along the path determined not only by fate, but also by free will. The Fool card is the immediate example of this point.

It is the journey of The Fool that will help you to gain the most fundamental understanding of tarot, the system of tarot as an illustrative metaphor for the journey of life, and the need to balance emotional impulses against a restrained mindfulness.

Prior to the development of the Rider-Waite tarot deck, The Fool remained unnumbered. Pamela Coleman Smith added the number zero to the card, which was adapted in publications to be either zero (0) or twenty-two (XXII). This book focuses on the standard modern print version of the deck, which depicts The Fool as zero. The Fool card was always intended by the creators of the Rider-Waite deck, to remain distinct from the other twenty-two cards of the Major Arcana suite, to reflect the card's unique role in tarot as a symbol of unlimited possibilities, infinite potential and a blank slate that is free to become anything.

The Fool card differs from other Major Arcana cards, all of which are labelled using roman numerals. The Fool is numbered zero, which is of Arabic derivation. As we progress through the symbolism of each card within the deck you will begin to see a pattern forming in this regard, in that the Rider Waite deck makes generous use of different languages and beliefs to exquisitely describe The Fool's journey with a series of symbols and images. This is not a haphazard decision on the part of the deck's creators, but a subtle reminder that all of us, regardless of where we come from or what we believe, experience a journey through life. The Fool's journey has just begun, and so its progression point is zero.

First impression

A young man steps forward, or backward, upon the precipice. He is casually, or shabbily dressed, and appears relaxed, innocent, naïve in his demeanor. He has stockinged feet, and a feather in his cap. He carries a white rose in one hand and a stick in the other. Tied to the stick is a small sack of the young man's possessions, which are few. An excited dog tries to get his attention nearby. Above him is a white-hot sun, and below is the ravage mountains or sea.

Basic Definitions

In the upright position, The Fool represents taking a risk, gaining a fresh perspective, and possessing faith in the universe.

In the reverse position, The Fool represents foolishness, keeping bad company, and making unwise decisions.

Interpretation of symbols

This book examines each card from a variety of vantage points, consisting of the macro point, in which the dominant colors, symbolized proportions and general mood of the card are explained. A closer, micro examination also takes account of individual symbols that appear in each card. This may help you, the reader, to absorb the overall intention of individual cards. Absorption of new knowledge is a far easier and more sustainable way to learn, than attempting to memorize individual components.

In the first instance, the Fool Card contains a high percentage of yellow. The central character is a young man, almost surrounded by sky, indicating a deeply immersed experience of human consciousness. His awareness is heightened, and he is ready to learn and grow from everything he is subsequently exposed to in his journey. The proportionate largeness of the central figure relates to the young man's sense of self, which is likely to be the very first and only thing of which he is aware.

A white, oversized sun shines near the young man's head, its rays partially penetrating the meagre belongings he has tethered to a stick. The closeness of the sun, yellow sky and cliff face all hint at potential danger, should something go wrong. The whiteness of the sun shows an empty mind, lack of forethought, or purity of spirit. The small and humble sack of possessions alludes to a lack of life experiences, and an equal lack of emotional baggage.

The blue and white landscape may be mountainous range, or icy waters. They represent the adrenalin thrill of embarking on something new, which is pure and without ulterior motive. The peaks of the icy horizon reach towards the heavens, denoting limitless possibilities, idealistic outcomes, or potential dangers ahead.

The young man's life force appears as the red feather he wears upon his head. Throughout The Fool's journey, look out for changes in the appearance of this symbol of life force. In this image, the young man's life force denotes vibrancy and optimism, and points towards the heat of the sun as if to declare a lack of fear or even awareness of its existence.

The Sun is The Fool's intended destination in his journey; however, this young man is facing the opposite direction. His colorful, patterned clothing combines red, white, green, and black, denoting enthusiasm, innocence, freshness, and mystery, respectively. He may not know where he is going, or he does not care. His posture is open and inviting, and he appears oblivious to the potential dangers that surround him. His stockinged feet and the white rose in his hand reinforce the idea that this young man is naïve, which may derive from innocence, or equally correlate to arrogance.

An enthusiastic small white dog rears up to gain the young man's attention. There is a possibility that the dog is attempting to warn the man of potential dangers, but an equal possibility exists that the dog is trying to distract the man.

When The Fool card appears in reverse, the positioning of certain symbols changes. The dog appears above the man, demonstrating that he may be falling for a distraction, or following the directions of a dog. There is a shift in perspective. Innocence is more likely to become foolishness, with all its trappings.

Symbols matching other Major Arcana cards.

Where relevant, symbols in The Fool are also in other Major Arcana cards. A dog also appears in The Moon. A white rose appears in Death. A sun appears in The Lovers, Temperance, Death, The Moon, and The Sun. A red feather appears in The Sun and Death. A yellow sky appears in The Magician, The Empress, The Chariot, Strength, and Justice.

Overall theme

The overall theme of a card is the generalized message that may apply to a single card spread. The overall theme of The Fool is as follows:

The journey has just begun, and so far, the load is light. It is time to move forward from zero, relying on instinct. The path of a lifetime awaits you and as you step toward your destiny there will be choices to make, each of which takes you one step closer to a positive or negative outcome. This is only the first of these choices, and the choice is yours.

CHAPTER 9

THE MAGICIAN

Just as we may observe during a magic show, The Magician card represents the manifestation of outcome that may otherwise appear to be impossible. The Magician draws his manifesting power from all

THE MAGICIAN.

four Minor Arcana suites of the tarot deck. His powers are unconstrained, other than by the limitations of confidence, inspiration, and desire that he may possess.

The first numbered card in the Major Arcana, The Magician, represents a readiness to manifest an unlimited range of desires, by unifying the physical and spiritual realms. The Magician reminds us that the universe is a single being, and all which exists in the universe is merely a component of a single creation.

To consider The Magician in context of the journey, he once travelled as The Fool and possesses a primal readiness and potential to manifest as conduit between earth and heaven. He is yet to arrive at the wisdom of the High Priestess, and the commitments he has made to his passions may be ego-based or selfish.

First impression

A man stands upright with limbs extended to demonstrate his vitality. One hand points to the ground, the other hand holds a double-ended white wand which points to the sky. The man wears a white robe with red mantle, he looks directly at whomever looks directly at him. On the table before him are a wand, sword, pentacle, and cup, which represent the elements of fire, air, earth, and water respectfully. Above and below him are roses and lilies and the background is clear, but for the yellow rays of the sun.

Basic Definitions

In the upright position, The Magician represents confidence, magic, and having the tools, resources, and power to manifest at will.

In the reverse position, The Magician represents deception and trickery. There may be a lack of empathy, or a personality disorder to consider.

Interpretation of symbols

The proportion of yellow sky has increased beyond that of The Fool card, indicating that the man in this scene has an increased awareness of his own power to manifest.

The Magician is the first encounter in The Fool's journey, and there have been no prior experiences to temper a highly active ego or sense of self. This is neither a positive nor a negative inference about The Magician himself. Rather, it is an example of the limitations of the card's range of definitions. There is a sense of self, with no consideration for what sits outside of self.

Each of the four earthly elements sits atop a table. They are readily available and within reach, demonstrating the vast potential for good, or evil. An infinity symbol floats in suspension above the man's head, and a serpent belt wraps around his waist. These two symbols provide a perpetual cycle of balance. Alternatively, they may denote repetition or obsession.

The man's red and white robes demonstrate that he is inexperienced, but enthusiastic. There may also be a practical or material connection to the earth. The man's posture is alert and forward-facing. He points a double-ended wand upward towards the sky with one hand, and down towards the ground with the other hand. This makes him appear as though a conduit between heaven and earth. The double-ended wand possesses the power to manifest heaven (or hell) based outcomes. The man's headband represents the mind and the manifestation of thoughts. Overall, The Magician is a character who unifies the spiritual mystery of heaven with the material reality of earth. He is aware of himself and his power.

The red roses and white lilies in The Magician provide a filter between material and spiritual, earthbound, or heavenly. The roses represent passion, growth, and transformation. The lilies offer innocence, purity, but are also the flower denoting the return of innocence after death. Their relevance as a filter beneath The Magician may imply a selfishness or isolation when the card is in reverse.

Symbols matching other Major Arcana cards.
Where relevant, symbols in The Magician are also in other Major Arcana cards. The infinity symbol appears in Strength. A serpent appears in The Lovers and Wheel of Fortune. A magic wand appears in The Chariot and The World. Red clothing appears in The Emperor, The Hierophant and Justice. Roses appear in The Hierophant and Strength. Lilies appear in The Hierophant. A yellow sky appears in The Fool, The Empress, The Chariot, Strength, and Justice.

Overall theme
The overall theme of a card is the generalized message that may apply to a single card spread. The overall theme of The Magician is as follows:

You are the conduit of energy which you draw beneath you from the earth, and above you from heaven. It is a time for action and your opportunity to transform. Harness your skills and step confidently into the power you possess. Beware of tricksters, manipulators, and repetitive cycles.

CHAPTER 10

THE HIGH PRIESTESS

Our lives of earthbound existence serve as a constant reminder of the perceptions of polarity and individualism that distinguish us from each other and persist in keeping us divided.

The High Priestess card reminds us that we possess within our reach, source theologies and undiscovered realities, which demonstrate that all things are simply a varied and diverse representation of a single creation. There is more to life and our existence than what we know.

There is no other card in the Rider Waite deck that better illustrates the theory of a single creator than The High Priestess. This card embodies mystery, intuition, and inner wisdom, representing the divine feminine and our connection to feelings, instinctive truths, and the awareness of what lies beyond our own sense of self.

First impression

A woman sits upright between two stone lettered pillars. Behind her is a veil of palm trees and pomegranates which obscures the scene beyond it. Her horned headdress encases a full moon, and the crescent moon also rests at her feet. The woman wears a large cross affixed to her blue and white robes and holds a lettered scroll in her lap.

Basic definitions

In the upright position, the High Priestess represents intuition, knowledge, secrets, and mystery. There is a sense of looking within, for answers not found in the material realm.

In the reverse position, the High Priestess represents experiencing a release or reveal of tightly held secrets, or an emergence from depression. There may be issues with confidence, or an element of superficiality. The card may also indicate a predatory risk.

Interpretation of symbols

In contrast to its predecessor cards, The High Priestess card includes a clear blue sky. The sky's color relates to truth being ever-present. However, a veil of pomegranates and palm trees obscures the sky, as an expression of hidden truths or unsolved mysteries. What sits beyond the veil is the other world, beyond the reach or comprehension of a material-focused mind.

The central character is a woman, sitting in a relaxed but attentive pose, looking directly forward. She is wearing flowing blue and white robes and a full moon headdress. There is also a crescent moon positioned at her feet. The moon features and color of the robes, relate to the rhythm of the moon and tides, life's cycles or stages, the mysteries of darkness and the night, and the potency of spiritual awareness and the subconscious. The prevalence of blue and white in the woman's clothing also points to her as a character of truth and virginity.

The pillars on either side of the woman are lettered B and J. The letters are a reference to Boaz and Jachin, two pillars that once stood outside the First Temple of Jerusalem, as written in the Old Testament. The pillars are of importance to Masonic principles and teachings. They represent spiritual development, self-discovery, and personal growth. Most Masonic temples include representative pillars within their architecture.

The comparison of black and white coloring in the pillars is a layer of symbolism referred to as Yin and Yang, which is a Chinese philosophy of opposite but interconnected or balancing forces. This is a reference to the material and spiritual realms being unified and counterbalanced against one another in perfect alliance. Also, the relationship between the conscious and subconscious mind.

The lettered scroll shows the letters T O R A, which is a reference to the Torah, the sacred Jewish text. There is an inference that the woman has the knowledge of life in her hands or resting in her lap. She also wears a cross against her chest, demonstrating a deep spiritual faith, and awareness of religious values.

Symbols matching other Major Arcana cards.

Where relevant, symbols in The High Priestess are also in other Major Arcana cards. Pillars appear in The Hierophant and Justice. Pomegranates appear in The Empress. A moon appears in The Moon.

Overall theme

The overall theme of a card is the generalized message that may apply to a single card spread. The overall theme of The High Priestess is as follows:

You are what you know, believe, understand, value, trust, inquire of and reveal to yourself.

CHAPTER 11

THE EMPRESS

The archetype of fertility and abundance, The Empress often appears as a pregnant woman or is dressed and positioned in way as to imply pregnancy. Third card in the Major Arcana, The

Empress represents creation, womanhood, enterprise, and matriarchy. Representative of feminine strength, The Empress has the power to create and provide comfort. She wears as her gown, the pomegranates that once appeared as a veil by the High Priestess, to obscure that which is beyond our material world.

First impression

A young woman sits comfortably within a paradise of natural abundance. Her relaxed pose is supported by a cushion. A field of corn grows at her feet. A lush forest of trees stretches to the sky behind her, divided by a river that cascades into a waterfall.

Basic definitions

In the upright position, The Empress represents a new enterprise, fertility, motherhood, a dominant female, sensuality, growth, and abundance.

In the reverse position, The Empress represents famine or drought, smothering, neglect, vanity, infidelity, and failure.

Interpretation of symbols

The Empress card provides a sensory delight of color and creativity. Apart from the clear yellow sky, the entire card contains details of majesty, abundance, and generosity. The yellow sky relates to conscious awareness. It may provide a sense of the sun's warmth and its role in giving life to the natural abundance of earth.

The central figure is a young woman surrounded by a lush forestry, flowing river, and a field of corn. The landscape provides a blend of natural, free flowing beauty with a cultivated outcome. The message is one of nurture, replenishment, and successful or abundant harvest. The woman is comfortably resting against red and orange cushions. She wears a loose-fitting gown of pomegranates. These aspects of the card suggest that the woman is pregnant. The colors and flowers hint at warmth, passion, lifeblood, and fertility. There is a promise of blooming possibilities and the conception of something new.

The heart-shaped stone is a symbol of Venus and womanhood, impartial love, and the feminine spirit. However, upon closer inspection, the card demonstrates that there is more to The Empress than simply her roles of motherhood and nurturer of others. In her right hand she holds a gold scepter which she points towards the sky. Atop her head is a laurel wreath and crown of twelve stars. A string of seven pearls adorns her neck.

The scepter is a sign of the power that the woman yields, and specifically, the power of her youth and/or sexuality. The laurel wreath pertains to success and peaceful attainment of outcomes. The twelve stars of the crown coincide with the twelve months of the year, the astrological cycle, and may also be a reference to the coronation of the

Virgin Mary.

The woman's pearl necklace connects her earthly existence to heavenly wisdom. The necklace may relate to the seven classical planets, or the seven major chakras.

When The Empress card is reversed, the sky becomes a foundation of yellow that may depict sentiments of jealousy or greed. Every natural beauty within the card is at risk of transforming into a contrived vanity. There is an implied suffering, derived from abandonment, overwhelming restrictions, or failure to produce a successful outcome.

Symbols matching other Major Arcana cards.

Where relevant, symbols in The Empress are also in other Major Arcana cards. A laurel wreath also appears in The Chariot and The World. A yellow sky appears in The Fool, The Magician, The Chariot, Strength, and Justice. Pomegranates appear in The High Priestess.

Overall theme

The overall theme of a card is the generalized message that may apply to a single card spread. The overall theme of The Empress is as follows:

You are a goddess and possess the gift of creation and abundant harvest. You nurture and love, provide security and material comfort. You embody the feminine spirit inherited by the mother, grandmother, and a lengthy line of female ancestry. Life overflows with what you choose to embrace with a generous heart.

CHAPTER 12

THE EMPEROR

The Emperor is the fourth card in the Major Arcana suite and one of only three cards in which a bearded man appears. The Emperor represents the archetypal father, a symbol of male ego, virility, and power. He is a complement to The Empress that came before him and draws from opposite but interconnected elements as revealed by The High Priestess. The emperor's white beard establishes him as precursor to the nineth Major Arcana card (The Hermit) in The Fool's journey. He is positioned at the top of the secular hierarchy (ruler of the world) in the Rider Waite deck, just one card away from The Hierophant.

First impression

A mature man sits upright in a stark, high-backed, throne of stone. His posture is alert, as though ready to activate at a moment's notice. The background appears desert-like, with orange sky, and mountainous rocks devoid of vegetation.

Basic definitions

In the upright position, The Emperor represents rules and structure, organization and control, dominance, masculinity, security, and power.

In the reverse position, The Emperor represents a dictator or tyrant, obstruction, rigidity, misuse of power, greed, and excessive behaviors.

Interpretation of symbols

The Emperor primarily suggests that its central figure is a man who commands authority over his surroundings. In contrast to The Empress, who appears relaxed and surrounded by natural abundance, The Emperor sits upright and alert to everything around him. His white beard denotes wisdom and authority, and the rectangular shapes of his stone throne provide a sense of orderly conduct, controlling tendencies and stark materialism.

There is little detail in the card to detract from the imposing central figure, and this accentuates the significance of the masculine presence that dominates the card. This may be reassuring and denotes a strong protective presence when the card is upright. However, in reverse, it may translate into arrogance and egoism.

The imposing rock faces in the background give the landscape a desolate atmosphere. However, the height of the rocks also gives the impression of a hazardous mountainous range, providing security and protection from outside threats. The orange and gold tones of both rock and sky, along with the man's deep red attire, are all features of majesty, male virility, and momentum.

The man wears a suit of armor beneath the fabric of his clothing. The armor represents ability, chivalry, preparedness, and protection, when the card is upright. However, in reverse, there may also be a severity or inflexibility that relates to excessive restrictions or dominance.

Each corner of the man's throne includes a carved ram's head. This is a symbol which represents godly figures of ancient Egyptian mythology. The most relevant of these figures is Khnum, the ancient god of the River Nile, and of fertility and creation. Ancient Egyptians believed that Khnum created human bodies from clay on his potter's wheel and then placed them in their mother's wombs. He was also associated with the annual flooding of the Nile, which brought fertility to the land and allowed human settlement, development of the land, and commercial enterprise to occur in the Nile region. Khnum was consistently associated with the ram's head in Egyptian mythology, and his divine power is suggested in the slender stream of water that appears in The Emperor, along with the color of the rock face, which takes on the orange appearance of clay when it is affected by iron oxide.

However, rather than simply a suggestion of correlation with the ancient god Khnum, The Emperor provides an even stronger link with the inclusion of the emperor's golden crown, scepter, and globe. The head of the golden scepter is an ankh cross, which is the ancient Egyptian symbol for key to life and male sexuality. The golden globe represents power, domination, and secular hierarchy, and the crown refers to autonomy, self-governance, and materialism.

Collectively, the subtle suggestion of iron in clay rock formation, along with the supremacy features of specific golden symbols, provides The Emperor with the creative powers of Khnum, the material substance from which to harness the most barren earth, and the regenerative influences of water. The implication therein is that The Emperor has the ability and the passion to grow, and reign over, a powerful material empire, which he created from even the most challenging physical environments.

Whoever finds themselves under the guard of The Emperor can rest assured of being well protected when the card is upright. However, in reverse, The Emperor's powers can be overwhelming, oppressive, or authoritarian.

Symbols matching other Major Arcana cards.

Where relevant, symbols in The Emperor are also in other Major Arcana cards. A grey beard also appears in The Hermit. Armor appears in The Chariot. Red robes appear in The Magician, The Hierophant, and Justice. Crowns appear in The High Priestess, The Empress, The Hierophant, The Chariot, Justice, Death, and The Tower. Rectangular features appear in The Chariot, Temperance, and The Devil.

Overall theme

The overall theme of a card is the generalized message that may apply to a single card spread. The overall theme of The Emperor is as follows:

You are a pioneer in the world, unafraid to stake your claim and cultivate your environment. Your power is tempered by your ability to self-regulate your ego. You create order and follow your ambition with vigor and without fear. You embody the male spirit inherited by the father, grandfather, and a lengthy line of male ancestry. You explore new possibilities and remain undaunted. Despite the desert, you will grow a garden to harvest for those who rely on your protection and the security you provide.

CHAPTER 13

THE HIEROPHANT

The fifth Major Arcana card in the Rider Waite deck is The Hierophant. The immediate significance of The Hierophant is the progression it represents in The Fool's journey from secular dominance, towards a knowledge attained from within the spiritual realm.

The Hierophant is historically a reference to the position, power, and dignity of the Pope during the 15th and 16th centuries. Unquestionably believed to be God's human representative on Earth, papal influence over royalty, military and politics was a key aspect of the Italian Renaissance period.

The Hierophant draws from non-secular wisdom and pontification and travels beyond The Emperor's command of Earth, into the aspiration of spirituality. The Hierophant's position within the journey of life is yet to encounter the healing power of the soul, so whilst it may include elements of wisdom and kindness, it may also present elements of superficiality, dogma, and ostentation.

64

First impression

An apostolic figure sits between two grey columns. His left hand holds a gold scepter, and his right hand offers a blessing for two worshipers who kneel before him.

Basic Definitions

In the upright position, The Hierophant represents religion, spirituality, government, prominence or influence, and guidance or a path of greater learning.

In the reverse position, The Hierophant represents rejecting established ideas, rebelliousness, expulsion, and having ulterior motives.

Interpretation of symbols

The Hierophant speaks of establishing a societal framework, whether it be spiritual, religious, or governmental. The central figure acts as a representative of something higher than himself. He is not a ruler, despite his prominence among those over which he presides. For this reason, it may appear as though he sits upon a throne, like each of the King and Queen cards, plus The Emperor and Justice cards. However, unlike the Kings and Queens, the presiding figure in The Hierophant does not control his environment. Unlike the Kings and Queens of the Rider-Waite tarot deck, he has no kingdom to rule over. Unlike The Emperor, he has not conquered his material surroundings, and unlike Justice, he is not the highest form of justice in the court to which he presides. For this reason, what people sometimes assume to be a throne is a headstone. The telltale sign of the lack of armrest that appears in each of the cards for which a ruling force is the central figure. The presiding figure in The Hierophant has a job to do on behalf of the one who rules over others.

The Hierophant interprets and shares sacred mysteries as God's highest representative on Earth. This is evidenced by his papal crown and three-crossed scepter. The crossed keys that sit at his feet are the keys to the Kingdom of Heaven that Jesus gave Saint Peter, as described in Matthew 16:19 of the Bible.

The Hierophant appears as an exemplary example of humanity, righteous and open to God's wisdom, as illustrated by the predominance of V-shapes in the imagery. Righteousness differs from virtue, demonstrated by the creators of the card elevating The Hierophant's standing among men, on account of his service to God, rather than by him possessing any of the four essential virtues attributed to Strength, The Hermit, Justice, and Temperance. This aligns with biblical scripture in which righteousness refers to being morally right or justifiable in the eyes of God. It encompasses living in accordance with God's will and commandments.

The figure's red and blue robes denote his energy and passion, but also the pageantry or idolization of traditional frameworks. To visualize this aspect of the card's imagery, consider the elaborate ceremonies that align to pagan rituals, religious holidays, or official events of State. The elaborate spectacle indicates passion and faith, but it can also become a pompous or dogmatic evidence of idolization of the establishment, rather than what it represents.

Two worshipers or acolytes sit with their rear profiles visible. They represent the transfer of sacred knowledge, and the path towards education and greater learning. Their shaved heads demonstrate an openness to receive, and the central figure offers them a blessing with his right hand, or a warning. The gesture points two fingers upward, towards righteousness, and downward, towards damnation. The worshipers wear robes of lilies and roses, denoting purity, and truth.

The overall message of The Hierophant is that of humanity forming the governing or faith-based structures that include esteemed representatives who bring them together into a single collective entity of laws, rules, traditions, and beliefs. The inference of these structures is that they provide security, safety, and collective identity, in which the differences between people is superseded by what they share. The grey impartiality and safety implied by the solid stone structures and colorless sky reinforce this ideal.

Symbols matching other Major Arcana cards.

Where relevant, symbols in The Hierophant are also in other Major Arcana cards. Red robes also appear in The Magician, The Emperor and Justice. Crowns appears in the High Priestess, The Empress, The Emperor, The Chariot, Strength, Justice, and The Tower. Lilies and Roses appear in The Magician.

Overall theme

The overall theme of a card is the generalized message that may apply to a single card spread. The overall theme of The Hierophant is as follows:

You possess the key to proclaiming what is sacred. To unlock the door, you must first accept with an open heart and settle yourself within a pattern of recognizable truths.

CHAPTER 14

THE LOVERS

The Lovers is the first depiction of male-female unification in the Major Arcana suite. As we gain life experience, we come to realize that the partners we choose to accompany us in our life journey also contribute to the outcomes derived from our decision. Wise choices in love can result in blissful happiness and shared success. Unwise choices often end in heartache, betrayal, or even abandonment.

So says The Lovers, the sixth Major Arcana card. The Lovers represents decision-making and the importance of careful consideration to avoid potentially negative, lifelong, implications. Historically, The Lovers represents two-halves of a single soul and often appears as a turning point reference in tarot card spreads.

First impression

A naked man and woman stand on either side of a paradise garden, separated by a dark cloud and pointed mountain. An angel in violet robe and with red outstretched wings, presides over their union. Directly above, a massive sun fills the sky.

Basic definitions

In the upright position, The Lovers represents relationships and unions, joining two as one, life changing choices, and a turning point moment.

In the reverse position, The Lovers represents relationship failure, negative consequences, untrue love, betrayal, and stalking.

Interpretation of symbols

The Lovers is one of only few cards in the Rider-Waite tarot deck that includes nudity. Nudity in its artistic form relates to a tasteful interpretation of the human body, unclothed. This is the case in each of the Rider-Waite cards that include unclothed human figures. However, The Lovers also provides context for nakedness, which differs from nudity in distinct ways.

Nakedness depicts openness, innocence, vulnerability, power, and at times, shamelessness. All these interpretations may be relevant to either the naked man or woman in The Lovers. Despite being naked, the man looks directly at the woman. Near to the man is a tree with twelve flame-shaped leaves. The structure of the tree tells us that it is the Tree of Life.

The Tree of Life is a symbol that appears in various cultures and religions. The twelve leaves carry a variety of meanings, including the twelve months of the year, or the twelve signs of the zodiac, symbolizing the passage of time, and the cyclical nature of life. The flame-like appearance of the leaves signifies enlightenment and spiritual growth, as would result from a positive union.

The Kabbalistic Tree of Life presents the twelve leaves to mean the twelve tribes of Israel or the twelve apostles, which similarly symbolizes a connection to spiritual enlightenment, interconnectedness, and growth. The proximity of the tree pertains to the Male Principle or traditionally male behaviors, social structures, and physique. Consider the man's nakedness, his direct gaze towards the woman, and the proximity of the tree, and the overall message is one of male virility, power, and the initiation of a union. The man may also be vulnerable, as it relates to the power or influence that the woman has over him in her naked state.

The woman is also naked. She is looking up towards the angel, demonstrating that she does not have any deliberate intentions in the card, and does not even see the naked man standing before her. She is a passive recipient of any advancement, rather than the initiator. The tree near the woman is the Tree of Knowledge that appears in the Bible. This is confirmed by the appearance of a serpent that has wrapped itself around the tree and is whispering in the woman's ear.

The proximity of the Tree of Knowledge pertains to the Female Principle or traditionally female behaviors, social structures, and physique. The four fruits on the tree relate to the four classic earth elements. The serpent references the fall of Adam and Eve in the Garden of Eden, demonstrating that good and evil coexist. The decisions we make, the temptations we succumb to, and the company that we keep are the dividing lines between the two.

Other symbols exist in The Lovers to reinforce its central messages. The size and positioning of the sun and presiding angel relate to warmth, love, unity, and connection to the highest realm. The angel's violet robes and red wings use the colors red and blue in ways that symbolize innocence, truth, new beginnings, and passion. The high points of the mountain depict a heavenly union and the power of two people combining their strengths. However, when the card is in reverse the mountain may represent major challenges to a relationship, a nasty breakup, insurmountable obstacles, or an impossible match. Similarly, the dark clouds may obscure the truth, leading to betrayals in a relationship, unclear motives, and distorted perceptions.

The Lovers card is often underappreciated in its depiction of relationships and unions. Choosing to become united with another, whether in love, friendship or business provides a turning point towards a future that is yet unknown.

Symbols matching other Major Arcana cards.
Where relevant, symbols in The Lovers are also in other Major Arcana cards. A presiding angel also appears in Temperance and Judgement.

Nudity appears in The Devil, The Star, The Sun, Judgement, and The World. A serpent appears in The Magician and The Wheel of Fortune. The sun appears in The Fool, Temperance, Death, The Moon, and The Sun.

Overall theme

The overall theme of a card is the generalized message that may apply to a single card spread. The overall theme of The Lovers is as follows:

Your paradise union exists within the sun, and the soul who matches yours will know of practicality as the way toward blissful union. It is most practical to learn to know yourself first and to place expectations on another to know you second.

CHAPTER 15

THE CHARIOT

As the seventh Major Arcana card in the Rider Waite deck, The Chariot draws from each of its predecessor cards and appears as a culmination of The Fool's journey so far. Its purpose is to remind us that we each head towards a karmic outcome. Our path in life is determined by the past experiences we draw from during our journey. It is important, therefore, to learn from our prior experiences.

First impression

A young man of strength stands encased within a stone chariot. To his front are two sphinxes, both resting. Behind him lies a city, amidst a cultivated garden and flowing river.

Basic Definitions

In the upright position, The Chariot represents mediation, negotiation, determination, autonomy, self-control, and moving progressively forward.

In the reverse position, The Chariot represents stress, failed negotiations, bad business decisions, and misguided ambition.

Interpretation of symbols

The generous proportion of yellow sky indicates that The Chariot is a card of conscious awareness. Indeed, the card represents the lessons learned from The Fool's journey so far. In sequence, the relevant symbols begin with the youthfulness of the central figure, drawn from The Fool. Following this is the wand, which the man holds in his right hand. The wand, along with the man's alert posture, refers to the power to manifest earthly desires and readiness for what comes next, both of which are also present in The Magician.

The High Priestess influences The Chariot by introducing the concepts of cycles, mystery, and the potency of conscious awakenings, along with elements of character and truth. See the crescent moons that appear on the man's lapels, coupled with the blue and white cloth that drapes as a canopy above his head. The stars that appear on the blue cloth add a sense of liberty, independence, and the promise of possibilities ahead.

The laurel wreath and crown appearing in The Empress have reappeared in The Chariot, alongside a fertile landscape. The crown's eight-pointed star is a symbol of Freemasonry, denoting hope, and personal truth. The lessons drawn from The Empress combine with those learned from her complementary card, The Emperor. See the city landscape and orderly natural scene, which demonstrate the rewards achieved through a controlled cultivation of Earth's natural abundance. An abundance of rectangular shapes in The Chariot are reminiscent of The Emperor's controlled management of his environment. They include solid stone structures, towered buildings, and a square pendant on the man's clothing. The Hierophant's influence appears in these structures as well, denoting safe carriage, containment, and rules.

The contrasting colors of the two resting sphinxes draws from the complementary male and female figures that appear in The Lovers and relate to controlled instincts, diversity, and the power of opposites

73

uniting. The sphinxes in The Chariot display a similar reverence to that shown in The Hierophant.

The center of the card includes a crest of blue wings, representing victory when upright, and defeat when reversed. The accompanying red symbol is the Lingham and Yoni, a Hindu representation of unity between male and female, and the birth of something new.

The symbols of The Chariot are a collective statement on controlled instincts, peaceful negotiation, and the appreciation of complementary differences.

Symbols matching other Major Arcana cards.

Where relevant, symbols in The Chariot are also in other Major Arcana cards. Sphinxes appear in The Wheel of Fortune. An eight-pointed star appears in The Star. A magic wand appears in The Magician and The World. A Laurel wreath appears in the Empress and The World. A yellow sky appears in The Fool, The Magician, The Empress, Strength, and Justice. Armor appears in Death. Rectangular features appear in The Emperor, Temperance, and The Devil.

Overall theme

The overall theme of a card is the generalized message that may apply to a single card spread. The overall theme of The Chariot is as follows:

Your courage to face truth, respect differences and reach compromise, sets your guiding path towards shared victory with others.

CHAPTER 16

STRENGTH

The key lesson to learn from developing your deepest understanding of the Rider Waite tarot deck is that none of the imagery appears by chance. Each human figure, its posture, the

STRENGTH.

surrounding landscape, and accompanying symbols, appears for the purpose of communicating a message. It is therefore no accident that the eighth card in the Major Arcana suite is also the one with the greatest percentage of yellow sky.

Strength is a card of advanced consciousness, awareness, and the preparedness to remain open to continuous self-development. Strength is the card of higher purpose, and the last card in the journey towards the prudence of The Hermit.

Strength is also the first card in the Major Arcana Suite to acknowledge one of the four essential virtues. Personal strength is a virtue that empowers a person to face challenges and adversities with courage, resilience, and determination. Personal strength enables a person to stand up for their beliefs, make tough decisions, and persevere in the face of obstacles. Demonstrating strength of character inspires others and fosters a sense of confidence and hope. It contributes to personal growth and the ability to navigate life's complexities with grace and integrity. Personal strength is a virtue that a person must possess themselves. It is neither borrowed from another, nor achieved through outside means.

First impression

A woman adorned with flowers stands with a lion. She holds the lion's open jaw in her hands. The environment around them is a serene and natural landscape, with gentle mountains appearing in the distance.

Basic Definitions

In the upright position, Strength represents patience, compassion, self-awareness, self-development, and possessing the qualities of good leadership.

In the reverse position, Strength represents pettiness, obsession, cruelty, intolerance, mental illness, and disregard for others.

Interpretation of symbols

Here we see a woman dressed in humble attire. Her white robes denote her humility, preference for simplicity, and purity of spirit. There are no buildings, no gold fixtures, and the natural landscape is uncultivated. Instead, the woman is simply present in the moment, with no material factors, or earthly desires, to distract her or elevate her status. This is a sign that she is taking care in the moment, and values equity.

The woman has adorned herself with flowers. The garland of roses around her waist symbolizes her connection to earth, natural things, and the vitality of life. It also represents gentle, nurturing strength that people of good character and leadership quality possess. The flowers appear as a crown in the woman's hair. Note the visual differences between this and the laurel wreath worn by other figures, such as The Empress. This crown of flowers denotes beauty, gentleness, quiet confidence, and a connection to the natural world.

Accompanying the woman is a lion. The lion's orange coloring denotes warmth, vigor, and is a blend of red and yellow. This reinforces the conscious effort to subdue base instincts which may have represented anger if the lion were entirely red.

The woman strokes the lion's head and cups its open mouth with her hands. Despite the physical power and potential for danger that the lion represents, the woman is unafraid. She is calm, and gently keeps the lion under control. Not through brute force. Those who use force against others are compensating for weakness, or lack of leadership skills. True strength involves courage, compassion, and confidence, and derives from inner harmony and balance, rather than from coercion or physical power. Note that the lion is licking the woman's hand as a gesture of affection. As humble as the woman may appear, her method of approaching the lion is effective.

Consider the infinity symbol above the woman's head. It curves as does the number eight, in continuous motion. This also coincides with the number of the card, which is also eight. The symbol represents continuous learning and self-development, and the good fortune that comes from patience and respect towards others. However, when Strength is in reverse, there may be a pattern of repeated mistakes, overthinking, and failure to learn from experiences.

As mentioned earlier, the yellow sky is a dominant feature of Strength, and a reminder that conscious awareness of oneself, plus deliberation, are key to achieving positive outcomes. The predominance of yellow in the card may conversely alert us to the potential risks that are present in the moment. The gentle landscape of lush greens and clear blue are reassuringly calm, but may imply a hidden motive, or wolf in sheep's clothing when the card is in reverse.

Symbols matching other Major Arcana cards.

Where relevant, symbols in Strength are also in other Major Arcana cards. The infinity symbol also appears in The Magician. Orange features also appear in The Emperor. A lion appears in The Wheel of Fortune and The World. Yellow sky appears in The Fool, The Magician, The Empress, The Chariot, and Justice.

Overall theme

The overall theme of a card is the generalized message that may apply to a single card spread. The overall theme of Strength is as follows:

Accept that your base instincts exist, draw determination from your passion, and recognize the same in others, so that you may serve a higher state of purpose.

CHAPTER 17

THE HERMIT

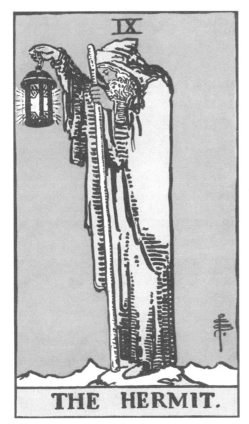

The nineth card in the Major Arcana suite, The Hermit may a grown version of The Fool, or a mature and wiser version of The Magician. Indeed, these beliefs about The Hermit exist. There is also a lesser-known aspect of The Hermit which is fundamental to the method by which I learned to understand The Fool's journey as depicted by tarot.

In the pursuit of spiritual fulfillment, The Hermit represents the arrival of one's journey along the material plain. In his travels, The Hermit has learned of instinct from The Fool, creativity from The Magician, intuition from The High Priestess, attainment from The Empress, progress from The Emperor, structure from The Hierophant, practicality from The Lovers, and courage from Strength.

The culmination of these experiences sits within The Hermit, who appears one step away from the halfway point in The Fool's journey. As the journey continues, its direction will be set by destiny and a karmic realization of all that came before within the material world. This second half of the journey leaves the material world behind and embarks on an expedition of the spiritual.

The Hermit also corresponds with the second essential virtue, which is prudence. Prudence is a fundamental character virtue that involves the ability to make wise and judicious decisions. It is often considered the mother of all virtues because it guides and regulates other virtues by ensuring that actions are taken with careful consideration and foresight. Prudence helps a person to discern the right course of action in any given situation, balancing moral principles with practical realities. This virtue is essential for leading a balanced and ethical life, as it promotes thoughtful decision-making and responsible behavior.

First impression

An old man with a long white beard stands alone in the night. He holds a lantern in his right hand, which he raises up to cast light ahead of him. In his left hand is a staff, which he uses to stand firm upon the snow-covered ground.

Basic definitions

In the upright position, The Hermit represents solitude, wisdom, self-reflection, and an awareness of the power of one.

In the reverse position, The Hermit represents a fear of being alone, paranoia and bitterness, and having trouble with the challenge of letting go.

Interpretation of symbols

The first thing to notice about The Hermit is that, apart from the snow on which he stands, the central figure is the only visual aspect of the card. This confirms the principle that the man himself, is the central message of the card.

The man stands upright, but with his head tilted in a half-down posture. His long white beard indicates that his journey of life has matured him, but his upright stance shows that he remains unburdened by past experiences. Rather, overall body posture demonstrates a stoicism that comes from gathering insight over a lifetime of encounters. The man is open to looking forward but is also reflecting upon the past with discretion and wisdom.

There is more than one way to interpret the man's white beard, which may pertain to masculine archetypes, or practical purposes. As a masculine archetype, the fullness and color of the beard relates to age, experience, and wisdom. From a practical perspective, the color white, which may also be relevant to the whiteness of the snow upon which the man is standing, relates to a new beginning. There is also the practicality of growing a full beard to hide an identity, isolate, or remain undetected. In some instances, this man may be ready for a new leg in his journey. In other instances, and particularly when the card is in reverse, he may be lost and feeling isolated or attempting to go unrecognized.

The man is cloaked in grey robes, indicating a lack of pretense, objectivity, or indifference. Grey is neither white, which is clean and pure, nor black, which is unknown. The status of the man's situation, therefore, may be somewhere in-between, or uncertain. The snow beneath his feet is virgin white, indicating that he is about to embark on a leg of his journey that he, or no man, has yet travelled.

Other than The Hermit and all that he brings with him, there is nothing but a dark and empty sky. The lack of background features indicates that The Hermit stands on higher ground. Withdrawn from others, in a moment of concentration with nothing to distract him, he is illuminated as the central element within the card. He carefully considers the lantern that he holds, from which the light of a six-pointed star shines brightly.

The shape of the star combines two triangles, representing heaven and earth. The light is implied to be divine, illuminating the path of life experience.

The man exhibits the essential virtue of prudence as he reflects upon where he has been and what he has become. He is the light in the darkness, and he stands holding his staff, which will steady him as he continues his journey. The Hermit relies on himself for support when the card is upright. In reverse, the cloaked nature of his appearance, his beard, and the inability to steady his staff, may imply an identity crisis.

Symbols matching other Major Arcana cards.

Where relevant, symbols in The Hermit are also in other Major Arcana cards. A white beard also appears in The Emperor. Snow appears in Judgement.

Overall theme

The overall theme of a card is the generalized message that may apply to a single card spread. The overall theme of The Hermit is as follows:

You have travelled a long way, but the journey is not yet over. Stop to reflect upon everything you have learned, all that you are. The path you have followed is uniquely yours, the culmination of your past and your quest for what lies ahead, is the continuance of your journey.

CHAPTER 18

WHEEL OF FORTUNE

The tenth card in the Major Arcana suite marks the halfway point in The Fool's journey. Wheel of Fortune is where encounters from the material world transform into a karmic revelation. This sets the unique path to continue the journey onward through a spiritual plane towards completion and fulfilment of one's life purpose.

WHEEL of FORTUNE.

Whereas The Hierophant provided an early glimpse into the relationship between earthly and heavenly existence, Wheel of Fortune provides a first step away from one's relationship with the material world, to an inward-facing journey into spiritual enlightenment.

Wheel of Fortune is an opportunity to see how the Rider-Waite tarot deck provides insight into life's lesson in practice. We may not be able to escape our karmic destiny. We can, however, help to define its direction of travel with our free will. The free will exhibited in the material phase of our life journey now brings us to Wheel of Fortune, which marks the point of change wherein the luck we have attained, born in part from the choices we have made, points us towards our path of destination. Our destiny.

First impression

A wheel of character symbols sits suspended in the sky. Surrounding it are four clouds, each with an angel of different animal form. Atop the wheel is a sphinx, holding a sword. To the left of the wheel is a serpent. Beneath the wheel is a demon (alternatively referred to as a red jackal).

Basic Definitions

In the upright position, Wheel of Fortune represents change, destiny, and the greater influence of good luck.

In the reverse position, Wheel of Fortune represents change, destiny, and the greater influence of bad luck.

Interpretation of symbols

Wheel of Fortune is a card of luck and destiny, but also of hope and the search for clarity. For this reason, the figure of the wheel sits suspended in a clear blue sky. It is like the sun, connected to the highest realm, and appears between the clouds, just as the sun often does.

The wheel comprises of circles representing the hub, the inner, and the outer worlds. The lettering within the outer world circle alternates Latin and Hebrew characters. The Latin characters spell T.A.R.O., referring to the cycle of life's journey, which at the point of ending, begins again. See how the first letter, T, is also the last in a motion of continuous cycle. The Hebrew characters spell Y.H.V.H., referring to the true and personal name of God.

The inner world circle consists of wheel spokes and alchemistic characters. The characters refer to mercury (air), sulfur (fire), water (water), and salt (earth).

Four winged figures appear within the clouds at each of the four corners of the card. These figures relate to the Four Evangelists referred to in the New Testament. The man refers to Matthew, and corresponds with the element, air, and the Swords Suite within the Minor Arcana. The ox refers to Luke, and corresponds with the element, earth, and the Pentacles Suite within the Minor Arcana. The Eagle refers to John, and corresponds with the element, water, and the Cups Suite within the Minor Arcana. The lion refers to Mark, and corresponds with the element, fire, and the Wands Suite within the Minor Arcana. The Evangelists are a divine tetramorph, interpreted to be a single, perfectly balanced unit that personifies the most admired characteristics of Christianity. The books each is reading relate to the benefits of learning from one's own experiences, and from the experiences of others.

The blue sphinx sits atop the wheel. Its coloring relates to the search for clarity and truth, defined by the sword it holds. There is no direct relationship to the intellect and communication aspects of the Swords Suite within the Minor Arcana, and Wheel of Fortune. To infer a direct relationship with a particular suite would also infer a deliberate omission of other suites. Therefore, the sphinx and his sword are blue to represent similar elements of truth and justice that may appear in the Sword Suite cards, but without directly using, or relating to, any specific suite.

Below the wheel is a demon, although it may equally be a red jackal. In the upright position, the demon is positioned submissively below the wheel. In reverse it appears above the wheel, denoting a dominant position. This relates to the trickery of a demon force, and whether it has power over the future, or not. As the red jackal there is also a message of reincarnation, including a positive (optimistic) or a negative (pessimistic) construct.

The serpent is a reminder that life's experiences and learning opportunities are slippery. It faces downward in a slithering format, to demonstrate the negative elements of fate. Wheel of Fortune shows that fate is a mix of circumstances out of our control, and circumstances we create for ourselves.

Symbols matching other Major Arcana cards.

Where relevant, symbols in Wheel of Fortune are also in other Major Arcana cards. Latin characters also appear in The High Priestess. A sphinx also appears in The Chariot. Swords also appear in The Magician and Justice. A serpent also appears in The Magician and The Lovers. The Four Evangelists also appear in The World.

Overall theme

The overall theme of a card is the generalized message that may apply to a single card spread. The overall theme of Wheel of Fortune is as follows:

As your life journey continues, the ever-turning wheel of destiny is in motion. At this halfway point in the voyage, comes a time to travel beyond the material outer self and discover a spiritual inner world of experiences that will culminate to shape you as you continue your journey.

CHAPTER 19

JUSTICE

The eleventh card in the Major Arcana suite is also the third card depicting an essential virtue. Justice relates to fair and balanced judgement of material matters, using clear insight and divine guidance.

Clear insight, as a character virtue, involves the ability to perceive and understand situations, people, and oneself with clarity and depth. It allows a person to see beyond surface appearances and grasp the underlying truths and complexities that may exist. This virtue is crucial for making informed and wise decisions, as it helps in recognizing the true nature of challenges and opportunities. Clear insight fosters self-awareness, empathy, and a deeper connection with the world, enabling a person to navigate life with wisdom and integrity.

The Justice card is one of the easiest cards in the Rider Waite deck to interpret as its imagery closely resembles that which we learn to understand operates in a legal or judicial setting. The key difference, however, is that justice in a legal or judicial setting is described as 'blind,' whereas Justice in the Major Arcana delivers judgement of one's material existence, based on deservedness and retribution, the elements of which must be seen to be considered.

First impression

A female sits upon an elevated platform, flanked on either side by stone pillars. She wears red robes and a simple crown. In her right hand she holds a sword to the sky, and her left hand holds a set of scales. To her rear is a deep red veil which obscures an unknown background. A small segment of yellow sky is visible.

Basic definitions

In the upright position, Justice represents legal matter, fairness, karma, cause and effect, and the triumph of a deserving side.

In the reverse position, Justice represents unfairness or bias, excessive severity, disputes or legal battles, vengeance, and a poetic justice.

Interpretation of symbols

Justice is an example card in which the posture of the central figure infers a connection between Heaven and Earth, or spiritual and material realms. The female character in Justice points her sword towards heaven with her left hand, and her right points downward whilst holding a set of scales.

Justice also provides an example of how the positioning of a character's feet is relevant to the card's interpretation. In fact, central characters within the Major Arcana Suite often include the right foot positioned forward in comparison to the left. This symbolizes progress, action, and moving ahead. The right foot is traditionally associated with masculine or yang energy, even in female characters, and relates to assertiveness and initiative. The message is one of moving forward in life, making decisions, and stepping forward towards personal transformation. Characters in the Rider-Waite deck will often include a forward positioning of the right foot to emphasize the importance of self-discovery and spiritual enlightenment.

The woman in Justice sits upon a stone structure, with stone pillars on either side. The seat is an implied throne, but not a royal throne. This woman has full command of her courtroom, in a comparable way in which a King or Queen would rule their kingdom. Her decision within the realm of justice is final and her power therein is absolute. The pillars extend upward beyond the parameters of the card to demonstrate this point. Their grey stone appearance denotes balance, neutrality, or constriction when the card is reversed.

The woman's robes are red, with gold trim. This denotes drive, dominance, energy, and passion (red). Also, wisdom and hierarchy (gold). The upward pointed sword relates to a righteous resolution of challenges, truth, and successful outcomes. Just as the pillars extend beyond the card's boundaries, so does the sword. Closer inspection reveals that the sword also extends beyond the height of the dark red veil that conceals the background. The veil is a reference to free will, and the decisions that are given consideration within a process of justice. The obstruction of background means that the ultimate outcome is not yet known. When a judgement is made, the veil will drop, and all will become clear. The relevance of the sword's extension beyond that of free will is to demonstrate that a person's decisions may have brought them to a place where they are no longer in control of the ultimate decision on the matter. The ultimate decision follows clear insight, consideration of all sides, and comes from a power higher than that of any vested interest.

The fairness denoted in Justice appears on the scales. They represent balanced consideration and equity. The woman's crown carries a single blue jewel, denoting the third eye of higher intuition, order, and an ability to resolve all manner of contradictions.

Symbols matching other Major Arcana cards.

Where relevant, symbols in Justice are also in other Major Arcana cards. Stone pillars also appear in The High Priestess, The Hierophant, and the Chariot. Swords appear in The Magician and Wheel of Fortune. A crown appears in The Hierophant, The High Priestess, The Empress, The Emperor, The Chariot, Strength, and The Tower. A yellow sky appears in The Fool, The Magician, The Empress, The Chariot, and Strength. The third eye appears in Temperance.

Overall theme

The overall theme of a card is the generalized message that may apply to a single card spread. The overall theme of Justice is as follows:

To form a preconceived idea of what is, and then forever call it an experience, is flawed. You must first experience yourself, and second experience others, and then, with the clarity of all experiences you will travel forward into righteousness.

CHAPTER 20

THE HANGED MAN

The Hanged Man is a card which strongly aligns to Christian teachings of how Jesus hanged from a cross so that he may pay a penance for the sins of others. As with the biblical descriptions of how Jesus surrendered to his fate, as a sign of his surrender to God, the overall message of The Hanged Man is quite similar.

The twelfth Major Arcana card, however, does not relate to punishment or penance, but to surrender and acceptance of what will be. The Hanged Man has allowed himself to willingly hang in suspension of what may happen next. His material values have been assessed by Justice, and he accepts his fate as he approaches the stage of ending the earthly phase of his journey and embarks on a phase of spiritual enlightenment.

First impression

A man is hanging upside down, tethered to a t-shaped tree. His arms are folded behind his back, and a golden halo surrounds his head.

Basic definitions

In the upright position, The Hanged Man represents powerlessness, letting go, or being on hold, or stuck in a situation.

In the reverse position, The Hanged Man represents unfinished business, hidden motives, being held back, or leaving others.

Interpretation of symbols

The upside-down positioning of The Hanged Man, along with his relaxed posture and serene facial expression, are all signs of his willingness to surrender. However, the act of hanging upside down also denotes the readiness to see things from a new, or unfamiliar, perspective. Despite his precarious placement, he remains calm. He may be a willing martyr, or simply ready to progress beyond his comfort zone.

The t-shaped tree, to which the man is tethered, consists of a vertical trunk which is squared off by a horizontal beam. The tree's shape represents having reached the final stage of material development, or alternatively, the act of preventing further development. The tree also consists of new budding leaves, which grow in abundance as the horizonal beam continues to travel outward. This indicates a promise of new beginnings, or a new life path.

The cards of the Rider-Waite deck often use blonde hair to infer that a human figure is young. While this may also be the case in The Hanged Man, the primary purpose of the man's blond hair is to associate it with the golden halo that surrounds his head. The halo depicts spiritual enlightenment and provides immunity from danger to the man, who has almost become one with the halo. The golden hair in this instance represents intellect, wisdom, and a higher state of consciousness.

The directional pose of the man's legs and arms align with each of the alchemistic Hebrew and Latin characters that appear in the Wheel of Fortune card. This is an acknowledgement of the inner and outer world qualities that exist within life's journey. There is a greater good to the process of life, and the man's pose may be a sign of his acceptance to sacrifice material desires to achieve heavenly outcomes.

The lack of background features in the card indicates a departure from the earthly perspective, and a progression into the spiritual realm. The color of the sky is indeterminate, potentially white, grey, blue, or none or all of these. This depicts an emptiness, lack of prejudice, or openness to experience something new.

The Hanged Man may have tethered himself to the tree or may have been placed there by another force. However, the overall message of the card is an acceptance of powerlessness, and the act of spiritual enlightenment achieved through sacrifice.

Placing the card in reverse often helps to reveal its reverse meaning, and The Hanged Man is an excellent example to explore. A relaxed pose when the card is upright, suddenly seems contrived when the card is upside-down. Is the man balancing on the tree? Are his legs posed artificially? Are his arms defiantly pressed into his waist, or tightly holding onto the tree's trunk to prevent him falling? The gold halo and upright pose of the man when the card is in reverse alludes to a deliberate pose that may be hiding the truth, or not yet willing to surrender completely. Is there more to do? Is the man unable to separate himself from the tree?

Symbols matching other Major Arcana cards.
Where relevant, symbols in The Hanged Man are also in other Major Arcana cards. A halo, and the indefinite sky color, also appear in Temperance.

Overall theme
The overall theme of a card is the generalized message that may apply to a single card spread. The overall theme of The Hanged Man is as follows:

You are in a moment of pause, with nothing more than your free will, and the time in which to reflect on the suppositions you have been dependent upon. Acknowledge them, and what they may be worth to you, if worth anything at all.

CHAPTER 21

DEATH

The thirteenth Major Arcana card can often be misunderstood to relate to something sinister or unsavory. Although Death represents the end of all things, including life, it tends to signify a cyclical death. This may or may not include the physical death of a person.

DEATH.

It should also be noted that the lifespan of a cycle is infinite, its new beginning always occurs at the precise point of its ending. The cycle of Death is also inevitable and relates to everything and everyone. Whether young or old, rich, or poor, Death is a rite of passage that impacts every person.

In the sequence of the Major Arcana, Death once the entire material aspect of the Fool's journey is experienced, assessed for virtuosity, and then left behind to acquire a directional rebirth. Death is therefore the birth of a new leg in the journey of life, and its direction of travel points towards successful completion of one's spiritual fulfilment.

First impression

A skeletal figure dressed in black armor, sits atop a white horse at the bottom of a deep valley. Before him are the living and the dead. Beyond the valley, the sun rises between two pillars.

Basic definitions

In the upright position, Death represents endings and new beginnings, transformation, transition, and death.

In the reverse position, Death represents near death experience, chronic illness, an accident, or trying to avoid the inevitable.

Interpretation of symbols

The imposing size of the skeletal figure, along with the blackened features of the card, give Death an ominous look, and it is easy for tarot beginners to automatically consider the appearance of the Death card in a reading as being a sign of terrible things to come. As with all the cards in the Rider-Waite deck, however, Death has a far broader scope of messages, and once the detail of the symbols is examined, those messages easily reveal themselves.

The imposing size and general blackness of the skeletal figure speaks of how life's journey, its beginnings, and endings, are often unanticipated. They arise from mysteries that we may never fully understand. Those mysteries of life are part of something much bigger than us, and inevitability cannot be prevented. The skeletal figure refers to the grim reaper, and the fated cycle of beginnings and endings that form part of all earthly things.

The varied mix of people that have encountered the skeletal figure include a small child, a fair maiden, a bishop, and a king. Each person has a unique response to the figure. The king has succumbed, his material wealth laying discarded on the ground. His royal crown has fallen from his head, demonstrating that status and wealth, as defined by material laws, have no value in the spiritual realm.

Similarly, the bishop, whose gold attire infers a heavenly association, has dropped his golden staff. He speaks directly to the figure, but his posture is undetermined. Is he so close to God's wisdom that he fearlessly looks death in the eye? Or is he attempting to plead for privilege? He has abandoned his staff, a possession that had once been a symbol of his purpose as representative to God.

The fair maiden turns away from the skeletal figure. She is young and still naive and so she is unable to, or in denial of, the inevitability of her own death one day. The small child, however, makes an offering of white flowers. This represents a blessed purity, innocence, and the complete surrender to one's fate.

The skeletal figure wears armor, demonstrating the invincible, unstoppable, and inevitable cycle of life and death. The end of the cycle is in motion, depicted in the wilted lifeforce feather in the figure's helmet. The white/grey horse is a reference to beginnings, which in a cycle arise from every ending. It also signals lack of judgement, to remind us that all are equal, whatever the material interpretation of their standing. The figure carries a flag of rose and five ears of corn. The black, square features of the flag relate to darkness, loss, endings, and the reliability of inevitable cycles. The rose is a symbol of rebirth, and the ears of corn depict a new harvest.

In the background, a ship travels upwards towards the sun, which appears between a stone gateway atop a soaring, distant clifftop. Although its point of entry is obscured by the imposing size of the skeletal horseman, there is a slender river which flows downhill from the stone pillar gateway, until it merges into the valley. Note the tiny arrow-like spur that protrudes from the horseman's foot. As a spur, it represents forced movement. As an arrow it signals the way. The ship relates to the Ship of Souls in Egyptian mythology, which carries souls from death to reincarnation. The stone pillars relate to the heavenly gates and transformation from end of life to the afterlife.

It is not clear whether the sun is rising or setting in Death. This demonstrates that the dusk of an ending cycle, or the dawn of a new beginning, is in play.

Symbols matching other Major Arcana cards.

Where relevant, symbols in Death are also in other Major Arcana cards. The sun also appears in The Fool, The Lovers, Temperance, The Moon, and The Sun. A stone gateway also appears in The Moon. A horse appears in The Sun. A flag appears in The Sun, and Judgement. Armor appeals in The Chariot. A red feather appears in The Fool and The Sun.

Overall theme

The overall theme of a card is the generalized message that may apply to a single card spread. The overall theme of Death is as follows:

Discard that which does not serve you well and see that by surrendering the past, you may finally achieve clear sight of a future that may otherwise appear impossible.

CHAPTER 22

TEMPERANCE

In The Fool's journey, Temperance appears immediately following the discarding of material attachments and outward-facing perspectives. As fourteenth card in the Major Arcana suite, Temperance pertains to the fourth of the essential virtues of mind and character.

Temperance, as a character virtue, signifies self-control, moderation, and balance. It encourages individuals to manage their desires and impulses, fostering a harmonious and disciplined life. By practicing temperance, one can achieve inner peace, make thoughtful decisions, and maintain healthy relationships. It is a cornerstone of ethical behavior and personal growth.

The imagery within Temperance, as a virtue, links biblical references of diluting wine with water, to the concept of deliberate self-restraint. As the card immediately following Death, Temperance suggests a promising perspective beyond worldly constrictions. This promise is achieved through moderation of free will, balancing the conscious and unconscious influences we are subject to, and then harnessing this newfound harmony so that it may propel us along the path towards enlightenment.

The promise is conditional however, as Temperance immediately precedes The Devil and The Tower cards, both of which must be navigated as one progresses through life's journey.

First impression

An angel stands by field of lilies, pouring water from one chalice to another. One of the angel's feet submerges in a pool of water. The other foot, rests upon a rock.

Basic definitions

In the upright position, Temperance represents balance, moderation, economy, frugality, chemistry, and getting things right.

In the reverse position, Temperance represents lack of balance, unrealistic idealism, non-cooperation, conflicting ideas, and competing interests.

Interpretation of symbols

Angels are often depicted as androgenous, and the angel in Temperance lacks any clear identifying gender features, which indicates that a message of androgyny is implied. This indicates that the concepts of the card apply equally to all.

The angel wears a long white robe, representing truth, and has large, overstretched wings, which extend beyond the parameters of the card. The colors, size and extension of the wings indicate a balance between life's unknown possibilities, divine intervention, and the connection between the earthly and spiritual realms. In the upright position, the angel's wings allow guidance and support of higher powers to maintain the angel's balance. When in reverse, the wings may indicate overcomplications and torments.

The angel's appearance includes two symbols that are key to understanding the card's meaning. The astrological symbol for the sun appears on the angel's head. This represents enlightenment, clarity, and divine guidance. This symbol is also the alchemical symbol for gold, which infers a purity and perfection. The position of the symbol on the forehead is a reference to the third eye. In Hinduism and Buddhism, the third eye symbolizes intuition, enlightenment, and the ability to perceive beyond ordinary sight.

The angel's breastplate comprises of a red triangle inside a white square. This is a symbol of complementary opposites, including femininity and masculinity, spirituality and materialism, or Heaven and Earth. Although sometimes difficult to see, the Hebrew letters (Y H V H), meaning God or Jehovah appear directly above the breastplate. This adds a layer of divine significance to the card and emphasizes its spiritual message.

To the angel's left is a field of yellow irises. This is a reference to the goddess, Iris, who used the rainbow as a bridge between Heaven and Earth. To the angel's right, a slender and lengthy pathway cuts between mountains and towards a rising sun. The path is narrow to demonstrate a direction of travel which is the virtuous exercise of free will, along the pathway of life's plan. When the card is in reverse, the pathway may symbolize overcomplication, and false or competing ideals.

The positioning of the angel's feet provides a balance. This may relate to the matters of the past and present, emotions and intellect, or conscious and unconscious. Similarly, the pouring of water between two cups represents a balance, relating to moderation, matters of equality, reconciliations, or simply maintaining emotional stability.

Temperance is a card of heavenly potential, but can also represent unrealistic idealism, particularly when read in reverse.

Symbols matching other Major Arcana cards.

Where relevant, symbols in Temperance are also in other Major Arcana cards. A sun appears in The Fool, The Lovers, Death, The Moon, and The Sun. A halo appears in The Hanged Man. A third eye also appears in Justice. An undefined color of sky appears in The Hanged Man. A presiding angel appears in The Lovers and Judgement. The position of the feet also appears in The Star. Rectangular features also appear in The Emperor, The Chariot, and The Devil. A pathway also appears in The Moon.

Overall theme

The overall theme of a card is the generalized message that may apply to a single card spread. The overall theme of Temperance is as follows:

A new dawn promises new insight. Make peace with the past, moderate the present and enable your future. See things as they are and harmonize your will with that which must be, for the path is narrow and requires steady footstep.

CHAPTER 23

THE DEVIL

The imagery of the fifteenth card in the Major Arcana suite has been known to evoke feelings of anxiety, for the Querent of a tarot card reading, and even for the inexperienced tarot card reader. If this is the case, and The Devil appears in a reading, it could result in a skewed outcome.

The reader may decide to direct attention for the card away from the Querent, and erroneously towards an outside influence. Alternatively, the reader may misinterpret the card as relating to the Querent's character, which could lead to a distorted perception of the entire reading.

The Devil is, in most cases, a gentle nudge towards greater vigilance. When reversed, it is true that The Devil has no redeeming qualities, however, it is rare that it will ever relate to something as sinister as the card's imagery may lead some to believe. Nonetheless, the following deconstruction of The Devil card's derivation and symbolism should help to demonstrate the proper significance of its inclusion in The Fool's journey.

In the Rider-Waite tarot deck, The Devil is derived from a famous illustration by the French occultist, Éliphas Lévi, called Baphomet (circa 1861). Despite earlier references to Baphomet appearing as far back as the late 14th century, Lévi's visual representation was found for the first time in his book, which when translated from French to English, was called Transcendental Magic: Its Doctrine and Ritual. Baphomet was shown as half-human and half-animal, male and female, good and evil, and was intended to represent the goal of perfect social order.

One notable similarity can be found between The Devil and two of its preceding cards. The first of these is The Hierophant, in which a presiding figure, an earth-bound representative for God, provides blessing to two worshippers. The communication of the blessing travels from Heaven, through God's representative, to Earth. The communication is see Heaven.

The second similarity appears in The Lovers, wherein an angel presides over the union of two people. In this instance, the communication also travels from Heaven, through a heaven-bound representative of God, to Earth. The communication is see yourself.

Just as The Hierophant and The Lovers show a supervisory connection between Heaven and Earth, so does The Devil. However, the key difference is that the presiding figure in The Devil seeks to block, rather than transfer, information between Heaven and Earth. The Devil presents a roadblock that attempts to divert from the continuation of a progressive life journey, by focusing one's attention, even obsessively, to distractions and temptations. Its communication is see only Me.

Following Death of unnecessary things, comes the birth of spirituality as shown in Temperance. However, a journey does not reach its desired destination until it has concluded. The Devil offers clarity of vision as to how material desires and complacency serve to obstruct the door to spiritual enlightenment.

First impression

A bearded figure presides over a naked man and woman, both chained by their necks to a rectangular box. The presiding figure is half man half animal, with beastly facial features, a ram's horns, bat's wings and clawed feet. Atop his head sits an inverted pentagram cross. He gestures upward with his right hand and his left hand holds a fired torch, which he points downward. Both the man and woman have tiny horns growing from their heads, and tails protrude from behind them. The background is entirely black.

Basic definitions

In the upright position, The Devil represents addiction and bad habits, materialism, complacency, and co-dependency.

In the reverse position, the upright definitions are magnified and include severe addiction, abusive behavior, the desire for ultimate control, and psychopathy.

Interpretation of symbols

When considering the symbolism of The Devil, it is helpful to compare it to The Lovers card which preceded it. The presiding angel has been replaced by a grotesque figure, and the imagery has morphed from gloriously abundant, to bleak and oppressive. We are reminded that one lesson from The Lovers was to consider the blended consequences of attraction (a primal instinct) and partnership. The beastly features of the presiding figure in The Devil refer to the confining nature of falling victim to primal instincts, in which our animalistic tendencies take control of us.

Negative energy, dark forces and cruelty are all implied in The Devil's imagery. An example of this appears with the use of an inverted pentagram, and the similarly shaped ears and jaw of the presiding figure. An inverted pentagram is a five-pointed star that, positioned upside-down, demonstrates the overturning of the good and proper order, and thus represents blasphemy, corruption and evil.

The man and woman remain naked, but any reference to innocence implied by The Lovers imagery, has been replaced by shamelessness, or the denial of one's own culpability. Both are now chained at the neck. This represents a form of slavery. However, upon close inspection the chains are loose and can be slipped off at any time. The oppression may be imposed by others, but may also be self-imposed through addiction, denial, or complacency. This allows for a conscious decision to walk away from enslavement.

The woman's tail includes a fruitful tip, which links directly to the Garden of Eden, and Eve's consumption of forbidden fruit. The man's tail includes a tip of fire, having caught the corruptive flame of the devil's torch, representing complacency, and a willingness to corrupt.

The box to which the man and woman are chained comprises of the same rectangular features of other manufactured structures in the Rider Waite's imagery. The box's relevance links the desire for materialistic safety, but to the point where it may provide a false sense of security (if the box is empty). Alternatively, the beastly figure is sitting on the box, preventing reveal of its contents (if the box is full), which represents the nature in which addiction can blur or obscure our ability to see the truth.

The beast's hand positions are purposeful. His right hand is raised to gain attention. The hand gesture is like a benediction, which Christian clergy use to offer a blessing. However, in this instance it is a mockery or inversion of the traditional blessing, symbolizing the perversion of spiritual power. The message is to see only what he intends for us to see. The left hand lowers the torch, obstructing vision and preventing the light. What remains is an entirely black background, representing mental or emotional darkness, and the unknown.

When The Devil card appears in a tarot card reading, the message is likely to relate to the importance of remaining vigilant to avoid common pitfalls that occur when we become complacent. When the card appears in reverse, the warning is more urgent.

Symbols matching other Major Arcana cards.

Where relevant, symbols in The Devil are also in other Major Arcana cards. Rectangular shapes also appear in The Emperor, The Chariot and Temperance. A black sky appears in The Tower. Nakedness appears in The Lovers, The Sun, Judgement and The World.

Overall theme

The overall theme of a card is the generalized message that may apply to a single card spread. The overall theme of The Devil is as follows:

If you are trapped in the darkness, you need only find the light to be free.

CHAPTER 24

THE TOWER

THE TOWER.

To help develop a sound understand of the sixteenth card in the Major Arcana suite, one needs only consider the mantra adopted by every 12-step program in the world. The Serenity Prayer speaks of courage, clarity, and surrender, at a time when most commonly, addiction has brought a person to their lowest state. The original wording of the prayer, as first written by Winnifred Crane Wygal in the Santa Cruz Sentinel of March 15, 1933, is as follows:

"Father, give us courage to change what must be altered, serenity to accept what cannot be helped, and the insight to know the one from the other."

Having travelled three-quarters of The Fool's journey so far, opportunities for courage and clarity have been fruitful. The Fool's courage to embark on the journey, The High Priestess's courage to seek wisdom, and The Devil's opportunity for unclouded vision, are examples. Each card in the Major Arcana suite provides a message of how our free will contributes to the direction of our destiny.

To travel the final few steps of the journey, The Tower shows that free will must also include the will to freely surrender. The serenity to accept what cannot be helped opens the passageway for enlightenment to greet us.

Often, it is at the point of rock bottom when we finally must acknowledge our powerlessness of certain things, that we are ready to surrender to our awakening.

First impression

A tower on a hilltop has been struck by lightning and is ablaze with a raging fire. Smoke billows from every side and the tower's massive crown-shaped dome has been blown away. Two people plummet to their fate.

Basic definitions

In the upright position, The Tower represents chaos, destruction, upheaval, and unwanted or unexpected change.

In the reverse position, The Tower represents slight setbacks, pressure, stress, or illness.

Interpretation of symbols

A key feature of The Tower is the height of the grey-white tower which sits upon a cliff topped hill. This represents ivory tower ideals, in which ideas or beliefs are developed in a state of privileged seclusion. Grey denotes detachment, white denotes purity. The privilege provides safe shelter from reality, and thereby a disconnect from the practicalities of everyday life. There may be an out-of-touch perspective, or a preoccupation with egotistical pursuits.

At the top of the tower, a dome, shaped like a massive crown, is blown away by a sharp lightning strike. Once a sign of majesty, wisdom, and closeness to Heaven, it is now a worthless aspect of the material past and is no match for nature's power. Its vulnerability and weakness are further denoted in the tilted angle in which it flies away from its once safe positioning. It has lost any sense of control.

The lightning strike appears as a flash of awakening, enlightenment, and purification. The tower's artificial purity was misleading, and nature's purity arrives with overpowering and indisputable force. The twenty-two golden droplets that fall from the tower are curve shaped. This links them to the Hebrew letter "J," which relates to fire. They are divided into ten droplets, representing the ten points of the Tree of Life, and twelve droplets, representing the twelve signs of the zodiac. They relate to the distraction of chaos and confusion that intimidates our intuition and tantalizes our imagination.

Two people are plunged from the tower, and tumble downward to meet their fate. Their attire demonstrates that they were each regarded to be of high standing in the material sense. They are now powerless, their former state irrelevant. There is no indication as to whether these people have fallen, were pushed, or willingly jumped. They dive down from their cocooned safety, nonetheless.

Symbols matching other Major Arcana cards.
Where relevant, symbols in The Tower are also in other Major Arcana cards. A black sky also appears in The Devil. Crowns appear in The High Priestess, The Empress, The Emperor, The Hierophant, The Chariot, Strength, and Justice. Golden droplets appear in The Moon. Fire appears in The Devil.

Overall theme
The overall theme of a card is the generalized message that may apply to a single card spread. The overall theme of The Tower is as follows:

Egotistical pursuits can only take you as far as you can see. To view what lies beyond that which you know, accept that more exists than you can currently see, and allow change to bring forth a shift in awareness that transcends your current orbit.

CHAPTER 25

THE STAR

The end of every cycle is also its beginning. This is true for every creation. There is the creation, followed by the destruction, followed by the rebirth. Source is life, and life appears as a cycle. The seventeenth card in the Major Arcana suite reminds us that, despite every experience and encounter in The Fool's journey, the cycle of life as created by Source is eternal.

To surrender one's preconceptions of power is to free oneself from self-imposed constraints. Therein appears an unobstructed path in which a higher state of consciousness may travel. The Star brings hope, and splendid revelations, born from that newfound state of higher consciousness.

First Impression

A naked woman kneels towards a pool of water, holding a jug in each hand. She pours one jug of water into the pool, and the other onto the land. Eight stars are in the sky, one is almost sunlike in its size and appearance. It is not clear whether it is day or night.

Basic definitions

In the upright position, The Star represents hope, serenity, another chance, spiritual love, and joy.

In the reverse position, The Star represents low self-esteem, lack of clarity, futility, disappointment, failure, and lack of love.

Interpretation of symbols

The woman's nakedness represents her rebirth, which renders her pure, and reconnects to the truth. When The Star is in reverse, however, the woman's nakedness may be a representation of shame or vulnerability.

The woman's posture of kneeling with her right foot on the water, and the left on the ground is like the representation made in Temperance. In both cards, the foot on ground represents practicality, and the foot in the water relates to intuition. However, there is one subtle difference between the two cards. In Temperance, the figure's right foot sits submerged in the body of water. In The Star, the figure's right foot sits on top of the water. This demonstrates the Fool's progression into a later stage of development, in which the intuitive senses denoted by Temperance have advanced into an ability to harness intuitive abilities. The placement of the woman's feet suggests that while she remains grounded, she is also in touch with her higher self and the divine.

Water in tarot represents life and energy. The Star is a card that represents these aspects of water in several ways. Firstly, the woman's right (conscious) hand, pours water from a jug, into the pool. Her left (subconscious) hand pours water from a second jug onto the ground behind her. Five rivulets of water flow from the second jug. These represent the five earthly senses. One of the rivulets flows back into the pool. This is a suggestion of the eternity of life but may also refer to futility.

The landscape is lush and green with small seedlings or flowers scattered across the ground. The scattering of new vegetation is a sign of new beginnings, along with the youthful sense of coming back to life, and the freshness of a new experiences.

In the distance, atop a tree on a hill, a lone bird watches on. The bird is an ibis, which is a breed of bird associated with the ancient Egyptian god Thoth. Thoth, the god of wisdom, knowledge, and the moon, was often depicted as a man with the head of an ibis. The ibis, with its distinctive long beak, symbolized Thoth's writing tools and his mastery of knowledge and celestial wisdom. Birds are also symbols of freedom and spirituality.

In the sky are seven small white stars, and an eighth massive, guiding star. The smaller stars represent the seven chakras. Their radiant glow signifies cosmic alignment, linking spiritual energy to a divine source. The large, guiding star represents the inner, indestructible essence that resides within every living being. The eighth star's resemblance to the sun is a signal that the card validates neither day nor night specifically. It is eternal.

The Star is a card of hope and second chances, after having experienced a spiritual rebirth or awakening.

Symbols matching other Major Arcana cards.
Where relevant, symbols in The Star are also in other Major Arcana cards. The position of feet also appears in Temperance. An eight-pointed star also appears in The Chariot. Nakedness appears in The Lovers, The Devil, The Sun, Judgement, and The World. A day/night sky also appears in The Moon.

Overall theme
The overall theme of a card is the generalized message that may apply to a single card spread. The overall theme of The Star is as follows:

Your inner truth is eternal and effortless. Life is hope and spiritual surrender clears the path for truth.

CHAPTER 26

THE MOON

The Moon appears as the eighteenth card in the Major Arcana suite. It is also the card that carries the deepest and often the most disregarded message for the tarot reader. The clue is in the keyword, illusion, in which one's own imagination allows them to believe things that are not true.

Earlier in this book I talked about the difference between a person who proficiently reads tarot cards, and a psychic who uses tarot as an instrument through which to receive a message from Source. Learning a clear and consistent range of definitions for each card and practicing the art of gently expanding those interpretations to satisfy contextual differentials is something anyone can do, even if they do not consider themselves to be psychic. Building your intuitive muscle so that it becomes strong, and the card readings become more accurate, achieves the purpose intended by the cards.

By holding on too tight to the I am psychic mantra, a person who is attempting to understand the message of the cards is continually refusing to let go of their own sense of power. This causes confusion with messaging. What is the meaning of each card if that meaning can be overridden by a vibe, a hunch, or a feeling? How can I discern between genuine intuitive messages from Source, and imaginative glimpses that satisfy my sense of psychic ability?

The Moon reminds us that we are of the material world and therefore we are flawed. We are subject to illusion and distraction when we fail to surrender fully and wholeheartedly to our inner truth, which is universal and thereby sits outside our individual sphere of influence. The key to becoming a true psychic is to forego the earthly desire to be exceptional, in favor of a humble openness to receive.

The Moon shows us that we are approaching the end of The Fool's journey. The Sun lies just beyond the horizon. As with any threshold worth passing, there will be a final challenge in which those who complete the journey have indeed achieved a higher state.

First Impression

A wolf and a domesticated dog stand at a riverbank, barking at an eclipse. To the left and right are pillars of a stone gateway, between which a narrow path travels towards the horizon.

Basic definitions

In the upright position, The Moon represents secrets, illusion, imagination, fear, anxiety, health issues, infirmity, and acting under cloak of darkness.

In the reverse position, The Moon represents self-delusion, lack of spirituality, having a closed mind, or being stuck in an old pattern of repetition.

Interpretation of symbols

The Moon is a card that deeply connects to the concept of illusion, and all the distractions that may keep us from seeing the truth. Nonetheless, the primary color in The Moon is blue, denoting truth.

The achievement of the deep blue that appears in The Moon is due to its blackened tones. The deepness of color, therefore, suggests hidden truths, and the mystery and vastness of the subconscious mind. Note that despite the preponderance of blue, the dog and wolf are only concerned with the eclipse. This eclipse combines the sun and a crescent moon. The moon represents our emotions, which hides the sun's representation of truth.

Golden droplets fall from the sky. The shape of the droplets relates to the Hebrew letter "J" which relates to fire. There are fifteen droplets, linking The Moon to the fifteenth Major Arcana card, The Devil. The droplets provide a distraction from inner truths that exist within each of us. There is also a comparison between intuitive truths and imaginative constructs.

The dog and wolf present a caution and warning. The wolf relies on wild instinct, and the dog represents the taming of the self. There is also a crayfish at the riverbank, which denotes the old ways, or a crustacean reminder of ancient times, primal instincts, and subconscious fears. It is unclear whether the crayfish is climbing out of the water or is slipping back into the water. This suggests the power of illusion, and how lack of clarity can lead to superstitious beliefs, conspiracies, and anxiety.

The stone gateway represents transformation from end of life to the afterlife, and the threshold that must be passed to achieve spiritual fulfilment. Note the mystery that exists in the landscape beyond that which is the solid ground, and the necessity for the pathway to extend beyond the earthly landscape, far beyond and into the unknown. The path is narrow to demonstrate a direction of travel which is the virtuous exercise of free will, along the pathway of life's plan. When the card is in reverse, the pathway may symbolize overcomplication, overwhelming anxiety, self-delusion, and having fallen for distractions and temptations.

Symbols matching other Major Arcana cards.

Where relevant, symbols in The Moon are also in other Major Arcana cards. Moons appears in The High Priestess and The Chariot. The sun appears in The Fool, The Lovers, Death, Temperance, and The Sun. Golden droplets appear in The Tower. A dog appears in The Fool. A stone gateway appears in Death. A narrow pathway appears in Temperance. A day / night sky appears in The Star.

Overall theme

The overall theme of a card is the generalized message that may apply to a single card spread. The overall theme of The Moon is as follows:

Where hope guides the way, fearfulness and doubt prevents you from seeing the path of truth.

CHAPTER 27

THE SUN

O ften described by tarot readers as the "best card" in the Rider Waite deck of cards, The Sun is the nineteenth card in the Major Arcana suite and signifies the completion of the Fool's journey.

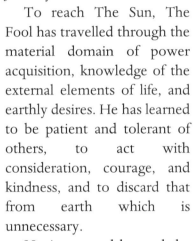

To reach The Sun, The Fool has travelled through the material domain of power acquisition, knowledge of the external elements of life, and earthly desires. He has learned to be patient and tolerant of others, to act with consideration, courage, and kindness, and to discard that from earth which is unnecessary.

Having passed beyond the material domain into one which is spiritual, The Fool's journey became an inward-facing series of experiences. Maintaining balance, recognizing the constrictions of addictive, controlling behaviors, letting go of fear and insecurity, and possessing faith in a power greater than that of the individual.

The journey of life as described by tarot is a circular one. It begins with The Fool who embarks on his journey, with a fresh expectation of everything and nothing. The journey is subsequently long and winding, assessing every aspect of the conscious and unconscious mind. Arrival at The Sun, with Judgement and The World, still to come. Nonetheless, the Sun is anthropomorphized and smiling, to indicate that the tests of the journey have concluded with success.

There is no negative way to read The Sun, depending on its position and direction in reading, its meaning sits somewhere on a broad range of positivity. The Sun is unique in this regard.

First impression

A naked infant sits atop a white horse, in a walled garden of sunflowers. A large sun brightly illuminates the entire scene and has taken on a human face that smiles serenely. The infant holds a massive red flag.

Basic definitions

In the upright position, The Sun represents exposure, light, improvement, positivity, joy, success, love, and enlightenment.

In the reverse position, The Sun represents a weaker sense of enlightenment, and a mediocre success or happiness.

Interpretation of symbols

The sun dominates the clear blue sky, radiating truth, warmth, love, and joy. Its twenty-one rays of light represent each of the Major Arcana that, along with The Sun, completes tarot's journey through life.

An infant of no determinate gender sits atop a white-grey horse. The infant's nakedness denotes purity, truth, and vulnerability. Whilst vulnerability can infer risks, in an infant child, vulnerability signifies a beautiful openness to the world, a willingness to learn, grow, and connect with others. It reflects their innate courage to trust and embrace new experiences, fostering resilience and empathy. Supporting this is the walled garden environment, which denotes protection and security. The wall sets boundaries and maintains safety. The infant's posture makes it clear that no fear or apprehension exists in this place, only joy, trust, truth, and love. The infant is a character representing perfect innocence, purity, simplicity, and wholeness.

The white-grey horse marks the successful completion of a journey, and the beginning of a new one. The horse's color shows a lack of judgement.

Tall sunflowers peek from behind the walls of the garden. Sunflowers represent glowing energy, growth, strength, and reaching up to heavenly outcomes.

The infant's red feather life force is a sign of renewed life and rebirth. The life force is at its strongest, reinforced by the massive red-orange flag that the infant is holding. The colors and proportionate size of the flag indicate a welcomed openness, fearlessness, and abundance of energy.

Symbols matching other Major Arcana cards.

Where relevant, symbols in The Sun are also in other Major Arcana cards. The Sun appears in The Fool, The Lovers, Death, Temperance, and The Moon. A horse appears in Death. A red feather appears in The Fool and Death. Flags appear in Death and Judgement. Nakedness appears in The Lovers, The Devil, The Star, Judgement, and The World.

Overall theme

The overall theme of a card is the generalized message that may apply to a single card spread. The overall theme of The Sun is as follows:

Your life is not regulated by habits and routines, but rather by your deliberate and conscious free will. Innocence is renewed by the discovery of yourself, and your hope for the future. You have arrived and therein you prepare for your departure.

CHAPTER 28

JUDGEMENT

The twentieth card in the Major Arcana suite is traditionally modelled after the last judgement or universal resurrection theories found in some form, within Christianity, Judaism, Islam, Buddhism, Hinduism, and other less populous faiths.

Whilst theories vary in detail, the eschatological concept is the same – that life in its many forms ends, following which a measurement of good and bad it taken. Life is then renewed in its purest sense, and in perfect unity with its creator.

In Judgement, evil is destroyed. Sins are forgiven but not forgotten, for they hold in their memory important knowledge, earned through experience. What remains is a freedom and acceptance of renewed life. The soul has been awakened, without judgement and ready to begin again.

First impression

An angel blows on a trumpet, calling all to awaken. People of all ages rise naked from caskets which are floating in an expansive body of water. Gazing in awe, the men, women, and children gaze upward to see the angel.

Basic definitions

In the upright position, Judgement represents forgiveness, letting go of the past, assessment, finding your calling, and rebirth.

In the reverse position, Judgement represents alienation, rejection, harsh judgements and criticism, resistance, and being stuck in old ways or patterns.

Interpretation of symbols

The scene for Judgement takes place in a large expanse of water, amidst snow-covered mountains. This reflects the Book of Revelation's chapter twenty which states that the sea gives up its dead. The white snow-topped mountains represent virgin ground, the fulfilment of a task, and new beginnings.

It should be noted that apart from the president angel figure, the remainder of the card is colored blue, grey, and white. This represents the passages within scripture of truths revealed after life, divine judgement of all who have passed, and the meaninglessness of prior status, privilege, or other defining characteristics in life. Everyone is equal after death, and the grey pallor of the people in Judgement, not only represents the rising of the dead, but also an indifference or lack of judgement, other than that which appears in each person's Book of Life.

The people are rising from caskets. The blackness of the interior caskets denotes the restrictions and confinement from which each is rising. There is one exception, an infant in the distance. Whilst it is likely that they too would rise from a casket, Judgement shows them as remaining pure in life, as in death. The nakedness of the people relates to the naked truth of their judgement, along with innocence, and warnings of shamelessness when the card is in reverse. The caskets also dominate the card when in reverse, implying that the people are trapped within the confined space of judgement and criticism.

The presiding figure represents Archangel Gabriel, who is the messenger of God depicted in all Abrahamic religions. Scripture describes Gabriel as having announced the births of Jesus Christ and John the Baptist and is often depicted with a trumpet. The trumpet signifies an awakening, a proclamation, or a call for action.

The red cross flag is an inclusion that is relevant to the time and place in which the Rider-Waite tarot deck was created. It is the Cross of St George, the patron saint of England, and centers on a legend of when St George slayed a dragon that was terrorizing a town. He saved the townsfolk and a princess, and his story symbolizes the triumph of good over evil.

Over time, the red cross adopted other significance, relating to neutrality, humanitarianism, separation, reconciliation, and unification.

Symbols matching other Major Arcana cards.
Where relevant, symbols in Judgement are also in other Major Arcana cards. Snow appears in The Hermit. Flags appear in Death and The Sun. A presiding angel appears in The Lovers and Temperance. Nakedness appears in The Lovers, The Devil, The Star, The Sun, and The World.

Overall theme
The overall theme of a card is the generalized message that may apply to a single card spread. The overall theme of Judgement is as follows:

Forgive yourself and others and you will be reborn.

CHAPTER 29

THE WORLD

Earlier in this book we discussed the halfway point of The Fool's journey, depicted by The Wheel of Fortune. This was where the journey shifted from earthly outward-facing reflections to the inward reflections of a spiritual awakening. The Fool's journey has since concluded. The World marks the fulfilment of all four essential virtues. It is the achievement of one's destiny and the knowledge and experiences attained throughout the journey, and which bring a new beginning of fresh optimism and vitality.

The World is the twenty-first, and final, card in the Major Arcana suite. It reminds us that karmic travel towards destiny cannot be avoided but can be redirected with the power of free will we each possess. The World reflects of the wholeness with which we begin each cycle, and the continuity of life beyond that of simply birth or death.

The journey is about to begin again. The World is where the soul appears, as if for the first time, in acknowledgement of the completion of a journey, and in readiness anew.

First impression

A woman floats in a dance-like posture in the sky, surrounded by a large laurel wreath. She is holding two double-ended wands and her otherwise naked body is loosely draped with a violet shawl. Beyond the wreath, are a man, an eagle, an ox, and a lion. Each float on a grey cloud.

Basic definitions

In the upright position, The World represents accomplishment, completion of a task, triumph, a new beginning, anticipation, deservedness, and being in the right place at the right time.

In the reverse position, The World represents mediocre accomplishment, overdue birth, delayed results, limbo, doubts, apprehension, and stalled progress.

Interpretation of symbols

In the first instance, note that the central figure is naked, except for a violet shawl that drapes around her torso. This is the only instance in which a naked form is covered in the Rider-Waite illustrations. The card contains numerous hints of gender neutrality.

For example, the figure is holding two double-sided wands. A double-side wand provides the power to manifest conscious and unconscious, earthly, and heavenly, material, and spiritual outcomes. There is no purpose for which two wands could be relevant, other than to imply the embodiment of more than one physical manifestation of energy. The wands, therefore, relate to both male and female embodiment, symbolizing the harmony of opposites.

In esoteric traditions, androgyny is a symbol of spiritual wholeness and enlightenment. Esoteric writings describe the androgynization of Humanity as a sign of progression towards a new age of existence. The World card, being the final card of the Major Arcana, signifies the culmination of a spiritual journey, where the seeker achieves a state of unity and completeness that rises above gender.

124

The floating of the figure, their ambiguous gender, posture, and nakedness, all infer that the figure is reintegrating into the whole. The violet shawl combines free will, fire, and energy (red), with openness to the unknown and spirituality (blue).

Laurel wreaths are a symbol of triumph. In The World, the large wreath separates the conscious and unconscious, the earthly and heavenly, the material and spiritual realms. The wreath is tied with red ribbons, which are each wound into a figure eight. This represents the cyclical continuance and infinite nature of life. When The World appears in reverse, the ribbons may refer to repetitiveness, or lack of growth or progress.

On grey clouds, the four evangelists from Wheel of Fortune are present again. They emphasize the card's message of completion, balance, and the interconnectedness of all things.

Symbols matching other Major Arcana cards.
Where relevant, symbols in The World are also in other Major Arcana cards. Nakedness also appears in The Lovers, The Devil, The Star, The Sun, and Judgement. A laurel Wreath appears in The Empress and The Chariot. Four Evangelists appears in Wheel of Fortune. A magic wand appears in The Magician and The Chariot.

Overall theme
The overall theme of a card is the generalized message that may apply to a single card spread. The overall theme of The World is as follows:

Pause for a moment to celebrate your success because the moment you step forward a new journey shall begin.

CHAPTER 30

THE WANDS SUITE

The Wands Suite comprises fourteen cards and represents one of the four elemental suites of the Minor Arcana (Fire). There are four Royal cards (Page, Knight, Queen, and King), plus ten numbered cards (Ace, and II-X). The key phrase which corresponds to the Wands Suite is, *I desire.*

There are two specific aspects of the Wands Suite which will assist you in developing a firm understanding of the language of tarot. Firstly, each numbered card from the Wands Suite aligns with one of the Major Arcana cards numbered I-IX. Examples of the numerical relationship become clear as we discuss the Minor Arcana cards individually.

Secondly, the Wands Suite's representation of fire relates fiery passion, base instinct, and primal urges. When a card from the Wands Suite appears in a reading it may represent propulsion of energy, motivation, and action. Matters of will and ego may also be present.

Consider fire as a standalone element. Fire is hot, spontaneous, and can be unpredictable. The energy of fire as a driving force can melt, cook, and ignite a motor. Without fire there may be a lack of stimulation, desire, or inspiration. However, fire also has the potential to be destructive when left to rage unabated.

Wands in a tarot card reading.

When a card from the Wands Suite appears in a reading, it is likely to signify an aspect of the Querent's core being. Impulse, desire, and what makes them tick.

If a tarot card reading mostly comprises of cards from the Wands Suite, the situation may be volatile, uncertain or at its earliest conceptualized stage. The reading may be a call to action, or a warning to slow down and give greater regard to potential consequences. Alternatively, the reading may reflect the Querent's passion for the subject, their wish to resolve an unsettled issue, or the acknowledgement that action may exist but is otherwise meaningless.

Relying on the Wands Suite and element of fire alone can lead to rash decision making, chaotic relationships or messy outcomes. However, cards from the Wands Suite may also demonstrate creativity, genuine interest and enthusiasm, and an abundance of energy to get things done.

To proficiently read a card from the Wands Suite, take account of its symbolism, numerical value, placement in the reading, whether it sits upright or in reverse, and proximity to other wands cards. Consider that life comprises of all four earthly elements, and that energy from surrounding cards representing other Minor Arcana suites may be relevant.

CHAPTER 31

ACE OF WANDS

Ace of Wands denotes a newly inspired beginning. Ace of Wands appearing in relative proximity to any other Minor Arcana card may serve as an override to the other card. This may be a positive thing, denoting a powerful inspiration, or a positive injection of energy. Conversely, it may denote a dangerous impulsiveness. Ace of Wands can inject a sense of rapid momentum into a reading, which may be positive or negative, depending on the context.

All Ace cards in the Minor Arcana suite can be read as yes/no cards. Upright tends to represent Yes, and reverse appears as No. The interpretation of yes or no is not absolute however and should reflect the symbolic references that appear in the card.

First impression

A colorless hand emerges from a cloud, holding a single wand. The wand has budding leaves, eight of which are detached and falling. The cloud and its surrounding sky are grey, and beyond the natural landscape lies a distant castle and mountainous range.

Basic definitions

In the upright position, Ace of Wands represents the ultimate inspiration, a rush of energy, passion, desire, and action or momentum.

In the reverse position, Ace of Wands represents a lack of growth or expansion, failure to commit, or an inappropriate attraction or affair.

Interpretation of symbols

The first thing to note about Ace of Wands is that, as with all Ace cards, the most prominent color within the card is grey. The grey sky and clouds are neutral to the eye and represent a lack of foresight and/or judgement. Ace is the first number in the Wands Suite, and it marks the beginning of something new, which so far has produced nothing to judge. However, the hand's position within a cloud lacks logic, and represents the risk of having jumped forward without considering consequences.

The hand is making an offering of a new achievement, enterprise, relationship, or adventure, any of which appear as a fresh bud. Violet mountains in the distance symbolize spiritual goals, and the castle, a dream of success or material achievement.

The enthusiastic motion of the hand from the cloud has dislodged eight leaves. The Ace of Wands is the only card in its suite in which the leaves have dislodged from the wand. In Chinese numerology, eight represents wealth and success, and the leaves provide a glimpse of what is achievable. There is a need for balance and perspective in all new ventures however, and eight also represents knowing one's own boundaries and having respect for limitation or orthodoxy.

Almost every card in the Rider Waite tarot deck includes people, in their full body form. The inclusion of simply a hand in the Ace of Wands card is a warning not to become too carried away in the pursuit of passion. Should a loss of identity occur in the process, this may prove counterproductive to the desire.

There is, however, the acknowledgement of what is achievable through inspiration. The layers of pink-red and green-yellow landscape, plus the river, all demonstrate the fruitfulness of harnessing passion, and the possibility of cultivating positive outcomes from emotive pursuits.

Overall theme

The overall theme of a card is the generalized message that may apply to a single card spread. The overall theme of Ace of Wands is as follows:

A brand-new opportunity awaits you, along with a reminder that more than an instinctive craving will suffice to reap the desired reward.

CHAPTER 32

TWO OF WANDS

Two of Wands represents the broad considerations that form part of the planning process. It connects the past, present, and future, and demonstrates that more than a single space in time is relevant to any issue.

When Two of Wands appears in a reading, consider what helps to move the matter forward in a positive way, and any issues that may provide obstacles.

First impression

A young man stands atop a rooftop, holding a globe in his right hand. He has two wands, one he places on the raised wall beside him, and the other is secured inside a bracket to his rear. The man looks ahead, over a lush landscape, modest dwellings, roads, and an expanse of water surrounded by sandy shoreline. The sky is grey, and in the distance lies a violet mountain range.

Basic definitions

In the upright position, Two of Wands represents planning, decision-making, delays, and partnerships or the consideration of other viewpoints.

In the reverse position, Two of Wands represents an unexpected turn of events, reluctance, self-restriction, and gaining new perspectives.

Interpretation of symbols

Firstly, note the color of the sky, which is pale grey, just as it appeared in the preceding card, Ace of Wands. The rectangular stone rooftop and walls are also grey, but their combined color and form signify safe, supportive boundaries and careful, structured decision-making.

The man stands elevated upon a rooftop. This, along with the globe he holds, shows a broadness of perspective that may include the needs of others. The globe infers an attempt to achieve a universal perspective. The roundness of the globe, however, means that no matter how closely we examine our options, we will never see everything at once.

The man's side-tilted profile, between two wands, acts as a reminder that he is looking into something yet undetermined, and he stands between two sides of a portal that will lead him to a new experience. The wand he holds signifies the way forward, and wand left behind is tethered to a stable, reliable past. Together the wands signify the balance between unlimited possibilities and sensible outcomes, and reflects the interdependencies between the past, present and future.

The need for balance is reinforced by the man's clothing. The red cap represents his passion and eagerness to proceed forward, but is tempered by his brown robe, which marries him to the realistic or sensible nature of the earth.

Below the man is a fertile landscape of green fields and forests. Although the land is inhabited by people, as evidenced by roads, and scattered dwellings, there appears a harmony between man and earth, and the interruption of nature is minimal. Mountains in the far distance represent a spiritual aspiration. The blue mountain in particular links purity of the heart, or good intentions, to heavenly outcomes.

Water is a symbol of emotions, and the body of water in Two of Wands appears as a lake. There is also a sandy shoreline, which provides a practical filter (or barrier) that tempers (or prevents) achievement of what the heart wants.

The lily and rose cross derives from Christian esoteric traditions, including Freemasonry and provides a link to alchemy, or the transformation of energy to produce masterful outcomes.

Overall theme

The overall theme of a card is the generalized message that may apply to a single card spread. The overall theme of Two of Wands is as follows:

Carefully consider how you wish to proceed forward and whether you have taken contingencies into account. Delay may be an option to include in consideration, if the outcome benefits from a slower, more deliberate pace.

CHAPTER 33

THREE OF WANDS

Three of Wands represents embarking on an adventure. Three of Wands is an encouragement to go boldly forward, but it also reminds us to remain mindful of what may lie ahead and what we can learn from past experiences that may help us to navigate new experiences.

First impression

A man stands with only his back profile in view, on a sandy hill overlooking a yellow body of water. The sky is also yellow, with only violet mountains in the far distance. Three boats are sailing in the water, just as there are three wands accompanying the man. He leaves two behind him, and takes a firm hold of the third.

Basic definitions

In the upright position, Three of Wand represents enterprise and opportunities, a new job or business venture, ambitious spirit, and taking responsibility.

In the reverse position, Three of Wands represents investment anxiety, delayed results, distrust, overcaution, and feeling blocked.

Interpretation of symbols

Unlike the preceding card, Two of Wands, the sky in Three of Wands has turned from grey to yellow. However, it is not simply yellow. To understand in full, the meaning of the sky's hue, compare it to the yellow sky that appears in the next card, Four of Wands. A yellow sky represents conscious awakening, and transition from neutral lack of judgement to conscious desire, and at times, even envy. Yellow denotes energy, vitality, and enthusiasm. A blackening of the yellow tone warns of risks unknown, mystery, and negative potential consequences.

Another notable comparison to make is that the man's clothing has gone from brown tones to a vibrant red. He is about to embark on an enthusiastic adventure, and he is no longer fully grounded. He may also be naïve in his optimism about the future, which is represented by his green cape.

The man is holding firmly onto one of three wands, which represents a fixed commitment to move forward. The two wands left behind may return to him later as consequences of his actions.

The three wands, three leaves on every bud and three boats in the water are all reinforced messages of change, development and breaking new ground.

The man's headband is a reminder to remain attentive and aware, and the armor which is visible on his arm, and which drapes his body, is a reminder to act with courage.

Overall theme

The overall theme of a card is the generalized message that may apply to a single card spread. The overall theme of Three of Wands is as follows:

Good fortune awaits you if you learn from what you have known before and bravely face that which you do not yet know.

CHAPTER 34

FOUR OF WANDS

Four of Wands relates to the protection of being part of a group or society. Whether upright or reversed, Four of Wands is a message of relationships between people. This may include an intimate relationship, such as a marriage or close friendship, or within the wider concept of groups and society.

First impression

A couple rejoice as they hold bouquets of flowers high in the air. Ahead of them is a lush garland of fruit and flowers, hanging between four upright wands. Behind them is a castle with a small group of people gathered nearby. The group may be dancing or sharing a celebratory drink together.

Basic definitions

In the upright position, Four of Wands represents community, celebration, domestic comfort, congratulations, a wedding, or a job well done.

In the reverse position, Four of Wands represents building a

136

foundation, cultivating relationships, reunions, or taking a well-earned break.

Interpretation of symbols

Unlike the blackened yellow sky of its preceding card, the Four of Wands shows an entirely clear and vibrant yellow sky. Is the sun shining so brightly on this scene that its happiness has transformed the community? Whether the celebration depicted in Four of Wands relates to a wedding, a successful harvest, or the triumph of having won a battle, it is clear from the scene that the happiness comes from being part of a group of people, rather than being alone.

The proportion of the people who are small, against the wands and background features, which are large, relates to the idea that each of us belongs to a larger group, or that something bigger than ourselves is in play. As observers, we may feel a sense of invitation to join the group and their celebration. All it takes is for us to step through the gateway of wands.

The contrast of red and blue robes worn by the couple at the center of the card points to love and passion (including wrath if warranted), but also sentimentality and longing. Blue can, at times, also relate to inebriation, which is a reasonable expectation for some, during periods of festivity. The garland contains fruit and flowers, representing a fruitful outcome.

The large stone castle represents the safety and security of having shelter. Its imposing size in the scene emphasizes the message of safety, along with the adjacent bridge, which relates to the coming together of opposites so that they can join and give strength to one another.

Overall theme

The overall theme of a card is the generalized message that may apply to a single card spread. The overall theme of Four of Wands is as follows:

You are not alone and live in a world where others are searching for the same things as you.

CHAPTER 35

FIVE OF WANDS

Five of Wands represents egotistical pursuits. A temper tantrum designed to cajole another into compliance, a fake apology, a person who drains the energy of others, brinksmanship, or ego-based conflict are all examples of what may be represented by the card.

When the Five of Wands appears in a tarot card reading, it refers to a self-focused desire for triumph.

First impression
Five adolescent young men gather in disorderly confrontation. Each waves a wand, having little regard for what the other is doing.

Basic definitions
In the upright position, Five of Wands represents arguments, tension, competition, and strife.

In the reverse position, Five of Wands represents reaching resolution, refusing to argue, and inner demons.

Interpretation of symbols

The sky has changed color to a light blue hue for the Five of Wands, which represents cool indifference to each other's point of view. It may also relate to a light-hearted or performative disagreement, such as a game. In fact, Arthur Edward Waite, who first commissioned the creation of the Rider Waite deck once said that the Five of Wands depicted "mimic warfare" and "a sham fight."

Each young man is holding his own wand, which denotes his egotistical interest in his own desires, paying little interest in the desires or wishes of others. The ground beneath the young men is flat and continues into the horizon as though indefinitely, a muddle of assorted colors including green, yellow, orange, blue and violet. This represents turbulence and a lack of reliability. If the card appears in reverse, the muddled colors dominate the scene, evoking a sense of an ego that continues to feel bruised, long after agreement has been reached.

Similarly, each youth wears a distinct color clothing, which represents the individualism of the scene, and differing or selfish ideals. It can also represent the free will of every person, and the power they have, to exercise their will independently.

Five of Wands is the only card in the Rider Waite deck that includes only people of adolescent ages, this is to emphasize the self-centeredness of the message, which is often attributed to a childish mindset, particularly when describing a person who is no longer a child. When Five of Wands appears in reverse, it may signal appeasement, passive aggression, or lingering doubts. The dispute may seem resolved, but an underlying, covert, or disguised, issue remains.

Overall theme

The overall theme of a card is the generalized message that may apply to a single card spread. The overall theme of Five of Wands is as follows:

Your life is a constant interplay that allows free will to develop. To master the game, you must learn which battles are real, which are winnable, and which are a waste of your will.

CHAPTER 36

SIX OF WANDS

Six of Wands relates to victory and good news. Whether related to work or career, a legal matter, or a relationship, it provides the declaration of a desired message. It also warns of problems that may arise from arrogance and undeserved pride.

When Six of Wands appears in a tarot card reading, the message may be one of victory or public acknowledgement.

First impression

A young horseman presents a laurel wreath of battle victory. A crowd of other men surrounds him.

Basic definitions

In the upright position, Six of Wands represents victory, achievement, public acknowledgement, good news, and positive results.

In the reverse position, Six of Wands represents treachery, betrayal, public humiliation, embarrassment, and pride before a fall.

Interpretation of symbols

The power of free will is depicted in a light blue sky, which runs constant for the remainder of the Wands suite of cards. There will continue to be elements of coolness and indifference, but as the cards progress in rank towards the King of Wands, the power of the will continues to grow and intensify, as does the connotation of the need to demonstrate willpower. This is a recognition of the steely determination of the will that maintains inspiration and the desire for action, whilst also controlling willful impulses to achieve greater outcomes.

The man at the center of the image is the victor. He is admired and respected, as evidenced by those who congregate around him. Several symbols reinforce the point that this man is confident, self-controlled, and determined to deliver a positive message of triumph (depicted by the laurel wreath on the wand, which is likely to have once belonged to an adversary, now defeated). The man holds the horse on a tight rein, and the horse's color demonstrates its animal instinct is controlled by a dignified passivity.

The green rug that envelopes the horse signifies fruitful bounty, positive outcomes, and good news, but its freshness can dominate the card in reverse to depict an immaturity leading to false hope and potentially devastating outcomes.

Overall theme

The overall theme of a card is the generalized message that may apply to a single card spread. The overall theme of Six of Wands is as follows:

You deserve success and for matters in which you have worked hard and are deserved, you will succeed and can be proud that you have done well.

CHAPTER 37

SEVEN OF WANDS

Seven of Wands relates to challenges, courage, and prolonged effort. Seven of Wands is about standing your ground, being confident in your purpose and balancing a strong will against the will of others (some of whom may prove you wrong).

First impression

A giant man stands at the edge of a waterfall or cliff face. Beneath his feet lie mountains and a waterway that appear dwarfed in his presence. He holds a wand with both hands and tilts it towards another six wands that jut out of the ground before him.

Basic definitions

In the upright position, Seven of Wands represents being ready and willing, accepting a challenge, and not giving up.

In the reverse position, Seven of Wands represents refusing to negotiate, obstinance, and being biased or unfair.

Interpretation of symbols

The disproportionate largeness of the man in contrast to the landscape denotes his massive courage and his willingness to tackle any obstacle. He may be fighting against six adversaries that are out of view. Alternatively, he may be attempting the unlikely feat of standing all seven wands upright. Either way, he has been presented with a challenge, and he has readily accepted.

The color of the man's clothing hints at his age and state of mind. The browns denote a grounding, an awareness that nothing is gained unless an attempt is made. The green relates to a freshness or youthful immaturity that may be overly optimistic of its own abilities.

The cliff face is easy to miss and appears in the bottom left corner of the scene. It relates to the hazardous nature of prolonged challenge, and the possibility that remaining rigid in your viewpoint may be your ruin. The cliff becomes a dominant feature of the scene when the card is in reverse, turning courage into willful obstinance.

Whether upright or reverse, the man is confident in his position. However, his shoes do not match, which hints that confidence does not prove purpose. It may also relate to the inequity and bias. The heavier shoe is safely positioned on stable ground, whereas the lighter shoe may slip from the cliff at any moment.

Overall theme

The overall theme of a card is the generalized message that may apply to a single card spread. The overall theme of Seven of Wands is as follows:

If you know who you are, and can prove who you are, then you are and should continue to be as you are.

CHAPTER 38

EIGHT OF WANDS

Eight of Wands represents change, movement, and motivation. When Eight of Wands appears in a tarot reading, it may be a prompt to do what is necessary to achieve a requirement, an outcome, or to reach a destination.

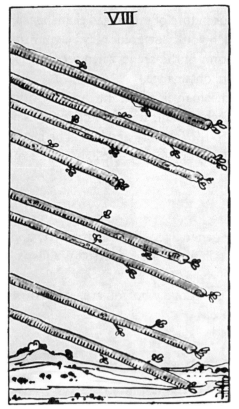

First impression

Eight wands, each with green buds, appear from a clear blue sky. They tilt forward diagonally, from the sky to the earth. The background is simple, with greenery and a river of still water. Atop a faraway hill is a dwelling, which appears tiny in the distance.

Basic definitions

In the upright position, Eight of Wands represents change, motivation, travel, and getting your ducks in a row.

In the reverse position, Eight of Wands represents family or business problems, and an unforeseen difficult effect.

Interpretation of symbols

Other than the four Aces, Eight of Wands is one of only two Minor Arcana cards that do not include people in its imagery. The other is Three of Swords. This is a deliberate omission. Its purpose is to emphasize the primary meaning of the card, which is movement.

To accentuate this point, the wands are disproportionately large when compared to other imagery in the card. The most important message is the act of moving, or traveling, towards a potential outcome.

It is implied that the beginning of the movement took place beyond the left-hand parameters of the card, out of view and at the other end of each wand. The decision to act is inspired, and therefore tilts downward from Heaven. The right-hand view of the scene is where potential outcomes are achievable on Earth. This is depicted by the buds of potential which appear near the end of each wand.

If we examine the card in its reverse position, the potential is replaced by obstacles, challenges, or an inability to proceed further. Alternatively, the wands appear to have come from the opposite side. This may suggest that an opponent has the upper hand.

The parallel proximity of the wands shows that more than one action, whether supportive or challenging, is in play at once. There may be many separate actions necessary to achieve a single outcome, or numerous problems that must be put into perspective.

The background landscape consists of green and blue. This reflects an open-minded freshness, and the possibilities of having everything in place to achieve success. The small white dwelling in the far distance atop a hill relates to man's ongoing desire to own a home, a long-time symbol of his achievements.

Overall theme

The overall theme of a card is the generalized message that may apply to a single card spread. The overall theme of Eight of Wands is as follows:

Your motivation is a combination of inspiration and action. To manifest change, you will need both components.

CHAPTER 39

NINE OF WANDS

Nine of Wands relates to having courage in the face of adversity. Nine of Wands is about possessing the longevity to ride above any single event, and turning every experience, whether good or bad, into an advantage.

First impression

A man stands upon a solid, grey platform. He holds a wand upright, and tightly close to his body. Another eight wands stand upright behind him in a field of green. The man's expression is notable. He may be fearful, suspicious, or hyper-aware of what is around him.

Basic definitions

In the upright position, Nine of Wands represents courage, resilience, and determination.

In the reverse position, Nine of Wands represents illness, over-analysis, feeling overwhelmed, or wanting to give up.

146

Interpretation of symbols

As in the preceding card, Nine of Wands includes paralleled wands. The central message of their positioning is the same. More than one matter may be relevant to the circumstances. The man may have access to multiple supportive resources, which he is willing to draw from to survive a demanding encounter. Alternatively, there may be multiple challenges facing the man at once.

The demanding circumstances of this card are unspecified. There may be an adversarial confrontation, requiring tremendous bravery. Alternatively, it may be an opportunity to achieve something great, which does not come easy. Either way, the man is determined to overcome the challenge, and to prevail in his experience.

His determination and resilience are evident in the solid ground upon which he stands. The smooth, grey platform is likely to be manufactured. It represents the solid foundation the man has built for himself with previous experiences, and the learning acquired during those encounters.

There is an acknowledgement of the natural environment which appears behind the man, but to prevail he cannot draw from outside his own inner strength. For this reason, he stands on a foundation of his own making, rather than within the landscape provided by his creator.

When Nine of Wands appears in reverse the solid ground seems overly weighty. If made of stone, it would be an overwhelming burden for any man to bear. The man's headdress may be a bandaging of his wounds from previous battles. Alternatively, it may be a bandana worn during a contest sport. Its inclusion in the imagery denotes pride and value of the previous experiences that have given the man the bravery he now possesses.

Overall theme

The overall theme of a card is the generalized message that may apply to a single card spread. The overall theme of Nine of Wands is as follows:

In challenging times, your ability to persevere and recognize the opportunity and learning points of every experience will add to your ability to withstand the next, and then even more so, the next.

CHAPTER 40

TEN OF WANDS

Ten of Wands relates to the heavy burdens of a life experienced. Ten of Wands is about nearing the end of a task but having the sole burden of achieving the outcome, and the risk of taking on too much burden.

First impression

A man awkwardly carries a collection of wands. He makes his way to a distant dwelling, his vision obscured by the wands.

Basic definitions

In the upright position, Ten of Wands represents stress, tough times, burden, responsibility, and using overly complicated methods.

In the reverse position, Ten of Wands represents wasted labor, letting go of a dream, and facing a tough reality.

Interpretation of symbols

The man's posture shows that he is putting earnest effort into his task. Is this a sign of determination, or diminished strength? His clothing color is like that of the wands. The warm orange may relate to the man's vitality and conscious decision to complete even the most arduous task. Preoccupied with his wands, he may have forgotten why he decided to carry them in the first place, or where he was planning to take them. Indeed, the wands obscure his vision, and although he is travelling forward, there is no guarantee that he will arrive at his destination without losing some, or all, of his wands.

A distant dwelling sits within a fertile landscape. This denotes security, ownership, and accomplishment of material wealth. The surrounding trees afford the dwelling a sense of privacy. There is also a small area of cultivated land which shows that the man is relying on his own ability to harvest crops to feed himself and his family.

The man is walking on a manufactured platform, rather than nature's ground. This represents a situation that may be of his own making, or a challenge that he can choose to delegate to others, so that he has less to shoulder alone. He has, however, chosen to proceed alone, blinded by his wands. He is about to step from the platform. Is the ledge elevated from the ground? Is it possible that he may in fact stumble?

Compare the platform against the platform in Nine of Wands. In contrast to the solid stone in the card which precedes it, the platform in Ten of Wands is colored a murky, blackened yellow. This infers a risk of overburdening yourself unnecessarily (with the maximum number of wands) and losing sight of the big picture while you fuss around with petty details.

Overall theme

The overall theme of a card is the generalized message that may apply to a single card spread. The overall theme of Ten of Wands is as follows:

In matters that seem complicated, remain focused on the destination and whether it continues to be worth the required effort. In all matters deemed worthy, a wholehearted approach will ensure that you never have to look back and wish you did better.

CHAPTER 41

PAGE OF WANDS

Page of Wands relates to autonomy and the free spirit. There are two shared features of all four Page cards in the Rider Waite deck. The imagery of each depicts a young man, and each carries a message. The message provided by Page of Wands is one of enthusiasm or encouragement. It also appears as good news.

First impression
A young man stands within a desert landscape with pyramid structures in the distance. The man looks upward at the buds growing from the top of a wand he is holding.

Basic definitions
In the upright position, Page of Wands represents exploration, limitless potential, no ties, a message, and good news.

In the reverse position, Page of Wands represents childishness, tantrums, reprimand, and lack of determination.

Interpretation of symbols

The young man's expression is positive and optimistic. His posture, standing in a relaxed, upright pose and looking at the budding leaves of his wand represents an enthusiasm for new or fresh possibilities. The direction of his sight is upward, inferring that his ideas may outsize the wealth of his experience. However, his inspiration is the limitless range of possibilities before him.

Notice the red feather in his cap, this denotes vitality and supports the idea that the man is enthusiastic about his possibilities. He may even overestimate his prospects for success and display an immature response to disappointment.

The burnt orange ground can denote a passion and eagerness, or a fiery envy and expectation of unearned rewards. It is easy to become disoriented in such simple surroundings, and the landscape warns not to get lost, or lose oneself, amid one's enthusiasm. Alternatively, the ground may be so barren as to mean that nothing is present that could prevent moving forward.

The uniformity of the pyramids distinguishes them from mountains. They point towards the sky, representing a closeness to otherworldliness, but also wisdom and grand aspirations. Too grand to be realistic?

The yellow and red of the young man's clothing shows his passion to proceed forward, and the salamander cloth represents a legend of creatures that can pass through fire without sustaining injury. The Page of Wands is ambitious and may not have awareness of his own lack of experience or limitations.

Overall theme

The overall theme of a card is the generalized message that may apply to a single card spread. The overall theme of Page of Wands is as follows:

Trust your inspiration to achieve things greater than you once believed possible. You need not feel the limitation of your circumstances, for you are capable of more than you know.

CHAPTER 42

KNIGHT OF WANDS

Knight of Wands represents flamboyance and volatility. Each of the four Knights in the Rider Waite deck relates to a distinct influence that helps to shape one's personality and manner of response to a variety of situations. Knight of Wands is influenced by a fiery impulse to act.

First impression

A young man dressed in armor sits atop a rearing horse. In his right hand the man holds a wand upright. In his left hand he attempts to control the horse with a tight rein, to no avail. In the background there is a desert, with three pyramids in the distance.

Basic definitions

In the upright position, Knight of Wands represents lust, enthusiasm, scattered energy, and lack of focus.

In the reverse position, Knight of Wands represents a rogue, philanderer or cheater, prone to bad temper, violence, or fighting.

152

Interpretation of symbols

Throughout the Rider Waite tarot deck, the depiction of a young man is often associated with impetuousness or lack of mature consideration of the circumstances he is faced with. An example of this occurs with the Knight of Wands. He is indeed alert and his upright posture and tight grip of both wand and reins shows that he is enthusiastic. However, there is no enemy in sight, which implies that the Knight is eager and lustful but without purpose or clear direction. He may not even realize that he is about to enter a battle. The desert environment provides nothing to battle over. It is possible that the Knight will put on a show of fighting, but his motives, mission, and even his fighting strategy may be lacking.

Close inspection of the Knight shows that his eyes lack focus. This may be a sign that he lacks confidence, and despite being easily activated, has not fully grasped the reason he is excited. Alternatively, he may be prone to acting out for reasons that may seem illogical to others.

Despite his tight hold of the reins, the Knight does not appear to have control over his horse, further suggesting that the messages of command he gives the horse are uncertain or confusing.

Other symbols pertaining to the heightened energy of the scene include enlarged red plume that cascades from the Knight's armor, the upright way he holds his wand, as though it is a lighted torch.

The man's yellow robe adorned with images of salamander refers to a conscious attempt to appear brave. In reverse, this courage may spill over into brashness or a harsh aspect of the man's personality, in which his lust for action leads him to perform roguishly.

In the far distance there is a heavenly wisdom depicted in the pyramids, which the Knight is yet to see. When the card is in reverse, these same pyramids, which are often filled with the earthly treasure of the noble departed, point towards hell, and the skullduggery of badly behaved men.

Overall theme

The overall theme of a card is the generalized message that may apply to a single card spread. The overall theme of Knight of Wands is as follows:

Things are moving at the pace which is set by your desire. Be mindful that action alone does not guarantee success. Your challenge is to draw from more than one element.

CHAPTER 43

QUEEN OF WANDS

Queen of Wands represents inspiration towards action. Each of the four Queens in the Rider Waite deck is an aspect of The Empress and provides insight into an influence affecting personality.

Queen of Wands represents the soul aspect of The Empress, her protectiveness towards others, and her passion. The appearance of a Queen in the tarot reading relates to a person in the querant's life, or a person of influence that may not be immediately apparent but is somehow relevant to the circumstances.

Queen of Wands relates to a person or influence that inspires action and may be controlling (even indirectly) the outcome of a situation.

First impression

A majestic woman sits atop her throne on a solid manufactured foundation. Her body faces forward but her head tilts to the side. She holds a wand in her right hand, and a sunflower in her left.

Accompanying the woman is a small black cat, and the background is almost entirely sky. The woman's throne appears in the center of two distinctly different landscapes, one grey desert, the other yellow mountains.

Basic definitions

In the upright position, Queen of Wands represents warmth, vibrancy, earthiness, delegation, and oversight.

In the reverse position, Queen of Wands represents jealousy, rivalry, infections, fever, extravagance, and promiscuity.

Interpretation of symbols

Unlike her counterparts, who sit with their knees pushed together, this Queen's posture is more relaxed. She sits with her knees apart, and her arms are comfortably laid upon the armrests of her throne. Her posture signals the awareness she has of the power of her majesty. As Queen of Wands, this Queen inspires others to act on her behalf, or on behalf of the principles of her kingdom. She is therefore mindful to demonstrate that she does not scare easily, nor does she act prematurely out of base instinct or pointless enthusiasm.

This Queen's throne is also the only matriarchal throne that reaches beyond the boundaries set by the card. This signifies a stretch of her potential and power towards the heavens – a privilege ordinarily reserved for Kings. This adds to her credibility as Queen. Men will act in accordance with her command, even in the absence of her counterpart, the King of Wands.

To the Queen's left is a barren, grey landscape, a wasteland. The sunflower she holds, also to the left, represents the potential of growth, energy, and strength, which reaches upward towards a limitless sun. The power of the sunflower's symbolism is magnified by other sunflowers appearing in the Queen's throne, and the pin she uses to secure her cloak. The inference is that this Queen can draw from the energy of the sun to produce mountains out of a dry and barren wasteland.

The lions carved into the base of her throne represent courage and strength. The red lions add passion, which could also turn to ferocity when the card is in reverse.

The small black cat represents an unpredictability, cunning, and propensity for survival, such as the cat has with its nine lives. However, when the card is in reverse and the cat dominates the imagery, this Queen takes on qualities like that of an alley cat, willing to scratch, bite and ruthlessly play with its prey. The black cat is also a reference to witchcraft or magic and provides the Queen with an intuitive sense of how to touch others with her warmth or afflict them with her wrath.

Overall theme

The overall theme of a card is the generalized message that may apply to a single card spread. The overall theme of Queen of Wands is as follows:

Inspiration adorns you from head to toe. Should you trust in your intuitive sense of how to proceed, you are almost certain to succeed.

CHAPTER 44

KING OF WANDS

King of Wands refers to having mastered the will. Each of the four Kings in the Rider Waite deck is an aspect of The Emperor and provides insight into an influence affecting personality. The appearance of a King in the tarot reading relates to a person in the querant's life, or a person of influence that may not be immediately apparent but is somehow relevant to the circumstances.

King of Wands relates to a person or influence that inspires action, and who may be energetic, talkative, visionary, or entrepreneurial by nature.

First impression

A majestic man sits atop his throne on a solid manufactured foundation. He holds a wand in his right hand, and his left hand is balled into a fist. A salamander appears before the man, and others are depicted in his throne and his clothing.

Basic definitions

In the upright position, King of Wands represents a leader, visionary, role model, with a healthy ego, possessing bravery or an earthy demeanor.

In the reverse position, King of Wands represents an arrogant leader, with an inflated ego, prone to extreme anger, hearth problems, stroke and who may be prepared to misuse their power.

Interpretation of symbols

This King, like his counterparts, is sitting in a relaxed position, with knees apart and arms rested comfortably. This is an indication of his unquestionable power, and his awareness of his own majesty. As King of Wands, this King inspires others with his bravery and acts of courage. His ego is grounded however, just like his wand is secured onto the earth, rather than the manufactured platform that elevates him above other men.

The King's throne reaches upward, beyond the boundaries set by the card. This signifies a stretch of his potential and power towards the heavens – a privilege each of the Kings may enjoy, but only King of Wands and King of Swords have chosen.

The King sits in a tilted half profile position. This reflects his self-awareness and confidence. He does not need to stare down an opponent to prove that he has courage. The fiery reds and oranges of his clothing reflect the fiery passion within him. His cloak and throne are adorned with salamander, which are known in folklore to be the only animal with fireproof skin. The additional salamander that appears before the King reinforces the message of his bravery. The green adornment of his shoulders and footwear represents freshness and favorable outcomes. This is a man who inspires a kingdom to act in his name, on the promise that his reign will bring glory to all who inhabit the kingdom.

The lions carved into the base of her throne represent courage and strength. When in reverse, the courage and strength turn to arrogance and entitlement. The King's ego controls his actions and leads him to misuse his power or suffer from excessive passion, causing accelerated blood flow. This can lead to anger issues or cause circulatory distress.

Overall theme

The overall theme of a card is the generalized message that may apply to a single card spread. The overall theme of King of Wands is as follows:

You have a vision supported by your courage. Knowing what you want and being brave enough to pursue your passion will provide likely success.

CHAPTER 45

THE CUPS SUITE

The Cups Suite comprises fourteen cards and represents one of the four elemental suites of the Minor Arcana (Water). There are four Royal cards (Page, Knight, Queen, and King), plus ten numbered cards (Ace, and II-X). Just as each numbered card from the Wands Suite aligns to one of the Major Arcana cards numbered I-IX, so do each of the numbered cards from the Cups Suite. The key phrase which corresponds with the Cups Suite is, *I feel*.

There are two distinct characteristics of the Cups Suite which will help you to appreciate the relevance of seeing Cups in a tarot reading. In the first instance, Cups relate to emotions, feelings, and human connections of the heart, including intuition, relationships, and sense of self. To fully appreciate the second Cups Suite distinction, consider its corresponding element, Water.

Water is a fluid substance. Its dexterity allows it to reshape itself in accordance with its environment (or containment). Water can flow softly, like a gentle stream, or unleash itself with the power of a massive tsunami. Water is also cleansing and can help to heal wounds.

When water is flowing unabated, it has a habit of bouncing off everything it touches, and this can often result in spillage and mess. Consider the unregulated flow of water to be a metaphor for the unregulated flow of emotions. When left unchecked, spillage and loss of control of both emotions and water can lead to secondary issues, complex situations. A 'messy life' is one in which a history of unregulated emotion has occurred. The power of emotions, just like the power of water, can be harnessed to produce compelling results. Conversely, water or emotions, when left to flow without regulation, can end up wasted.

This is where intuition and emotions differ. To demonstrate this point, consider the Cups Suite in isolation, where no elements of intellect, inspiration or consideration of wellbeing exist. The outcome is unknown, unprepared for, and may prove wonderful, or may prove disastrous. Emotions, when left to bounce around unabated, leave the human heart to gamble on an outcome, alone, with nothing to aid it.

Intuition is also represented in the Cups Suite. Intuition differs from emotion, however, and is the perceptive, or intelligent use of emotional power. Intuition can recognize inspiration over base instinct to react. Intuition takes account of one's wellbeing amid a primal urge. Intuition appears in the Cups Suite when cards from other elemental suites are also present in a reading. Alternatively, a standalone card from the Cups Suite can be a reminder of the need to sense what is beyond base or reactional instinct. It may even be a prompt to lay another card to sit alongside the single Cups Suite card.

Cards from the Cups Suite represent creativity, love, healing, sensitivity, frailty, beauty, kindness, compassion, and a reminder to balance the emotional aspects of self with the intuitive wisdom that raises raw emotions into a higher sense of spirituality.

Cups in a tarot card reading.

When a card from the Cups Suite appears in a reading, it is likely to signify an aspect of the Querent's emotional consciousness, or spontaneous feelings that should be examined against intuitive awareness.

If a tarot card reading mostly comprises of cards from the Cups Suite, the situation may be messy, with hurt feelings, reactionary responses, and questions about identity or loyalty.

Relying on the Cups Suite and element of water alone can lead to rash decisions, damaged relationships, or emotional insecurity. However, cards from the Cups Suite may also demonstrate warmth and compassion towards others, imaginative ideas born from creative talents, and strong emotional connection to others.

To proficiently read a card from the Cups Suite, take account of its symbolism, numerical value, placement in the reading, whether it sits upright or in reverse, and proximity to other wands cards. Consider that life comprises of all four earthly elements, and that energy from surrounding cards representing other Minor Arcana suites may be relevant.

CHAPTER 46

ACE OF CUPS

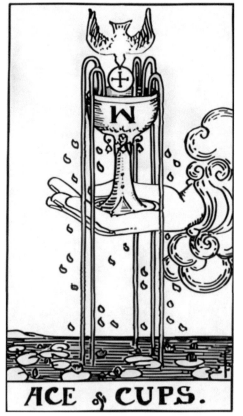

Ace of Cups denotes the life which derives from love. Ace of Cups represents connecting with your emotions, resolving any outstanding relationship issues, and acknowledging your innate value as a person. Ace of Cups appearing in relative proximity to any other Minor Arcana card may serve as an override to the other card. This may be a positive thing, demonstrating that love will prevail. Conversely, it may be warning to consider the emotional impact of the situation, defined by its context.

All Ace cards in the Minor Arcana suite can be read as yes/no cards. Upright tends to represent Yes, and reverse appears as No. The interpretation of yes or no is not absolute however and should reflect the symbolic references that appear in the card.

First impression
A colorless hand emerges from a cloud, holding a single gold chalice. A white dove appears to drop a eucharistic host into the cup, causing it to overflow into a large body of water below.

Basic definitions
In the upright position, Ace of Cups represents overwhelming love and emotion, friendship, compassion, and the ultimate sense of self.

In the reverse position, Ace of Cups represents lost love, losing love, sense of duty, a transition from romance to routine, and a drinking problem.

Interpretation of symbols
All Aces in the Minor Arcana Suite consist of grey sky and clouds which appear neutral to the eye and represent a lack of foresight and/or judgement. Ace is the first number in the Cups Suite, and it marks the beginning of something new, which may include the conception of life, a new or pure love, and spirituality. The hand's position within a cloud conceals the source from which the chalice came, which may be a reference to the divinity of creation, life, and love.

Ace of Cups is the only ace card in which the hand in question is debatable. Traditionally, an offer is given with the right hand and received with the left. Some people interpret the hand in Ace of Cups to be the right hand (giving love), but the contortion of the wrist makes this interpretation problematic. As with every other 'anomaly' in the Rider Waite illustrations, this is by design, and links to the card's divine references. The indeterminant hand may also represent the need to love oneself. Giving love and being open to receive love are equally necessary parts of acknowledging and embracing, without judgement, one's own sense of self.

The hand is offering and accepting love, borne entirely from emotion, depicted in the various forms of water. When pure, love is reciprocal, unconditional, it takes on a spiritual quality. Other symbols within the card support this message. The tiny bells that hang at the neck of the chalice represent generosity (giving) and prosperity (receiving).

The lotus flowers in the body of water below the chalice, appear in Buddhism and other East Asian traditions. Lotus flowers play a vital role in the representation of purity, fidelity, and spiritual awakening. The lotus often emerges from bodies of water that may otherwise appear swamp-like. In Buddhism, this represents love's ability to rise above any of life's challenges, and transport those who love purely towards enlightenment and spiritual wisdom.

The water features of the card are fundamental to its interpretations. Excluding a small distant mountain, the landscape is entirely water. This is a message that everything comes from love. The five streams of overflowing water represent the five earthly senses.

The twenty-six droplets of water coincide with the twenty-six letters of the alphabet. There are other interpretations for the inclusion of these droplets, such as with the manipulation of the Hebrew language and descriptions of God. However, the alphabetic connection is the simplest and therefore likely to be most relevant. My reason for this relates to the significance of the white dove, also included in Ace of Cups imagery. If each of the five senses are open to love, everything is borne from love, and love generates the language in which people speak to each other, then no obstacle realistically exists that could prevail over the peace, which is being offered in divine manner by the symbol of peace, the white dove.

Further support appears in the tiny but significantly placed green mountain in the distant landscape. Its relevance is to confirm that with love, anything is possible. Whilst shallow, the mountain represents the beginning of any number of outcomes that can arise from love.

Almost every card in the Rider Waite tarot deck includes people, in their full body form. The inclusion of simply a hand in the Ace of Cups card is a warning not to allow love to blind us to the other factors which may be in play, despite our inability to detect them.

There is also a little-known design element within Ace of Cups that is so difficult to see, that at the time of authoring this book, I am yet to find another reference to it in any tarot-related resources. Nonetheless, every single hard-copy product of the Rider Waite deck includes the detail, without explanation as to its relevance. Of the twenty-six droplets of water falling from the chalice, twenty-five of them are blue and relate to the relationship between water and emotions. One of the droplets is without color and sits isolated from the others by the combination of streaming water, hand, and cloud.

Note how the colorless droplet is positioned on the card. When Ace of Cups is reversed, it appears above the hand, in a position that could control the hand's movement forward. This droplet provides the basis for going through the motions of love, without a real sense of love. For example, a marriage of convenience, acting out of a sense of duty after love has passed, being kind toward a person you have no feelings for. This could also include peace talks between enemies for the purpose of ending war, or consciously reminding yourself that you matter when deep down you might feel as though you do not. The implication of a routine act of love that underived from emotion, is a reminder that acting with love does not require the emotion of love, but it is likely to produce the same result and is therefore of equal value as the emotional act of love.

Overall theme

The overall theme of a card is the generalized message that may apply to a single card spread. The overall theme of Ace of Cups is as follows:

You are whole, with the power to harness the divine, with which to heal, give kindness and bring peace.

CHAPTER 47

TWO OF CUPS

Two of Cups represents a soul connection. Twos in the Minor Arcana carry two, or more, considerations that should be balanced. As a single card for the day, Two of Cups may be a message of new friendship, relationship, or other emotional connection. It denotes the linking together of two or more kindred spirits. This may be romantic in nature, but may also be entirely plutonic, such is the case with people who share hobbies or personal interests.

In tarot, as in Chinese Numerology, two represents balance of two or more elements, along with harmony, and partnership. Two of Cups reminds us that creating a genuine and reciprocal bond with another person, or multiple people, is emotionally and spiritually satisfying.

When Two of Cups appears in a reading, consider the things you may have in common with others, rather than what sets you apart.

First impression

A young man and woman stand facing one another. Each holds a gold chalice. Presiding over the couple is a winged lion. The simple background provides a natural landscape with a single dwelling in the distance.

Basic definitions

In the upright position, Two of Cups represents attraction, commitment, and love.

In the reverse position, Two of Cups represents love obstacles, disconnection, separation, and losing love.

Interpretation of symbols

The connection between two souls does not necessarily relate to romance or physical intimacy. A soul connection may also be plutonic or familial, and shared between more than two people, say for example in family units, or among friends. However, it also applies to lovers and involves the spiritual bond that one person feels towards another. Two of Cups depicts the beginning of a new soul connection, along with the promise and risk associated with that new connection.

The woman in Two of Cups wears blue and white robes, like the attire worn by The High Priestess. This connects her to the passive intuitive aspects of the second Major Arcana card and supports the interpretation of The High Priestess as being complimentary partner to The Magician card.

The understated symbolism contained within the Rider-Waite illustrations is often underappreciated. Two of Cups includes an example in which this is the case. The man has the physical appearance of The Magician but is wearing attire more closely matched to The Fool. He is, in fact, a hybrid, or a midpoint between the two. The Fool's loud and colorful tunic supports the idea of his naivety. The clothing worn by the man in Two of Cups blends into the slightly more experienced Magician at the stage where a relationship with his Priestess is promised, but not yet realized. The message contained in the clothing is that a relationship or spiritual connection has sparked to life but has not yet rested into

169

routine.

Unlike Ace of Cups, the chalices that appear in Two of Cups take on an hourglass or double-sided shape. This is to show the reciprocal nature of unity, friendship, and love. In Two of Cups, the man is reaching out to give the woman her chalice. This represents a potential for, or emotional desire for intimacy. The green garland worn by the woman, as opposed to the red garland worn by the man, are respective of the traditional roles of gender. The man's passion and desire for physical intimacy, and the woman's passive virtue or sexual innocence, are reinforced by these colors.

The central staff, entwined by snakes refers to the Caduceus of Hermes, which relates to Hermes, messenger of the gods in Greek mythology. Hermes' staff is depicted as a winged staff entwined by two snakes, and represents commerce, negotiation, and trade. The Caduceus[i] symbol represents peaceful messaging. It is a symbol still used by emergency charities providing medical intervention to regions in severe conflict. The inclusion of the lion's head onto the Caduceus links the concept of commerce, negotiation, and trade to the spiritual. The lion refers to strength, ferocity, fire, and the fusion of spirit with brute force. The biblical aspects of the lion as seen in The Wheel of Fortune, The World, and other cards, also applies in Two of Cups.

The inclusion of a winged lion in Two of Cups provides a spiritual blessing and a promise of fiery passion when embarking on something new that may only be achievable through unified effort.

As seen in other cards, the distance dwelling symbolizes the attainment of a shared goal, to which unified effort provides a purpose for two or more souls to connect in profound ways.

Overall theme

The overall theme of a card is the generalized message that may apply to a single card spread. The overall theme of Two of Cups is as follows:

When you connect with another who shares your pure, honest, and reciprocal intent, you ensure that your joy is doubled, and your pain is halved.

CHAPTER 48

THREE OF CUPS

Three of Cups represents the pleasures of an abundant life. Three of Cups is an expression of how joyful life can be when people positively embrace the opportunities that come from others in

their life. This may include learning from one another's life experiences, sharing the burden, uplifting others, and creating a mutual sense of belonging. There is, however, a risk of overdoing things, or being too self-focused. Excessiveness, neglecting others, and feeling left out, can all apply when the card is reversed, as can other responses from people who feel marginalized from an abundant group dynamic.

First impression

Three young women raise their chalices in a celebratory toast. They appear connected to one another's joy, dancing together in unity. Surrounding the women is a natural landscape of flowers and signs of a bountiful harvest.

Basic definitions

In the upright position, Three of Cups represents friendship, community, celebrations, and the benefits of an easy-going perspective.

In the reverse position, Three of Cups represents over-indulgence, disenchantment, boredom, and lack of support.

Interpretation of symbols

The central message of Three of Cups is simple. We are stronger when we pull together and lift each other up. The simplicity of the message is supported by every aspect of the card's imagery.

The three women are each different, even direct contrasts to each other. This is portrayed through hair color, and the clothing they each wear. The white-grey robe represents purity and lack of judgement, the red robe represents passion, and the gold robe represents abundance. There is a deliberate colorization of gold in the third robe, rather than yellow or orange. This highlights the point that when a diverse group of people come together to achieve a shared goal, each may contribute differently, but each contribution should be valued. The combined contribution results in the collective success.

Also note the relaxed clothing each of the women wears. There is little in the way of adornment, and at least one of the women is barefoot. This emphasizes the way in which sharing a burden with others, lessens the burden for all. Further, relaxed perceptions tend to bring out the best in others, because they feel as though they can be themselves.

Each woman is holding her chalice high, towards the heavens. This is an expression of emotional unity. The centralization of the chalices denotes a shared sense of emotional support, given and received.

The background is simple and combines flowers and harvest vegetables to demonstrate the harmony of the moment, and the abundance of life when people are united. Each of the women supports the others, and each is supported by the group. There is, consequently, nothing to fear and a plentiful life to enjoy.

The reversing of the card provides clear explanation of what happens when people fail to support one another. The failure of a single unsupported person can negatively impact on the entire group. Feeling left out or disregarded, nitpicking, or resenting the success of someone else, makes it far more difficult for anyone, or even everyone, to thrive.

Overall theme

The overall theme of a card is the generalized message that may apply to a single card spread. The overall theme of Three of Cups is as follows:

Put aside any weight of the past and flirtatiously embrace the present, in all its glory. Now is the time for celebrating the joys of your life, and the people that you know.

CHAPTER 49

FOUR OF CUPS

Four of Cups relates to self-nurture and protection. Four of Cups is a card of looking inward and focusing on what really matters. Emotion can rule the card in reverse, which infers a destabilization of circumstances. In the upright position, Four of Cups is a reminder to balance emotions with intellectual enhancements, such as consideration of wellbeing, goal setting, or objectivity, to produce healthier, more sustainable outcomes.

First impression

A man sits with arms and legs crossed, under a tree. Three chalices sit before him on the ground, while a small cloud protrudes from the sky to offer him a fourth chalice.

Basic definitions

In the upright position, Four of Cups represents contemplation, inward focus, meditation, and emotional stability.

In the reverse position, Four of Cups represents looking for solutions, preparing for change, restlessness, tiredness, apathy, insomnia, and psychic experiences.

Interpretation of symbols

The cloud holding a chalice links to Ace of Cups but with two distinct differences. Firstly, the chalice in Ace of Cups is goblet-shaped, whereas Four of Cups includes a double-sided cup. The hand protruding from the cloud in Ace of Cups is indeterminate. The hand in Four of Cups is clearly the right, the hand of giving. The implication in Four of Cups is that the offer must be contemplated for its positive and negative consequences. The man is offering nothing. He is clearly the recipient, and the decision as to whether he accepts the cup is his. The crossed arms and legs, whilst comfortable, also show that he is focused on his own power to choose, rather than instructions from an outside influence, which may have its own agenda.

The three resting cups in a row depict the knock-on effect of what one decision can make on future outcomes. Alternatively, the man is weighing up his options considering choices he has previously made.

The slight raise of the hilltop on which the man sits represents a need to emotionally separate from things that require contemplation, to avoid making rash decisions that may lead to regret.

The lush green ground and the green of the leaves on the tree provide insight into the fruitfulness of good choices. However, the length of the tree's trunk, which extends up to the top of the card's perimeter, obscures most of the tree's greatest abundance. This is a reminder that sometimes we cannot know everything about what might happen down the line. Some choices are made with the best of intentions, and the complete pros and cons will be revealed as time progresses.

The ingredients for good self-management of emotions appear in the colors of the man's clothing. Brown represents realistic expectations. Blue represents inner truth. Red relates to the passionate self-protection, and grey is related to objectivity.

A tiny violet mountain is present in the distance, along with another far away tree. This represents the ongoing need for life's contemplations.

For as long as life continues there will be choices to make. There is however a way to achieve the most heavenly of outcomes, to which the violet mountain awaits.

Overall, the man is presented with one of many twists and turns of life. His role is to make sound choices, with the use of his intuition, tempered by the need for consideration beyond that of emotional impulse.

Overall theme

The overall theme of a card is the generalized message that may apply to a single card spread. The overall theme of Four of Cups is as follows:

Listen to your heart, and then listen to what your heart may not be telling you.

CHAPTER 50

FIVE OF CUPS

Five of Cups represents spiritual exhaustion. Five of Cups is a call for interpersonal connection, to help another person lift themselves out of their sense of grief.

First impression

A greying figure of indeterminate gender stands mournfully beside a flowing river. At the other side of the river sits a dwelling, and in a distance, a bridge.

Basic Definitions

In the upright position, Five of Cups represents loss, bereavement, hurt, disappointment, regret, and emotional challenges.

In the reverse position, Five of Cups represents healing a rift, acceptance, calmness, lessening the grief, and getting help from a friend.

Interpretation of symbols

The figure depicted in Five of Cups may be a man, due to the lack of adornment or traditionally feminine features. However, the black cloak that covers most of the figure's features obscures anything that may give clarification as to their gender. For this reason, the gender cannot be confidently determined. What is known of the figure is that they are shrouded in the darkness of their cloak, which represents grief, despair, but also mystery, the unknown, and the unfamiliar. Similarly, the indeterminate color of the sky is neither grey, white, or blue, but may in fact be all or none of these colors. The overall message related to the uncertainty of the figure and sky is that it does not matter, or is inaccessible, and that an air of hopelessness has taken over.

The figure's hair has turned grey, but not the white-grey of wisdom as seen in The Emperor or The Hermit. This figure's hair has transformed from worry or trauma, and takes on a darker, blackened-grey hue.

The barren ground on both sides of the riverbank depicts a sustained loss. Note the blackened coloring of the yellow ground. Three of the figure's cups lie overturned on the ground, their contents spilled. There is a deep, albeit narrow gouge, into which some of the cup's contents have spilled, forever lost to the dark and barren earth.

From the figure's perspective, the dwelling appears inaccessible. The figure's gaze is focused on what they have lost. There is nothing further that can be done to rectify a misfortune, which alludes to bereavement from death or other significant personal cost of enormous emotional impact.

Although it may not appear in all print versions, the figure's face is redder than the skin colors of many other Rider Waite figures. This is likely to represent the aspect of regret that appears in the card. There is the possibility of shame here, of loss and disappointment because something to damage the heart of another has been done.

Many of the subtle symbols within Five of Cups give relevance to the card's reverse definitions. The bridge in the distance has two arches. Similarly, two upright cups appear behind the figure. From the figure's perspective, neither of these figures is visible, however, when the card is in reverse, they represent the opportunities that arise when a problem is halved and shared with another person. Should the despondent figure represent someone who has been harmed, these same symbols can relate to the importance of apology, giving support to others, and offering gentle direction to a person who is blinded by their despair.

The liquid which has spilled from the cups is assumed to be blood and water (depicting life and emotions). However red liquid may equally relate to wine, which can be replaced, and the other liquid is not the same as the blue flowing river of emotion that appears in the card's imagery. Once again, newer print versions of the Rider Waite deck may depict water having spilled from the third cup, but it is in fact a green liquid rather than blue in most print versions. The meaning of the color difference is related to green, which relates to fresh opportunities, calmness, a renewed simplicity, and the growth of something new.

When the card is reversed the hopelessness is replaced by a sense of calm acceptance, room for healing, and assistance from others. The dwelling in the distance is indeed accessible, and once there, the figure may find the lushness of the opportunities that have been there all along.

Overall theme

The overall theme of a card is the generalized message that may apply to a single card spread. The overall theme of Five of Cups is as follows:

In the darkness of a tunnel, exists the way in of light and the way out of light. All you need to do is find the way.

CHAPTER 51

SIX OF CUPS

Six of Cups denotes fond memories of a simpler time. Six of Cups relates to cherished recollections of the past, including memories that may be flawed. When upright, the positive aspects of nostalgia

tend to appear. When in reverse aspects of childhood may turn sour or may raise the concept of a problem child. Alternatively, a harsh comparison between the past and the present may reveal a flawed perspective.

First impression
Two child-like figures stand in a village environment. The larger figure hands the smaller one a chalice of flowers.

Basic definitions
In the upright position, Six of Cups represents memories of the past, childhood, and nostalgia.

In the reverse position, Six of Cups represents failure to live in the present, obsession with the past, or problems relating to a child.

Interpretation of symbols

The softness of the two figures in the card immediately points to the idea of childhood. However, there is something amiss. The larger figure is too big to be a child, and the smaller figure is dressed like an old woman. This alludes to the fact that the memories of childhood belong to people who are older now. It is a clever use of proportions and clothing to show two moments in time – the present and the past.

Nostalgia about the past can be sweetened and flawed. Once trouble is overcome it is frequently forgotten. And hence the phrase 'the good old days,' during which everything is recalled as having been better than it is now. The white flowers that sit within each of the cups in this scene demonstrate the sweetness of the memory, whether real or simply a construct in the person's recollection.

Nostalgia can also have a bittersweet aspect and may result in feelings of loss, melancholy, or dissatisfaction. If idealized, the past can outshine the present. The safety, comfort and security of the village structures, whether it be the stone pillar and paving of the village square, the protection of the watchman in the distance, or the pleasant brickwork of the tower and dwelling, can be transformed into emotional barriers that prevent a person from fully engaging with the present, or planning for the future.

Six of Cups is certainly a card which translates emotion, relationships, and sense of self into a depiction of memory. However, note the subtlety of the yellow hue that dominates the card. Yellow represents consciousness, and in Six of Cups this means that everything is a matter of personal construct. Memories are what you remember them to be, but they may not actually be based on what was at the time.

Overall theme

The overall theme of a card is the generalized message that may apply to a single card spread. The overall theme of Six of Cups is as follows:

The past is a lovely place to relax, indulge and find wonderous souvenirs of experience. But the present is the only road that can take you to your future.

CHAPTER 52

SEVEN OF CUPS

Seven of Cups relates to reality, fantasy, and choices. When Seven of Cups appears in a tarot card reading, it may relate to fantasies and desires. Alternatively, it may be a warning of deceptions and wishful thinking.

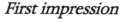

First impression

A dark figure conducts an orchestra of cups in the sky. Each cup is filled with a different object, and floats upon a mass of clouds that collectively obscure a sizeable proportion of the background.

Basic definitions

In the upright position, Seven of Cups represents fantasy, imagination, illusion, delusion, and having too many choices.

In the reverse position, Seven of Cups represents thinking for yourself, trusting your feelings, intuitive insight, and overcoming confusion or doubts.

Interpretation of symbols

To best understand Seven of Cups, imagine that all the imagery was absent. The only remaining feature is a clear blue sky. This would represent the truth.

The first layer that obscures the truth is the mass of clouds. This is a representation of intellectualism and provides a containment of any information that is available to view. Nothing beyond the clouds is visible, so for the viewer, nothing else exists.

The next layer is the series of cups that are floating within the cloud mass. Rather than allow the viewer to see the objective truth so that they may use their own judgement to reach a conclusion, the truth is obscured, and the cups represent a play on emotions, with a constructed set of alternative facts[ii].

The illusion in Seven of Cups relates to the concept of emotional triggers, marketed as intellectual choices. The variety of items that sit within each cup may or may not be logical, but each also has its own meaning.

The curly-haired head depicts beauty and eternal life.

The shrouded figure relates to mystery and enigma, but with an aura of light and power that alludes to the promise of religious virtue which may be fraudulent.

The snake is sly and stealth-like. It can represent wisdom, or flattery.

The castle is a promise of security, even though it is floating in the sky and therefore insecure.

The jeweled treasure depicts the choice of riches and material reward.

The laurel wreath represents victory and the promise of revenge or collateral damage.

The dragon can be a monster to fear, or a representation of the promise of power.

The items in blue blend into the blue sky, demonstrating that none of the assumed rewards in these cups really exist.

Each of the items serves as a distraction within a constructed reality. They represent the variety of ideals and mortal desires that commonly influence people. For example, disinformation often hides the positive aspects of reality and replaces it with fear-based messaging. In another example, the promise of riches or eternal life are forms of bribery that may or may not transpire, but, equal to fear, can be extremely persuasive methods of control.

The dark figure has their back turned and is unidentifiable. We do not know if they are young or old, male, or female, friend, or foe. The figure may be an outside force who is controlling the narrative. Alternatively, the figure may represent the things we tell ourselves, which feed our emotions, propel our imagination, but are not necessarily the options in life that will fulfil us.

In reverse, the cloud obscuring the truth becomes less relevant, the miscellaneous items fall away, and what dominates the card is an emotional or intuitive sense of what is true.

Overall theme

The overall theme of a card is the generalized message that may apply to a single card spread. The overall theme of Seven of Cups is as follows:

Be certain that your wishes and desires serve you, and not the other way around.

CHAPTER 53

EIGHT OF CUPS

E ight of Cups relates to emotional intelligence. Eight of Cups is about calmly trusting your intuition to help navigate you through situations as they occur. Eight of Cups in a tarot reading may serve as a reminder to remain open-minded, to carefully consider your options, or to bravely enter unfamiliar circumstances. Eight of Cups may also caution against rash decision-making or volatile emotions.

First impression
A man walks with his back turned, away from a body of water. There is a solar eclipse in the sky, and the landscape appears rocky and uncertain.

Basic definitions
In the upright position, Eight of Cups represents leaving home (or what you know), the end of a relationship, departures, and emotional choices.

In the reverse position, Eight of Cups represents returning home (to what you know), an embrace by family, and facing an emotional dilemma.

Interpretation of symbols

The night sky provides an indication that the mood of Eight of Cups is one of uncertainty. A solar eclipse provides for the moon to obstruct the illumination of the sun. This indicates that the way forward involves a potentially hazardous voyage towards something unfamiliar.

The man is cloaked in red and uses a staff to stabilize and pace himself as he navigates the low-level rock path before him. The Hermit also uses a staff, which provides grounding and stability of mind as he gathers wisdom. In The Hermit's example, he appears as a lone figure with nothing to guide him other than his own sense of prudence. The figure in Eight of Cups uses the power of his soul to move beyond that which gives him comfort, into a new and unknown territory, but shares the Hermit's calculation and insight to navigate difficult emotional territory patiently, to avoid potential setbacks wherever possible.

Behind the man are the cups he left behind. There remains an opening between them, big enough for the man to perfectly fit, should he decide to stay. This is likely to represent the familiar, or even family. The man is choosing to leave what is familiar and pursue something new.

The rock-faced mountains in the landscape represent future adventures and challenges. Emotional highs and lows are expected when the future is uncertain. By staying grounded the man can make his choices, one by one, as they are presented to him. Each step forward is an emotional triumph, each step back is a painful learning experience. But with the use of learned wisdom, the man will eventually reach the illumination of the sun, despite its present state of opacity.

When Eight of Cups appears in reverse, the familiar aspects of the card become dominant. The message may become one in which remaining close to the familiar is key to the circumstances. Alternatively, it may relate to a failure to make decisions in the past, which have now piled up, resulting in a much bigger dilemma.

Overall theme

The overall theme of a card is the generalized message that may apply to a single card spread. The overall theme of Eight of Cups is as follows:

You possess the bravery to keep yourself in check. Slow and steady, careful consideration, and tempered emotions will result in a satisfactory outcome.

CHAPTER 54

NINE OF CUPS

Nine of Cups represents comfort and satisfaction. Nine of Cups is a sign of contentment, satisfaction, and gratitude, and it often appears as a sense of emotional fulfilment related to various aspects of life, such as work, relationships, and wellbeing.

First impression

A man sits squarely on a timber bench, encircled by his cups. He appears happy and proud.

Basic definitions

In the upright position, Nine of Cups represents emotional comfort, satisfactory outcomes, emotional security, and happiness.

In the reverse position, Nine of Cups represents fleeting satisfaction, overcoming obstacles or mistakes, and a weakened sense of contentment.

Interpretation of symbols

Eight of Cups provided insight into what it takes to navigate the emotional complexities of life, and the importance of remaining steady and grounded. The Nine of Cups takes this concept further and demonstrates the liberation of feeling as though you can conquer any emotional challenge.

There is an air of radiance to Nine of Cups. The confident and happy posture of the man, the simple bench that he sits upon, which he may have made himself, represents the perfect simplicity of feeling emotionally settled and secure. Victories do not have to be major; they are victories that satisfy the soul.

The elevated cups represent a wall of security around the man's heart and the freedom to aim high. The blue table cover conceals the workings of the table onto which the cups sit. The details of how or what gave this man happiness are not important. What is important, however, is the combination of mind, body and spirit symbols that appear as a perfectly satisfactory outcome.

The man's head, symbolizing his mind, is wrapped in a red cap, demonstrating his pride and passion. His body is clothed in simple, sturdy attire and gives freedom for the man's movements. There is a glimpse of red hosiery, which denotes vigor in the man's step. The spirit is on display, high above the height of the man's physical or intellectual presence. This can relate to wishes and dreams that sit within the soul and can sometimes be deeply personal.

The Nine of Cups is sometimes referred to as the Wish Card. Depending on the circumstances of the reading, it can represent the freedom to aim high, and to believe that the deepest of desires can come true.

Overall theme

The overall theme of a card is the generalized message that may apply to a single card spread. The overall theme of Nine of Cups is as follows:

If you give yourself permission to dream big, then the door will open to permit big things to enter your life.

CHAPTER 55

TEN OF CUPS

Ten of Cups refers to the perceived or real achievement of life's purpose. It represents appreciation for family, home and other aspects of life that reflect harmony and prosperity.

First impression

A man, woman and two children are rejoicing. They stand beneath a rainbow arc of cups, among a pleasant scene of natural landscape and distant dwelling.

Basic definitions

In the upright position, Ten of Cups represents family, harmony, fulfilment, peace, and love.

In the reverse position, Ten of Cups represents the breakdown of an untroubled home, factures in family or group dynamics, shameful secrets, and relationship discord.

Interpretation of symbols

A sizeable portion of the scenery pertains to a manufactured platform of earthy colors. Depending on print cycles, the platform can range from a pale orange, brown and green, and a combination of all three. The relevant aspect of the platform is that the life being celebrated is a reward for hard work, honesty, and dedication. The people have the life they deserve, because they made it so with the choices that they made along the way.

The man and woman are father and mother of the children and live in the home that appears in the distance. The home sits within a pleasant natural setting of gentle hills, ample river, and lush vegetation. The ideal place to live. The home is half hidden behind trees. This relates to the trust in relationships that keep them strong, and the fact that we cannot know what is inside any other person, even a family member, which may break or impact on us later in life. It may also represent a harmonious relationship with the natural landscape.

The rainbow in the sky comprises red, blue, and yellow, the primary colors to which all others derive. The red denotes passion and vitality, blue represents truth and honor, and yellow relates to the conscious awareness of what it takes to stay on the positive path. It is relevant to consider that a rainbow only appears after the rain, and so the appearance of a rainbow in Ten of Cups shows that over time, the family has experienced good and bad and has worked to overcome any emotional challenges with which they were presented. The positioning of the cups within the rainbow means that spiritual attributes have ruled the favorable outcomes depicted in Ten of Cups. Living with love and friendship or family, and in harmony with the earth, is a spiritual pursuit that often pays high dividends on life.

When Ten of Cups appears in reverse, the platform becomes a dominant feature of the card. It represents the heavy weight of family or relationship issues on each of the individuals involved. There may be family secrets or skeletons in the closet. Alternatively, the relationships, shared outcomes, and individual or shared dreams of the group may be at risk of fracture. The sense of trust is broken.

Overall theme

The overall theme of a card is the generalized message that may apply to a single card spread. The overall theme of Ten of Cups is as follows:

There is no perfection in life and to wait for perfection guarantees an empty life. There are, however, opportunities for harmony in every moment, and each moment brings you closer to the brink of perfection.

CHAPTER 56

PAGE OF CUPS

P age of Cups is an invitation to be true to self. There are two shared features of all four Page cards in the Rider Waite deck. The imagery of each depicts a young man, and each carries a message.

PAGE of CUPS.

The message carried by Page of Cups is one of creativity, personal insight and information that may have an emotional impact.

First impression
A young man stands holding a chalice. Within the chalice is a live fish. Behind the man is a body of flowing water.

Basic definitions
In the upright position, Page of Cups represents introspection, creative insight, and arrival of a message.

In the reverse position, Page of Cups represents gender confusion, feeling like an outsider in the world, and an upsetting message.

Interpretation of symbols

Page of Cups depicts a young man whose posture is relaxed, gentle, with an air of curiosity. The overall sense of the card is light-hearted and playful. The Page's clothing demonstrates this with the use of colors, the most notable being pink. The most obvious relevance of the use of a non-traditional male color on a young man, is to demonstrate combined purity (white) and vitality (red). However, there may also be direction towards the prospect of gender awareness, or even gender discretion, reversal, and uncertainty. The relevance to gender, and other aspects of identity, is therefore one of the dominant features of the card when in reverse.

The fish that protrudes from the chalice is a reminder of the abundant life that is born from water. Depending on the context of the situation, this can relate to fertility, spiritual awakening, the depth of the psyche, opportunity, creativity, and the balance between conscious and unconscious mind. Page of Cups refers to all of these, and in making eye-contact with the Page, the fish is a reminder to know and celebrate oneself. The fish implies an invitation to love freely, enjoy the opportunity to create and live open-heartedly.

In Christianity, fish denotes faith, and in particular the secret sign of one's faith in Jesus Christ in persecution during the period of the Roman Empire. This is likely to translate into a secret, heartfelt faith in oneself in Page of Cups. When reversed, it is reasonable to expect the fish to fall out of the chalice. This infers a loss of faith in oneself, or a lost sense of identity.

The Page's clothing is adorned with waterlilies, which signify purity, innocence, and artistry. However, waterlilies are also a symbol of the female force, which reinforces the idea that a blurring of traditional gender identities was acknowledged by the creators of the Rider-Waite deck and accounted for in Page of Cups.

The body of water that flows behind the Page is proportionate to the emotional relevance of the card. The Page's headdress includes a blue scarf, draped across his head and shoulders as though aligned to the flowing waters behind him. The scarf curves and blends into the blue aspects of the Page's tunic. This indicates an open heart, and someone who freely expresses their emotions to others.

The contrast between the body of water and the yellow manufactured platform on which the Page stands demonstrates a relationship between emotions, thoughts, and ideas. The equal proportion of these two aspects of the card should be noted. When the card is in reverse, the identity of the Page is questioned, and the dominant platform becomes a burden of uncertainty against the water.

Overall theme

The overall theme of a card is the generalized message that may apply to a single card spread. The overall theme of Page of Cups is as follows:

Remain youthful at heart to experience joy in all you do, everyone around you, and everything you are.

CHAPTER 57

KNIGHT OF CUPS

K night of Cups represents the grandeur of love. Each of the four Knights in the Rider Waite deck relates to a distinct influence that helps to shape one's personality and manner of response to a variety of situations. Knight of Cups is influenced by a romantic dream of love.

First impression

A man dressed in armor sits atop an elegant white horse. In his right hand he holds a chalice upright and forward, like an offering. In the background there is a sparsely vegetated desert, with a gentle river flowing through its center.

Basic definitions

In the upright position, Knight of Cups represents idealism and romantic ideas which may sometimes turn out to be unrealistic.

In the reverse position, Knight of Cups represents a deceitful lover, love obsession, unfaithfulness, or coming out to others.

Interpretation of symbols

The idealistic inferences of Knight of Cups appear throughout the card's imagery. The Knight sits proudly upon a playfully prancing horse. The Knight's armor is adorned with expressions of heroism and divinity, which are lovely ideals, but not entirely supported by the realities of battle. The Knight's helmet and boots include wings, both of which are a reference to the God Hermes[iii]. The blue patterns of water on the Knight's tunic relate to his heightened emotions. The red fish on his tunic are an expression of enthusiastic faith.

However, the blues and reds of the Knight's attire are contradictory. Red denotes fire, and blue denotes water. Together they cancel each other out, potentially leaving the Knight with nothing to fight with.

As proud and elegant as the Knight with his horse appears, it is far more likely that they are suited to a parade, or a show, rather than a battle.

The desert landscape includes heavenly expectations (mountain peaks), but little vegetation, like The Emperor. As in The Emperor, a body of water allows for success, however, the optimism of the card presents an ideal, rather than a solid foundation from which to achieve a sound result.

This is not to say that the romantic Knight of Cups is a negative card. It is certainly not. Idealism and romance are beautiful ingredients to include in life and its passionate pursuits. However, Knight of Cups should be considered in the context of other cards in a reading, to ascertain whether sufficient forethought or substance accompanies the dreamy aspirations of love expressed by the knight.

When in reverse, the desert landscape in Knight of Cups becomes a dominant feature of the card. Every emotional aspect of the Knight is cast into doubt. Every ostensibly heartfelt message may be a lie. The chalice, assumed to be filled with love, may in fact be empty. There may be a grand show of affection, but without substance. There may also be the possibility of excessive love, obsession, or lifting the veil to reveal an opposite of what was previously held close to the heart.

When Knight of Cups appears in a reading, expect a bewitching person or influence to appear, or for new love to begin its bloom.

Overall theme

The overall theme of a card is the generalized message that may apply to a single card spread. The overall theme of Knight of Cups is as follows:

Bewitching are the early days of love. Romance is the blossom of the spring. As summer approaches, the blossom that survives to produce fruit will sustain you through the harshest of winters.

CHAPTER 58

QUEEN OF CUPS

Queen of Cups relates to intuition and sensitivity. Each of the four Queens in the Rider Waite deck is an aspect of The Empress and provides insight into an influence affecting personality. Queen of Cups represents the heart aspect of The Empress, her maternal love towards others, the abundance of life she can create, compassion and kindness.

The appearance of a Queen in the tarot reading relates to a person in the querant's life, or a person of influence that may not be immediately apparent but is somehow relevant to the circumstances. Queen of Cups relates to a person or influence that inspires empathy, and may be a safe emotional confidant, friend, or protector.

First impression

A gentle woman sits atop her throne on a pebbled beach. In both hands she holds a giant chalice, which she respectfully gazes at with bowed head. Rippling waters surround her, and in the distance is a steep cliff.

199

Basic definitions

In the upright position, Queen of Cups represents intuition, compassion, and a good friend.

In the reverse position, Queen of Cups represents a vulnerability, emotional or physical frailty, and need for support.

Interpretation of symbols

Queen of Cups is the only card in the Cups Suite that includes a closed chalice. This represents the sacred or valuable nature of the chalice itself, and its contents. Further yet, it represents spiritual abundance and the importance of remaining humble (even if you are royalty). The downward tilt of the Queen's head is a sign of deference towards the chalice contents, which she glances up to view and admire.

There are references to maternity and childbirth in Queen of Cups. Three water-babies appear on the throne, one of which holds a fish[iv]. The enclosed chalice is topped with a cross and adorned with angel silhouettes. The angels appear on either side of the chalice, as though guarding something precious. This references the Ark of the Covenant[v], a significant symbol in Christianity, Judaism, and Islam. The valuable nature of the chalice and its contents infer similarity to the Holy Grail. This may be an alignment to the descendants of Jesus Christ, the source of eternal youth, or the cup from which Jesus drank at the Last Supper.

The abundance of water surrounding the Queen's throne relates to her relevance as the most emotional and intuitive of the Queens. The Queen's half tilted posture demonstrates that she is self-aware and willing to embrace everything around her. She is not a defiant Queen that faces forward to demonstrate her stature or confidence, nor is she distracted in a sideways pose. She is an emotionally intelligent Queen with empathic tendencies towards everything around her.

The Queen's blue-white attire denotes purity and truth, and fish scale design of her cloak relates to emotional abundance, faith, trust, and creativity.

When the card is in reverse, the pebbles become treacherous to the Queen and the cliff in the distance demonstrates the peril that may lead to physical or emotional frailty. By giving her whole heart, the Queen is the most vulnerable Queen to heartbreak, or weakness.

Overall theme

The overall theme of a card is the generalized message that may apply to a single card spread. The overall theme of Queen of Cups is as follows:

You are a generous spirit who feels for others and wants to offer true friendship.

CHAPTER 59

KING OF CUPS

King of Cups relates to the mastering of spiritual yearning. Each of the four Kings in the Rider Waite deck is an aspect of The Emperor and provides insight into an influence affecting personality. King of Cups relates to the heart aspect of The Emperor, his warmth, emotional stability, compassion towards others, and sense of self. The appearance of a King in the tarot reading relates to a person in the querant's life, or a person of influence that may not be immediately apparent but is somehow relevant to the circumstances.

King of Cups relates to a person or influence that represents compassionate power, emotional or practical security, steadfastness to his ideals, and who is a representation of trusting one's intuition.

First impression

A man of nobility sits comfortably upon a throne floating on a choppy sea. His right hand holds a chalice, and his left hand holds a scepter. There is a sailing ship in the far distance.

Basic definitions

In the upright position, King of Cups represents friendship, charisma, emotional support and stability, and a warm-hearted character.

In the reverse position, King of Cups represents emotional isolation, self-pity, and drug or alcohol dependence.

Interpretation of symbols

As King of Cups, this King demonstrates calm and socially appealing attributes related to emotional strength, which he offers as a comfort to others.

The symbols within the card collectively demonstrate that the King has mastered the spiritual forces of life, his emotions, and as such can defy natural laws, such as gravity, composition, and density.

He sits comfortably on a stone throne that is miraculously floating on water. The message is that management of one's emotions brings buoyancy to even the turbulent times depicted by the choppy water.

The water itself represents a moment of emotional turmoil, uncertainty, or danger. Note the comparison between the distant sailing ship, tilted by the water's waves, and the uprightness of the King's throne. The throne is made of stone, which represents solid, supportive structure. The King is not at risk of falling from his throne, despite any turbulence he may face. His emotional security keeps him safely protected.

The King's tilted half profile demonstrates his comfort and ease. He is self-aware and confident. He does not need to stare down an opponent to prove that he is strong. His strength is within himself, his deep intuition, which he follows and trusts.

The King's attire combines the three primary colors. This relates to the need to remain true to (or directed towards) one's primary aims, even during times of emotional upheaval. The sight of the King overall is of a steady ship in a storm, which is a key aspect of the card's relevance.

Various smaller illustrative features are larger in relevance than they appear. The red jellyfish objects within the King's crown are not literal jellyfish despite the occasional assumption that they are. This is because of the various references to water, the sea, and other sea creatures that appear in the card. It is most likely that the red features of the crown demonstrate the passion or emotion available to the King, but sit within his crown, representing his sovereignty over those emotions. He can master his emotional responses in any situation, and for this reason, the positioning of the red features appears as close as possible to his point of wisdom, his mind.

A golden fish hangs from the King's neck. This is a reference to Christianity, and the security of following and gaining comfort from one's faith. The sea creature that appears above the water to the King's right reflects the King's understanding of things normally hidden below. The sea-creature would not ordinarily be visible, akin to the inner processes which guide a person's actions. The King's intuitive prowess is a mark of his dignity and sovereignty.

The King's scepter, which he holds in his left hand, is an emblem of authority, or a symbol of royal power. It signifies the King's rule over others. He has the power to control, which is evident in his scepter, but with superior intuitive senses, he chooses to do so with compassion.

When the card is in reverse, King of Cups is at the mercy of the overpowering waters. His authority is challenged, or he is unsupported. He may feel vulnerable to his emotions or may have emotion-based frailties that lead to damaging behaviors, such as substance abuse. The heaviness of his throne is less supportive and appears more like a crutch or a prison.

The combined intelligence, logic, and grounding of the King, along with his justice-yielding qualities, makes him a formidable presence.

Overall theme

The overall theme of a card is the generalized message that may apply to a single card spread. The overall theme of King of Cups is as follows:

Your mastery over your emotions and reliance upon the quiet whispers from within, with settle any storm.

CHAPTER 60

THE SWORDS SUITE

The Swords Suite comprises fourteen cards and represents one of the four elemental suites of the Minor Arcana (Air). There are four Royal cards (Page, Knight, Queen, and King), plus ten numbered cards (Ace, and II-X).

Just as each numbered card from the Wands and Cups Suites aligns to one of the Major Arcana cards numbered I-IX, so do each of the numbered cards from the Swords Suite. The key phrase which corresponds with the Swords Suite is, *I think.*

There are two distinct characteristics of the Swords Suite which will help you to appreciate the relevance of seeing Swords in a tarot reading. In the first instance, Swords relate to perception, thought, intellect, truth (or facts) and communication. To fully appreciate the second Swords Suite distinction, consider its corresponding element, Air.

Air is invisible, except when mixed with something else, such as smog, gas, or steam. In isolation, air can suddenly appear, as if from an unknown source, and destroy everything in its wake, like the most powerful hurricane winds. Then again, air may exist as the gentlest breeze, or sit perfectly still, displaying no movement at all. This does not mean that the air is not present, simply that its force is unseen. Where life exists, so does air exist. It is the most fundamental element for all living things.

Perception, thought, intellect, truth can be overt or covert by nature, varying only in the degree to which they are communicated. The power yielded by air, as represented in the Swords Suite, can be equally overt and easy to see. However, the power of hidden, covert power should never be underestimated.

Consider the Swords Suite in isolation, where no elements of compassion, inspiration or consideration of wellbeing exist. Raw unabated power, whether openly yielded or manipulating events from behind a curtain, can be devastating. Conversely, such intense power may bring a form of justice to the issue at hand. Justice, however, is something that may be subjective. It may be considered a positive end, or an injustice, depending on who is perceiving the outcome.

Note that when truth and intellect combine with inspiration and compassion, wonderful things can happen. For this reason, a tarot card reading that includes other elemental suites, tends to demonstrate greater balance and consideration of the situation at hand.

Swords in a tarot card reading.

When a card from the Swords Suite appears in a reading, it is likely to signify an aspect of the Querent's thought process, or may represent obvious (or hidden) truths, opportunities for analysis and open communication.

If a tarot card reading mostly comprises of cards from the Swords Suite, the environment may be rife with tension or disagreement. Legality, over analysis, and issues relating to communication (including miscommunication and lies) are all represented by the Swords Suite. A reading filled with Swords may be a warning of hidden motives and manipulations. Alternatively, the reading may reflect the Querent's questions about life and even what their life's purpose is.

Relying on the Swords Suite and element of air alone can lead to a disregard for others and the impact of one's decision making. However, cards from the Swords Suite may also demonstrate superior skills in the areas of logic, rationale and communicating with others.

To proficiently read a card from the Swords Suite, take account of its symbolism, numerical value, placement in the reading, whether it sits upright or in reverse, and proximity to other wands cards. Consider that life comprises of all four earthly elements, and that energy from surrounding cards representing other Minor Arcana suites may be relevant.

CHAPTER 61

ACE OF SWORDS

Ace of Swords denotes a triumph of force. Ace of Swords appearing in relative proximity to any other Minor Arcana card may serve as an override to the other card. This may be a positive thing, denoting justice, and a clean slate, arising from an airing of grievances or exposure of truth. Alternatively, the sharpness of the sword can be a danger to all who play with its power, including the Querent. Depending upon the placement and position of the card, it can appear as a warning of harsh truths, manipulations of fact, or forced injustices.

All Ace cards in the Minor Arcana suite can be read as yes/no cards. Upright tends to represent Yes, and reverse appears as No. The interpretation of yes or no is not absolute however and should reflect the symbolic references that appear in the card.

First impression

A colorless hand emerges from a cloud, holding a single upright sword. Encircling the sword is a gold crown, draped with sprigs of red berry mistletoe and fishbone fern. Six golden droplets fall from the sword. Below a grey sky lie nothing but gentle mountainous peaks.

Basic definitions

In the upright position, Ace of Swords represents the ultimate truth or revelation, clarity and understanding, justice, and decision-making.

In the reverse position, Ace of Swords represents restraint and patience, the violation of truth, miscommunication, the conceptualization of truth, or a surgical procedure.

Interpretation of symbols

As with all Aces in the Minor Arcana Suite, the grey sky and clouds appear neutral to the eye and represent a lack of foresight and/or judgement. Ace is the first number in the Swords Suite, and it marks the beginning of something new, which may include the conception of an idea, a shock admission, or a cleanse by administration of justice. However, the hand's position within a cloud conceals the source from which truth or justice derives, and any motives that may apply.

The hand is making an offering of a revelation, superior intellect, or the power to create a just outcome, whether in secret or for all to see. The offering is one of ultimate victory over matters requiring superior intellect, and methods of communication. The mountains of blue, brown, and violet symbolize spiritual goals, conceived through intellectual analysis and raw power. The crown represents superiority, its four points representing each of the four earthly elements, and the ability to harness all which is materially possible. The crown may have belonged to an adversary, now presented as collateral damage.

The enthusiastic motion of the hand from the cloud has dislodged six golden leaves from the crown. The number six aligns with the decision-making aspects of the sixth Major Arcana card, The Lovers.

In Chinese numerology, six represents intelligence, and how well a person can deal with issues of legality and negotiation. Superior outcomes requiring intellect and communication skills are possible where balance is achieved.

Almost every card in the Rider Waite tarot deck includes people, in their full body form. The inclusion of simply a hand in the Ace of Swords card is a warning not to allow the gift of intelligence to forego complementary gifts such as compassion, inspiration, or the consideration of matters related to wellbeing.

Overall theme

The overall theme of a card is the generalized message that may apply to a single card spread. The overall theme of Ace of Swords is as follows:

A revelation is upon you, should you wish to embrace it. Clarity can be both kind and cruel, and a forced outcome can result in success, or can rebound and return upon you as a success for others.

CHAPTER 62

TWO OF SWORDS

Two of Swords relates to realistic decision making. Two of Swords reminds us that decisions have consequences. Fear of those consequences may be illogical and baseless, but they may equally be founded and intuitively predicted.

First impression

A woman sits on a bench seat, upon a manufactured platform of stone. She is blindfolded and holds two swords, in crossed position, against her chest. The natural landscape behind the woman consists of a large body of water, and puddles on a lush green bank. Rocks protrude from the water, and in the distance is an orange mountain range.

Basic definitions

In the upright position, Two of Swords represents indecision, avoiding the facts, self-defense, and fearing reality.

In the reverse position, Two of Swords represents sorting through conflict, decision-making, and having been the victim of lies, duplicity, or betrayal.

Interpretation of symbols

When considering the symbolism of Two of Swords, it is helpful to consider the imagery in the context of the card's contrasting features.

The woman sits on a solid structure, on a purpose-build foundation, but cannot (or refuses to) see beyond her blindfold. Close examination of the blindfold shows that she may in fact be able to see, because her eyes are not entirely covered. This hints at the idea that she does not want to acknowledge the reality around her.

The woman is safely elevated from harm but does not know what surrounds her and so is only aware of her uncertainty. She has two swords crossed against her chest, to protect her heart. Each sword carries equal value, and thereby the weight of each sword and the option it may represent is in direct competition with the other. The length of each sword extends beyond the parameters of the card, depicting the massive weight each sword potentially yields.

The natural landscape shows a vast body of water with rocky banks protruding. Only the tops of each bank are visible and there are likely to be more rocks beneath the surface of the water. This reflects a sense of trepidation and unknown emotional risks, or risks to the heart. When the card is upright, the emotional perils of making the wrong decision, or failing to avoid unfavorable things rules the card's imagery.

Even the relationship between water and the ground poses a dilemma. Does the water nourish the ground and provide its fertile greenness? Or are the puddles a sign of a rising tide that threatens to flood the shoreline?

In contrast to the natural landscape, the solid stone platform and bench seat are signs of practical support, logic, lack of judgement, material safety, security, and predictability. A solid footing from which to reach a decision. When the card is in reverse, the act of making a sound choice rules the card's imagery.

A challenge exists in the Two of Swords, between logic and emotion, the conscious and unconscious, material and intuitive, left and right, up and down. Even the grey clothing worn by the woman has no determination of color. The blindfold fails to prevent the power of her third eye (see the part in her hair above the blindfold). Everything the woman needs appears in the card. Her preoccupation with hiding makes her blind to the resources available, or which option to choose.

One feature of the card hints that the woman's inner conflict could be resolved with courage. A tiny red section of the woman's robe, between her hands, reflects the brave decision that could be made if the woman chooses to acknowledge it.

There should not, however, be an automatic interpretation of undue fear when it comes to Two of Swords. The crested moon signifies intuition and may in fact depict a premonition of what is about to come in the very next card, Three of Swords. The card merely demonstrates the competing aspects of choice and what may be at play in a complex environment that requires decision-making.

Overall theme

The overall theme of a card is the generalized message that may apply to a single card spread. The overall theme of Two of Swords is as follows:

Your fear of truth or deception may or may not be founded. The answer to your dilemma is to balance intuition and intellect. A practical choice appears to those who are informed and brave.

CHAPTER 63

THREE OF SWORDS

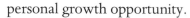

Three of Swords relates to learning from painful experiences. When the card appears in a reading, it may be a marker for a difficult moment that has the potential to become a positive personal growth opportunity.

Three of Swords is an experience of pain, but also an encouragement to exist beyond the pain. This may include learning how to improve the future, by learning from painful experiences of the past.

First impression

A heart appears suspended in a stormy sky. It has been pierced by three swords.

Basic definitions

In the upright position, Three of Swords represents miscommunication, rejection, hurtful words, and a painful realization.

In the reverse position, Three of Swords represents hiding the true extent of the pain or making a quick recovery.

Interpretation of symbols

The predecessor card to Three of Swords described a dilemma of conflicting choices, in which two competing ideas pose a risk to the decision maker. In Three of Swords, the intuitive premonition of doom may, in fact, be realized.

The intellect and communication represented by the Swords Suite has resulted in a triple stab to the heart. Three swords have entered from the left, the center, and the right, and protrude from the other side of the heart, demonstrating a complete perforation. There is no indication of how this occurred, but it is done, and the effects of the action are emphasized by the background scene of storm clouds and rain in an otherwise empty sky.

The act of impalement has historical context to consider. It was a method of torture and execution directed by Babylonian kings and Egyptian pharaohs (circa 1900-1200 BC) performed by others and out of view of the one who directed the order. A divine infliction of pain, communicated by someone or something unproven, for reasons unknown.

Similarly, Three of Swords is one of only two cards in the Minor Arcana suite, apart from Aces, in which no person appears in the imagery. The other card is Eight of Wands. The absence of a person is a reminder that the impact of the action is the only thing that matters, not the action itself.

The heart is wounded in an environment that is dismal. There is, however, a subtle color shift in the swords as they protrude from behind the pierced heart. Each of the swords in the Rider Waite deck comprises variations of white, grey, and blue. The purpose of this is to illuminate the shape and texture of a sword's metallic structure. There is also the indifference of a sword, purely pertaining to the process of thought, intellect, and communication, without consideration of any action, possession, or emotion.

The solid blue tips of the swords are not related to shape or texture, nor are they in keeping with the intellectual aspects of the Swords Suite, so the color itself requires examination.

Blue in tarot relates to air, expansiveness, breathing room, clarity, and is also the color of water, relating to emotions, relationships, and sense of self. The blue tips of the swords speak of a pain acquired through clarity or truth, or the manipulation and distortion of those things.

The proportions of the heart against the swords magnify the message of the card. The heart is central to the scene and large, while the swords that have resulted in so much pain, are comparatively small. This represents the emotional aspects of the card. A painful truth, an emotional realization, a sorrow from misunderstanding, or pain inflicted by lies, or hurtful acts.

Conversely, the oversized heart can also be testament to how small or temporary the damage can be, or appear to be, depending on how it is managed. Consider the implication of thought and communication and whether the pain is an honest reflection of the circumstances. Has a petty infringement been blown out of proportion?

When reversed, Three of Cups may mean that a person has not properly dealt with their emotional pain. They may be hiding the depths of hurt that they feel, or they may have bounced back without having healed their wounds. Alternatively, any attempt to hurt their heart has failed.

Overall theme

The overall theme of a card is the generalized message that may apply to a single card spread. The overall theme of Three of Swords is as follows:

When born from properly treated wounds, intellect and emotion are learned helpers that combine to provide you with enduring strength.

CHAPTER 64

FOUR OF SWORDS

Four of Swords relates to withdrawal and isolation. Four of Swords is a card depicting the withdrawal of a person, either way from others, or inward so that they may focus on themselves. Depending on which direction and position in a reading the card appears,

it may relate to a healthy mindset or attempt to restore a healthy perspective by pausing for a moment to regroup and reflect. Alternatively, the symbolism of the chapel and tomb-like resting place reminds us of death, and the card's message may be that of an unhealthy withdrawal, such as that of a troubled mind.

First impression

A knight lies upon a tomb in a stone chapel. His hands are positioned for prayer or meditation. His sword is set aside nearby, with others attached to the wall above him.

Basic definitions

In the upright position, Four of Swords represents holding back, taking a time-out, meditation, and resting the mind.

In the reverse position, Four of Swords represents loneliness, insomnia, self-neglect, and strange dreams.

Interpretation of symbols

The most prominent symbolism in Four of Swords is the starkness of the background, and the solid, stone structures. Apart from a vibrant, stained-glass window, the walls are pale grey. There is no visible sky. Similarly, the color of the knight, the stone structure he is resting upon are devoid of distinguishing colors. However, there is significance to the colors that do exist.

The greyness of the background, coupled with the simplicity of the hanging swords, represents composure, neutrality, and balance. Alternatively, grey can also represent clouded thinking, apathy, and indifference. Considering the color grey as relating to the conscious state, is the knight pausing to rest between battles, or hiding from the outside world?

The blackened yellow of the knight not only reflects his conscious withdrawal in the moment, but alludes to an element of mystery, which may reflect the mystery of the mind, and even offer a hint at disquieting or troubling thoughts.

The knight has laid one of his swords aside, and it appears as though part of the structure on which he sleeps. In this position, the knight's own sword is the most difficult to reach in the event he needs it. The other three are suspended on the wall, but would require careful removal, as the sharpness of their tips are positioned as though to skewer the knight at any moment.

Stained-glass symbolizes vision and perceptions. The perceptions may be mental, physical, or spiritual in nature, and may differ according to a person's beliefs. The origins of staining glass are relevant to the symbolism of the window, which appears in only two cards in the Rider Waite deck (also appears in Five of Pentacles). The staining of glass occurred as a form of ancient alchemy, for the purpose of creating a transformed appearance on what lay beyond the glass. Therefore, the inclusion of stained-glass in an otherwise muted scene, highlights the idea that conscious perceptions are in play.

The stained-glass window comprises of many glass panels, which collectively form a mosaic. This may reflect the need to solve a puzzle or gather one's thoughts about a complicated experience.

Finally, the stained-glass depicts a scene of people in vibrant color. This may reflect the knight's positivity about what lies beyond the confines of his chapel, or it may be a sign that he is in exile from a world that continues to flourish in his absence.

There is a symbol that hardly gets mention in Four of Swords, despite being quite relevant. To the right of the window there is the appearance of a long straight rod, with a handle within reach of the knight. If the rod controls a curtain, then the knight could control his perceptions by using the tools available to him which determine the source of what informs him. The end of the rod points towards the man's root chakra[vi], which is one of the seven major chakras, and associated with grounding and survival instincts.

Overall theme

The overall theme of a card is the generalized message that may apply to a single card spread. The overall theme of Four of Swords is as follows:

When life presents you with a mosaic of abstractions, allow yourself a moment to complete the puzzle before you, so that you may perceive the world with a refreshed, healthy perspective.

CHAPTER 65

FIVE OF SWORDS

Five of Swords symbolizes a ruthless victory, often at the expense of others, highlighting a willingness to sacrifice relationships and integrity for personal gain.

Five of Swords relates to the intellect of conflict and how strategy (planning) and tactics (method) can determine who wins the battle, and the war. An intellectual adversary may be calculating and cold or may be motivated by their own internalized dialogue that justifies winning at any cost. Key messages that appear in Five of Swords relate to recognizing that bullies fight unfairly, conflict is often sparked by misconception or bruised ego, and that the system does not always produce a justice-based outcome.

Because the Swords Suite points to issues of intellect and communication, Five of Swords may also be a reminder to work the system or cut your losses before things go too far.

First impression

A young man stands in an alert pose, holding two swords upwards against his shoulder, and another sword to the ground. He looks backward, into the distance, where two other men stand with their backs turned, and appear to be retreating.

Basic definitions

In the upright position, Five of Swords represents conflict, tension, and bullying.

In the reverse position, Five of Swords represents heightened conflict, upheaval, funeral, mourning, and taking it too far.

Interpretation of symbols

One of the smallest features of Five of Swords is also one of the most significant. The larger of the three men, is smiling. The scene depicts the moment of one man's victory over others, and the battle is likely to have been one in which the smaller men fell victim to a vicious opponent who aimed to dominate and control his environment, and anyone in it. They are defeated, or have surrendered, and have discarded their swords, which now lie on the ground for the victor to claim as his own.

The backward glance by the victor demonstrates an absence of dignity. He would rather gloat at the loss of others, than concern himself with appearances. For this reason, he possesses an air of arrogance. He points one sword downward to stake his claim and holds two additional swords upward against his shoulder, so that they elevate his stature and make him look even bigger than he is.

The dark grey clouds stretch across the entire span of water, as if to reinforce the tension that brought these men into battle in the first place.

In the far distances, a shallow mountainous range is visible. The violet color of the mountains comprises red and blue, which denote passion and indifference, respectively.

There is a separation of water and solid stone surface on which the men are standing. The water depicts what might have been an emotional trigger for the battle to occur in the first place, but the existence of the stone surface under foot shows that compassion has no place in this scene.

The colors that appear in the men's clothing signify envy (yellow), immaturity (green), energy, passion, will and wrath (red). The blackened-red clothing of the defeated men may relate to the bloodiness of the battle, defeat, death, and emotional darkness.

Overall theme

The overall theme of a card is the generalized message that may apply to a single card spread. The overall theme of Five of Swords is as follows:

Triumph and disaster balance on a slender thread, woven from your ability to choose your battles wisely. Enter the wrong battle and you may lose. Enter the right battle and you may lose. But if the battle is unavoidable, and regardless of whether you win or lose, fight only as far as to release yourself from the battle. Remaining whole and fully restored is your ultimate victory.

CHAPTER 66

SIX OF SWORDS

Six of Swords denotes a departure from troubling times. There does not need to be a departure to achieve harmony with Six of Swords, and it may relate to a rosier future, or a harmonious new enterprise. When reversed, Six of Swords may warn of difficulties that arise when a person is passive in their own life, or overburdened by stressful situations, represented by floods and/or storms.

First impression
A ferryman steers his boat, in which a child and adult sit as passengers. The boat travels towards a destination of shallow mountains and natural landscape.

Basic definitions
In the upright position, Six of Swords represents transition, moving on, travel, and recovery.

In the reverse position, Six of Swords represents travel delay, floods, and storms.

223

Interpretation of symbols

As with other cards in the Rider-Waite deck, there is significance in the positioning of the figures within the card. It is implied that the seated adult is the child's mother. Both are hidden by an enveloping cloak.

All three figures are all turned away from the viewer, and towards the distant landscape. The waters to the left of the boat are calm, whereas the waters to the right are choppy. The positioning of the figures, and the difference in the waters infer that the people are departing, fleeing, or being rescued from, a turbulent or challenging moment in time.

The pale grey-white of the sky depicts neutrality and a new beginning. There is no judgement of the past upon arrival, and the future promises a clean slate. Similarly, the shallow landscape of soft rolling mountains depicts serenity ahead, a place to recover from the past and transition into the new.

It is worthwhile noting that the scene also shows the man taking the active role, whilst the shrouded adult figure takes the passive role. Given the traditional roles ascribed to male and female figures in the Rider-Waite deck[vii], this aids in the assumption that the passive adult figure is a woman. The inclusion of a child in the scene further supports this point, as children are traditionally closer to the mother during early years of development.

The long pole that the ferryman is using to steer his boat is black or black-brown in color. The color may relate to the mysteries of what the future holds (black), or a sense of getting back to basics (brown). The length (or depth) of the pole refers to the concept of digging deep to resolve matters of the past. Notice that all the swords in this scene sit in front of the passengers. Everything from the past is resolved or left behind, and everything ahead is perceived as simplified, positive, and a move forward.

Keeping all the symbolism in mind, consider how the card may appear in reverse. No longer is the active figure in a dominant position, steering towards a calming future. Instead, a childlike helplessness and a passive lack of resistance, may be trying to navigate a stormy sea. All the swords that previously appeared as evidence of a promising new beginning could compound into an insurmountable obstacle of past prejudice, bad decisions, or unwelcome news that precedes the people's arrival at their destination. There may even be delays or prevention of travel altogether.

Overall theme

The overall theme of a card is the generalized message that may apply to a single card spread. The overall theme of Six of Swords is as follows:

Your free will provides you with the tools to achieve a harmonious future, regardless of what has preceded it. Resolve your mind, get back to basics, and move forward into the new.

CHAPTER 67

SEVEN OF SWORDS

Seven of Swords represents entitlement and responsibility. When Seven of Swords appears in a tarot card reading, it may relate to theft and deception. Alternatively, it may be a prompt for the Querent to pursue a reclamation of something deserved.

First impression

A man tiptoes away from a colorful campsite. He is carrying five swords and looks behind him, where two additional swords sit upright. In the far distance, a silhouette of people gathers in a group.

Basic definitions

In the upright position, Seven of Swords represents stealth, theft, trickery, betrayal, or reclaiming something lost.

In the reverse position, Seven of Swords represents regret, remorse, returning something, community service, or the ramifications of getting caught in a crime or act of indiscretion.

Interpretation of symbols

The principal aspect of this card is the contorted positioning of the central figure. To the observer, he travels from right to left but is looking, back towards to the right, behind him. The card's coloring is also highly significant. Apart from the color-filled campsite, the remaining imagery has hues of yellow and gold. Yellow relates to the consciousness, and the preponderance of yellow in the card denotes a clear and firm conscious decision to perform a certain task. The task performed by the man in this card is one of taking the swords of others, as they preoccupy themselves in the far distance. They have no idea of what is taking place in their absence.

The question is whether the swords are a reclamation of what the man believes he is entitled to, or whether he is acting in a deceitful way, as a thief. The golden landscape alludes to envy and greed. Gold can also represent a glimmer that acts as a distraction. This is supported by the colorful and open campsite tents. Each carries its own striking design. All the tents are left open and unmanned. Perhaps the temptation was too much for a greedy opportunist.

The man is smiling or smirking. A smile may represent his joy at having taken back what he believes has always been his. A smirk implies that he has stolen something that belongs to someone else.

The red, fur-lined cap and shoes that the man is wearing represent free will, passion, and lifeforce. This is not an accidental occurrence; it is a deliberate act. The ostentation of the fur may represent an outward display of foolishness, to disguise a hidden cleverness. The man may have put on a performance to others that he is simple-minded or innocent, whilst he was cleverly devising a plan right under everyone's unsuspecting noses.

Whether the card appears upright or in reverse, its meaning relates to a conscious decision to achieve a willful outcome. The purpose-built platform that the man stands upon, and its elevation above the landscape, support this. He perceives the desired outcome of his will to be higher than that of others. The decision made to take the swords outweighs the potential consequences in the mind of this man.

When in reverse, the weight of the platform becomes the dominant feature of the card, demonstrating a sense of regret, remorse, or even a sense of responsibility towards others.

The only other element of the card that remains questionable is that of the two remaining swords. Are they a flaw in the plan that will come back to haunt a thief? Are they a sign of his remorse or regret later? Are they a representation of the man's concern for others, or an offering from the seven total swords that were his to begin with?

Overall theme

The overall theme of a card is the generalized message that may apply to a single card spread. The overall theme of Seven of Swords is as follows:

Protect yourself from those who attempt to challenge your rights, encroach on your space, or take what is yours. Be mindful however, that trust is a mutual effort, and that you have as much responsibility as entitlement.

CHAPTER 68

EIGHT OF SWORDS

Eight of Swords relates to a person's decisions and actions, which are at risk of holding them hostage. It carries a reminder to trust oneself and focus on finding positive outcomes.

First impression

A woman stands in a rock pool, surrounded by swords. She is blindfolded and her body is bound by ropes. In the distance, a stone city sits atop a rock-faced mountain.

Basic definitions

In the upright position, Eight of Swords represents self-restriction, self-entrapment, Isolation, and perceived victimhood.

In the reverse position, Eight of Swords represents a re-imagined future, rewarding hard work, finding a way forward, and self-reliance.

Interpretation of symbols

The symbolism of Eight of Swords can easily mislead. The blindfold provides no sight, the rope-bound body allows no movement. The cage of swords demonstrates a further physical restriction and prevents an escape from one's circumstances. The distant city on a rock-faced mountaintop would be difficult to reach, even if full sight and movement were possible. The downward tilt of the woman's head shows that she may feel defeated, despite the passion suggested by her red and orange clothing.

So, is this woman really a victim? The answer is yes, but with one caveat. She is only a victim for as long as she allows herself to be. The key to understanding Eight of Swords is to remember that the Swords Suite is relevant to one's intellect and communication. We are in the position that we convince ourselves of, and if we restrict ourselves, or make unwise decisions, or consider ourselves to be helpless, then we become restricted or trapped within the confines of our own fears, or our sense of inadequacy.

The use of color in Eight of Swords accentuates this point. The grey sky denotes neutrality which can also translate into a conscious apathy or unwillingness to participate. Whilst the woman's attire has tones of red (representing energy and passion), the orange tones indicate that yellow also appears (as orange is comprised of red and yellow). Yellow represents consciousness, but also suggests that envy, or dissonance may be interfering with the energy, convincing us that the woman wants to be free but simply cannot be, for reasons that are within the scope of her own decision-making.

The orange rock pool provides an emotional challenge. The woman is standing on a foundation of base instincts and is likely to be making fear-based decisions. All hope for rescue (represented by the city) seems far away, and her swords become the cage from which she cannot find an escape.

The blindfold and body ties also warn of allowing your thoughts to rule your actions. If you convince yourself that you cannot, then indeed you cannot.

The only part of the woman's body that is free to move is her feet. When the card is in reverse, the bottom of her body becomes the top (and therefore a dominant feature of the card). It is suddenly possible for her to activate her bravery and self-reliance, so that she can find another way to proceed forward. A small movement may help to unravel what binds her and release her blindfold. What was previously a prison of swords may become a method of intellectualized self-support.

Overall theme

The overall theme of a card is the generalized message that may apply to a single card spread. The overall theme of Eight of Swords is as follows:

If you believe you can, then you can. If you believe you cannot, then you cannot.

CHAPTER 69

NINE OF SWORDS

Nine of Swords relates to an obsession with potentially unknown risks or other circumstances. It is a reminder that everything is transitional, and even the worst of circumstances can be overcome or surpassed by something positive. The only time hope for good is no longer available is when life is over. In tarot, life in some form, never ends.

First impression
A man sits upright in his bed. He covers his face with his hands, as though overwhelmed by worry. The background consists of nothing but rows of his swords amidst a black sky.

Basic definitions
In the upright position, Nine of Swords represents anxiety, depression, nightmares, and negative thoughts.

In the reverse position, Nine of Swords represents recovery, exploring possibilities, and being open to new ideas.

Interpretation of symbols

Eight of Swords showed parallel swords forming a prison-cell of self-restriction. The Nine of Swords takes this concept further, and once again illustrates its intention with the use of parallel swords.

The swords stretch from far left to far right, and from the top of the card, until the final sword appears to directly pierce through the man's heart. He is paralyzed by distress and anxiety, obsessed with the negative thoughts swimming endlessly through his mind. The swords represent the bars of the prison cell of worry that he finds himself trapped in.

The stark blackness of the night sky is equal to the bleakness of the man's existence. He cannot see beyond the uncertainty of the black sky, and in the absence of certainty his imagination plays tricks on his mind. He sees no way out and thinks of nothing but his tragic distress and negativity. The posture of the man, sitting upright in his bed, hints at a sudden awakening from a frightening nightmare, or the shock of learning tragic news that his fraught mind is yet to fully process.

A contrasting feature of the imagery in Nine of Swords is the bright and colorful, patterned quilt. The blue squares of the quilt include outlines of the zodiac signs. This represents the facets of life that collectively shape a person, and the instances in which life's experiences may leave a person feeling overwhelmed by circumstance.

In reverse, the zodiac features evidence the endless opportunities for hope and recovery, and the possibilities for sudden turning towards better times. The roses in alternating patterns of the quilt remind us that when the quilt becomes the dominant feature of the card (in reverse), life can turn on shift in circumstance. What previously felt impossible to bear suddenly becomes a blip in the road already travelled. Long forgotten, or merely a juncture for learning as we proceed forward.

In the upright position, the man is covering his eyes. It is the horror of all he must deal with. Alternatively, his obsession with negative aspects of life blinds him to life's beauty and signs for hope.

Overall theme

The overall theme of a card is the generalized message that may apply to a single card spread. The overall theme of Nine of Swords is as follows:

Everything in life is temporary, except life itself. When it ends, it begins, and so whatever ails your heart and your mind will vanish to the old as the new is born.

CHAPTER 70

TEN OF SWORDS

Ten of Swords represents completion and the end of what was. Whether it refers to the completion of a life, a task, defeat in battle, or the loss of a desired outcome, the message remains that the cycle has concluded and it now time to enter a new cycle.

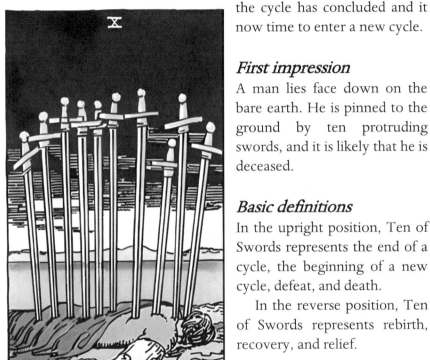

First impression

A man lies face down on the bare earth. He is pinned to the ground by ten protruding swords, and it is likely that he is deceased.

Basic definitions

In the upright position, Ten of Swords represents the end of a cycle, the beginning of a new cycle, defeat, and death.

In the reverse position, Ten of Swords represents rebirth, recovery, and relief.

Interpretation of symbols

The background of Ten of Swords demonstrates a shift, between day and night. The yellow aspect of sky may represent what we know, our conscious awareness of things we have already experienced, or the existing cycle. The black aspect of sky may be that of the subsequent new cycle that follows the old, mysterious, and yet to be experienced. There is also a middle sky, grey and thick. A blinding fog that further obscures the next phase or cycle, or a troubling and traumatic transition between life and death, as may occur when a cycle ends abruptly.

The yellow sky connects to a landscape of violet mountains and a body of water that stretches from far left to right. This infers that every emotion and passion has depleted. There is no more to give. The ground is barren, and the man's lifeforce, depicted by the red cloth that drapes his body, further supports the idea that the end has come. There are no further possibilities to extend the cycle.

The man is nondescript in his appearance, other than a few small features. His head is turned away from view, as though to confirm that he no longer exists. The color of his attire blends into the earth. Upon close inspection, the man's right arm is twisted into an unnatural pose. As appears in The Hierophant, two fingers point downward towards his palm, and two fingers point upward towards the sky. This is the sign of a blessing, or a warning.

The cycle has ended, and defeat has come, which now gives way to something new and unknown.

Overall theme

The overall theme of a card is the generalized message that may apply to a single card spread. The overall theme of Ten of Swords is as follows:

Let go of what was before. Your life remains and with it will come another cycle.

CHAPTER 71

PAGE OF SWORDS

P age of Swords represents a challenge to stagnant ideas. There are two shared features of all four Page cards in the Rider Waite deck. The imagery of each depicts a young man, and each carries a message. The message carried by Page of Swords is one of mental agility, and the ability to present an idea that may surprise or even shock others.

First impression
A young man stands alert upon a jagged hilltop on a windy day. He yields a sword and is poised to swing it as needed.

Basic definitions
In the upright position, Page of Swords represents mental agility, restlessness, experimenting or testing ideas, and a rapid message.

In the reverse position, Page of Swords represents slander, malicious gossip, personality disorder, or a difficult childhood.

Interpretation of symbols

The key aspect of Page of Swords is the indication of something about to occur. The blue sky, scattered with light clouds, depicts a new idea, with the possibility of risk or uncertainty. The flock of birds in the distance appear to be forming a shape, yet unknown. The man stands on higher ground, which may prove fertile and stable, but may alternatively represent the peril of self-elevation at the expense of others, when the card is in reverse.

The movement of the man's hair, the bend-like shape of the distant trees, the scattering of clouds and jagged hilltop all demonstrate that a strong wind is present. The wind refers to the uncertainty of the moment. Something unexpected is about to occur and the man is yielding the sword that represents his own intellectual pursuits.

Consider the wind in the clouds for a moment. Is the wind clearing the clouds from the sky, until only a fresh and true perspective remains? Is it gathering the clouds together so that they obscure the sky and hide what is real? When the card is in reverse, the clouds dominating the image are at their thickest, which may infer that the man's thoughts and words are designed to deflect and distract, rather than clarify or evaluate a new perspective.

Also examine the color transition from top to bottom. The highest point of the card when it sits in the upright position is the clear blue sky. The midpoint of the card is dominated by the violet clothing of the man (combining blue and red). The man's boots are red, denoting passion (but also ego and self-interest).

The man's legs and feet are relevant. One leg remains solidly positioned on the ground, while the other has a pointed toe. There is a hint of flirtation and quick wittedness in the pointed toe, which can turn to sharpness when the card is reversed. The man's face, and the intended movement of his sword, are both turned towards the side of his body that could range from an idea which is fun and experimental, or one which is vicious and cruel.

Overall theme

The overall theme of a card is the generalized message that may apply to a single card spread. The overall theme of Page of Swords is as follows:

You have the wind at your back and are powered with interesting ideas.

CHAPTER 72

KNIGHT OF SWORDS

Knight of Swords represents the ideological fight. Each of the four Knights in the Rider Waite deck relates to a distinct influence that helps to shape one's personality and manner of response to a variety of situations. Knight of Swords is influenced by a determination powerful enough to defy established ideas.

KNIGHT of SWORDS .

First impression

An armored knight on horseback gallops at full speed against a fierce wind. The knight swings his sword high above his head, as though to threaten an unseen enemy.

Basic definitions

In the upright position, Knight of Swords represents incisive, decisive, or impulsive behavior, and fighting for a political or ideological cause.

In the reverse position, Knight of Swords represents fanaticism, delusion, cruelty, and bad news coming.

Interpretation of symbols

The overall scene in Knight of Swords is that of conflict or surprise attack. The fierce winds, depicted by the bent-over trees and ragged clouds, demonstrate that powerful opposing viewpoints may be present.

The fully alert and tense posture of the knight and his horse, plus the full speed gallop towards a person, place or thing indicates a surge of power and determination is in play. The knight's armor is swamped in brilliant red cape, denoting fiery passion. Note the pointed toe, the sharp spur of his heel, the rod-straight leg, open helmet, high-held reins and billowing red plume. Each of these features of the card demonstrate that the knight is intensely preoccupied with his stance. There is no prospect for surrender.

Every facet of the card's imagery is intense, demonstrating that both knight and horse are fixated on a point beyond the boundaries of the card, and will not be prevented from reaching their target. There is no regard given to the barren, desert landscape, which represents an indifference to anything outside the driving force that has led to this conflict.

Despite the intensity of the imagery, the card consists of only four colors. Whilst the red clearly denotes passion and fire (even anger), the yellow ground relates to envy, which in the context of the card may also relate to conflict. The white horse denotes purity, which supports the ideological aspect of the fight. The light blue features may relate to an idolization of an idea, which in reverse becomes an obsession or delusion.

Smaller symbols add credence to the overall imagery. The birds and butterflies adorning the horse support light, air, and the ability of flight. The red plume in the knight's helmet denotes a raging lifeforce, and the predominance of armor in the knight's clothing relates to strength, impenetrability, and when reversed, a closed-off mind.

When Knight of Swords appears in a reading, it may relate to a desire to stand up for the underdog, or for ideals that are fiercely held, whether logical and fair, or not.

Overall theme

The overall theme of a card is the generalized message that may apply to a single card spread. The overall theme of Knight of Swords is as follows:

There are times when a person should defy the convention of others to realize their own aspirations. Now is your time.

CHAPTER 73

QUEEN OF SWORDS

Queen of Swords represents strategy towards truth. Each of the four Queens in the Rider Waite deck is an aspect of The Empress and provides insight into an influence affecting personality.

Queen of Swords represents the mind aspect of the Empress, the ability to focus, multitask and communicate with others.

The appearance of a Queen in the tarot reading relates to a person in the querant's life, or a person of influence that may not be immediately apparent but is somehow relevant to the circumstances. Queen of Swords relates to a person or influence that values truth and perceived justice, and who can directly influence outcomes through strategic methods or excellent communication skills.

First impression

A majestic woman sits in side-profile atop her throne on a solid yellow foundation. Her left hand stretches outward, as though to welcome others, and her right hand holds an upright sword. In the background is a blue sky with gathering billowy clouds, and a slender river.

Basic definitions

In the upright position, Queen of Swords represents perception, quick thinking, a seeker of truth and justice, and communicating in a straightforward manner.

In the reverse position, Queen of Swords represents bigotry, intolerance, narrow-mindedness, manipulation, and narcissism.

Interpretation of symbols

The Queen's posture is alert and upright. Both arms elevate upward from the armrests of her throne. The gesture of welcome that she makes with her left hand represents an openness to information and knowledge. The Swords Suite speaks of intellect and communication, and as such, Queen of Swords is highly intelligent, and thrives on information. It would be fair to conclude that information is power to the Queen. The more she knows, the more power she yields. Her alertness is a sign that she does not rest until she gets to the truth.

The overall imagery of the card coincides with the element air, wind, and flight. The top half of the sky is clear blue, with a single bird. The billowing clouds and distant trees suggest that the wind is present. The decorative aspects of the throne include a cherub with wings, and butterflies. Further butterflies adorn the Queen's crown, and further clouds appear on her sky-blue cloak. Air is the earth element that corresponds with the mind, and the prevalence of air, wind and flight features demonstrate the Queen as highly perceptive and quick thinking.

Note that the Queen's head and shoulders sit above the level of the clouds. This further reinforces the idea that she is clear-minded and highly intelligent. Also note the positioning of the single bird, directly above the Queen's crown. This symbolizes sharp focus and unlikelihood of distraction.

The more subtle imagery takes on greater relevance when the card is in reverse. The Queen's red veil covers her head and extends from the crown to the slender river. This links the Queen's intellect to the emotions of others, who may be dependent upon that supply of water. When reversed, the Queen uses her intellect as a weapon.

Similarly, the yellow platform supports the concept of a conscious mind. However, when reversed the yellow becomes a dominant feature of the card, denoting a rivalrous self-interest. The Queen's wrists are adorned with red bracelets. Are these broken shackles of her past, or a sign of her vanity that, when the card is in reverse, ignite self-serving interests that feed her sense of superiority?

The base of the throne includes what may appear to be crescent moons, however, on closer inspection they are sickles[viii]. The sickle is a superior cutting tool when compared to a straight-edged knife in the field. This is due to the sickle's curved edge, which gathers greater quantities of crops against the blade and therefore improves cutting performance. The inclusion of such an effective cutting tool infers a highly effective, and severe, cutting away of anything that might obscure truth or information,

The more subtle messaging within the card corresponds with the potential danger of a manipulative mind. This is a Queen who could use her greater intellect to fight in ways that you never see coming, until it is too late.

Overall theme

The overall theme of a card is the generalized message that may apply to a single card spread. The overall theme of Queen of Swords is as follows:

To derive success from the truth you must first know what the truth is, following which you must stand firmly upon it to achieve your success.

CHAPTER 74

KING OF SWORDS

KING ᴏꜰ SWORDS.

King of Swords relates to mastering knowledge. Each of the four Kings in the Rider Waite deck is an aspect of The Emperor and provides insight into an influence affecting personality. King of Swords relates to the mind aspect of The Emperor, his intellect, logic, and ability to skillfully communicate.

The appearance of a King in the tarot reading relates to a person in the querant's life, or a person of influence that may not be immediately apparent but is somehow relevant to the circumstances. King of Swords relates to a person or influence that represents power, expression of ideas and the attainment of a perceived justice.

First impression

A regal man sits comfortably on his throne. His right hand holds a sword upright towards the sky. The day is mild with a light blue sky, scattered clouds, and a serene, natural landscape.

Basic definitions

In the upright position, King of Swords represents truth, direct communication, authority, and powerful intellect.

In the reverse position, King of Swords represents perversion, control, a dangerous and ill-intended character, and sadistic or inhumane behavior.

Interpretation of symbols

As King of Swords, this King yields the sword of truth or justice. A variety of similarities appear between King of Swords, and Justice in the Major Arcana suite. Both men sit facing squarely forward, in structures that extend upward beyond the parameters of the card. Both men yield a sword in their right hands. Both men's right hands point upward, and left hands downward. Both wear full length robes, but in which the right foot is visible. These similarities confirm the justice elements of King of Swords.

Like his counterparts, King of Swords is sitting in a relaxed position, with knees apart and arms comfortably placed. This is an indication of his unquestionable power, and his awareness of his own majesty.

As with Queen of Swords, the King is surrounded by blue sky, which (depending on quality of print) will appear as a slightly paler blue. The subtle change in color is deliberate and demonstrates a diminished sense of uncertainty. Whereas the Queen of Swords seeks truth, the King possesses truth. There is an implied clarity and stability in the imagery. The winds depicted in previous court cards has died down and now the air is calm. There are two birds flying overhead, demonstrating that a more relaxed mindfulness is present.

As with Queen of Swords, the King's throne is adorned with butterflies and sickles, relating to openness and truth, respectively. On the left shoulder of the King, however, two fairies sit. When the card is upright, the fairies are linked to the King's violet cloak, and jointly represent his intuitive skill and ability to gain knowledge and wisdom from beyond the early plane. When reverse, the fairies become impish, whispering mischievous ideas that serve the King's interests.

The King's throne reaches upward, beyond the boundaries set by the card. This signifies a stretch of his potential and power towards the heavens – a privilege each of the Kings may enjoy, but only King of Wands and King of Swords have chosen.

The King's body is elevated against the clouds, demonstrating his superior clarity of mind. His throne sits on the natural earth, which is a mixture of green and orange-brown, representing the fertility of his ideas, the vitality of his spirit, and the logical way he exhibits his power, and which grounds him to the earth.

The combined intelligence, logic, and grounding of the King, along with his justice-yielding qualities, makes him a formidable presence.

Overall theme

The overall theme of a card is the generalized message that may apply to a single card spread. The overall theme of King of Swords is as follows:

Truth is power and the power is yours.

248

CHAPTER 75

THE PENTACLES SUITE

The Pentacles Suite comprises fourteen cards and represents one of the four elemental suites of the Minor Arcana (Earth). There are four Royal cards (Page, Knight, Queen, and King), plus ten numbered cards (Ace, and II-X). Just as each numbered card from the Wands, Cups and Swords Suites aligns to one of the Major Arcana cards numbered I-IX, so do each of the numbered cards from the Pentacles Suite. The key phrase which corresponds with the Pentacles Suite is, *I possess.*

There are two distinct characteristics of the Pentacles Suite which will help you to appreciate the relevance of seeing Pentacles in a tarot reading. In the first instance, Pentacles relate to material abundance, physicality, practicality, prosperity, and overall wellbeing. The physical aspects of life are key to understanding the Pentacles Suite. To fully appreciate the second Pentacles Suite distinction, consider its corresponding element, Earth.

Earth is a tangible element that offers a practical foundation and a sense of security and stability. Earth provides a tangible, solid base and can be proved and observed in a material sense. Its physical properties allow weighing and measuring, which supports its connection to the evaluation of prosperity and material wealth.

Earth as it relates to the Pentacles Suite, corresponds with manifestation, realization, material comforts, confirmation, and prosperity. Physical health is material in nature, and therefore also relates to a person's earth properties. For this reason, one's wellbeing, comprising of physical health, life stability, material comforts, and their general sense of prosperity, is all linked to a sense of earth grounding.

However, when taken in isolation, the material aspects of the Pentacles Suite can also carry unfavorable traits. Pentacles can represent greed, shortsighted or selfish pursuit of material wealth and comfort, or possessiveness in relationships.

When reading Pentacles, consider that physical, tangible things are both given and received. Other cards in a reading will help to ascertain whether the Pentacles card(s) are referring to material gain, or material gift to others. Also, the gain or gift may be material and relate to money or wealth, but may equally be of a physical nature, relating to health or a sense of security and safety.

Pentacles in a tarot card reading.

When a card from the Pentacles Suite appears in a reading, it is likely to signify an aspect of the Querent's relationship with the material world. Issues, such as reward for hard work, abundance, shortages, or scarcity, may be relevant.

If a tarot card reading mostly comprises of cards from the Pentacles Suite, the message may relate to a person's attitude towards wealth and possessions. There may be a need for greater practicality, or better balance between material and spiritual considerations. Further, if a reading consists of all, or almost all Pentacles cards, the message may relate to the Querent's limitations, based on a lack of non-material considerations.

To proficiently read a card from the Pentacles Suite, take account of its symbolism, numerical value, placement in the reading, whether it sits upright or in reverse, and proximity to other wands cards. Consider that life comprises of all four earthly elements, and that energy from surrounding cards representing other Minor Arcana suites may be relevant.

CHAPTER 76

ACE OF PENTACLES

Ace of Pentacles denotes a material manifestation. This may represent an actual gift, or the opportunity for attainment of great gifts. It may relate to a sudden windfall, a moment of exceptional good luck, or a chance to begin a new path towards successful attainment.

Ace of Pentacles appearing in relative proximity to any other Minor Arcana card may serve as an override to the other card. This may be a positive thing, denoting manifestation of positive outcomes. Conversely, it may denote an overly materialistic or possessive focus.

In Western and Chinese Numerology, the number one represents independence and beginnings, plus the wholeness of a single thing. It can also relate to business and intellectual pursuits, assertiveness, determination, and leadership.

All Ace cards in the Minor Arcana suite can be read as yes/no cards. Upright tends to represent Yes, and reverse appears as No. The interpretation of yes or no is not absolute however and should reflect the symbolic references that appear in the card.

First impression

A colorless hand emerges from a cloud, holding a single pentacle coin. Below is a cultivated garden scene, which includes an archway of roses. Beyond the arch, mountains are visible.

Basic definitions

In the upright position, Ace of Pentacles represents a gift, new home or project, prosperity, and the manifestation of wealth or wellbeing.

In the reverse position, Ace of Pentacles represents exaggerated treasure or wealth, prosperity without happiness, and corruption.

Interpretation of symbols

Along with all Aces in the Minor Arcana Suite, the grey cloudless sky appears neutral to the eye and represents a lack of foresight and/or judgement. Ace is the first number in the Pentacles Suite, and it marks the beginning of something new, which may include a new job, project, or place to live. However, the hand's position within a cloud conceals the source from which the manifestation arrives, and any motives that may apply. The hand is offering a material gift, which may be a physical item, wealth, or health. There is no judgement about from where the gift derives.

Ace of Pentacles is the only card within the Pentacles Suite in which the depicted coin has a double border. This is relevant in two ways. Firstly, the double border accentuates the apparent thickness or weight of the coin, which brings attention to its value. This is to infer that the coin is an ultimate manifestation, with the potential for immense value. Secondly, the double edging reminds us that a coin is double-sided. Consider that the motive of the gift-giver is undeclared. There may be no motive. The gift may indeed be deserved. Alternatively, the gift may be derived from greed, corrupt methods, and the acquisition of wealth may lead to negative consequences.

Consider for a moment a happy family, in which each member contributes in their own way to share a collective harvest, which is no more than satisfactory. What would happen if suddenly one of the members of that family acquired undeserved wealth, or simply great wealth of any kind? The family dynamic would change dramatically. The change may be positive, but it may also breed envy, and strain relationships. This is merely one example of the two-side elements of a coin, and how the double edging can be interpreted.

A row of hedged rosebushes run directly across the card, and grow into an archway, beyond which mountains are visible. A yellow pathway leads to the arch. The pathway provides the only way in which the mountains are accessible, and the color of the pathway alludes to a conscious determination to follow the path. The pale blue mountains peak upward towards a heavenly outcome, and whilst they appear in the distance, the message of their attainability is clear for someone who follows the path.

These elements of the card provide the message that a gift of opportunity has appeared Manifestation of the power provided by the opportunity will lead to attainment of a positive fulfilment.

An interesting aspect of the imagery relates to how the entire garden scene is cultivated. The rose hedges are shaped into a deliberate archway. The grass is neatly trimmed, and a display of cultivated lilies are present. Lilies denote purity and positive transformation. The green of the grass denotes freshness and new beginnings. The inference is that money can wash away prior sins. We have all come across spiritualists who seem to always focus on messages from departed famous people, or the rich and powerful. Recognizable names who spark our interest, and who have miraculously amassed a wealth of spiritual enlightenment, simply by passing away. The inclusion of cultivated lilies in Ace of Pentacles is not an agreement of this principle. Rather, it is a reminder of how our material perceptions can blind us to what appears in the distance. The placement of the lilies, along with the carefully grown hedging of roses, may serve as material decoys, which distract from spiritual truths that lay in the distance. Note the mountains are blue, and contrary to the cultivated garden area, the mountains are a divine creation and are therefore, the only truth.

Finally, the five-pointed pentagram symbol within the pentacle relates to the five elements of tarot. With the attainment of all five elements, anything is possible in a material sense, and there is also the added prospect of attainment in the spiritual realm.

Almost every card in the Rider Waite tarot deck includes people, in their full body form. The inclusion of simply a hand in the Ace of Pentacles card is a warning not to allow a material gift to forego complementary gifts such as compassion, inspiration, or the intellectualization of wisdom.

Overall theme

The overall theme of a card is the generalized message that may apply to a single card spread. The overall theme of Ace of Pentacles is as follows:

You will receive what you need, in abundance.

CHAPTER 77

TWO OF PENTACLES

Two of Pentacles refers to the juggling acts of life. It reminds us that decisions have consequences. One competing interest may overshadow another, leading to a lack of balance. Alternatively,

balance may be achieved. However, it is also relevant to note that simply balancing the priorities of the moment may be insufficient. There may also be ramifications further down the line that make Two of Pentacles far more complex than just a choice to be made.

First impression

A young man stands, balancing on one foot, with the other elevated. He holds two gold coins, wrapped in a green band. Behind the man two boats are rising and falling upon a turbulent body of water.

Basic definitions

In the upright position, Two of Pentacles represents making ends meet, balancing time and resources, and pondering available options.

In the reverse position, Two of Pentacles represents money shortages, learning difficulties, or an overload of work.

Interpretation of symbols

An important aspect of Two of Pentacles is the prevalence of blue that appears in the background. This relates to truth and clarity.

The man's attire consists of an unusually tall red hat, red and orange garments, and green shoes. The clothing colors reflect the man's youth and inexperience, the freshness of his ideas, his enthusiasm, but with a hint of the ridiculous. The hat is comically large and pointing upwards towards the sky. There are too many buttons on his tunic, denoting a risk of complication. The hem of the tunic is shaped like a Jester's, whose ability to juggle may be entertaining but lacks meaningful outcomes. There is a hint of ego and lack of credibility in the man's overall appearance. This man has taken on a mammoth task that may, or may not, be possible.

The man is holding two coins that represent two competing elements. They may work in partnership and harmony, or they may conflict. The green band relates to the continuous cycles of change, and the need to consider the wholistic nature of reality.

Two boats are attempting to navigate a turbulent body of water behind the man. His focus on maintaining his balance prevents him from seeing their strife. The waves of the water relate to the emotional ups and downs of life, which can sometimes be tumultuous. The boats, one large one small, must steer their way through something far more powerful than either can control. All they must do is try to stay afloat, regardless of what comes next.

Although it appears as a minor aspect of the card, the most promising message comes from the red belt around the man's waist. He is young and optimistic, and his energy is clearly apparent in everything he wears. However, the circular nature of his belt demonstrates his enthusiasm for what comes next, and his desire to succeed in finding a balance is genuine.

The truth is that life is filled with highs and lows. We may believe we can take on the entire burden, but it is not up to us. We just do what we can. The rest is up to fate. Although coins depict monetary matters, such as wealth or material prosperity, the Pentacles Suite also relates them to overall wellbeing, including health. Two of Pentacles is attributable to any competing aspects of life that must be harmonized or balanced.

When Two of Pentacles is reversed, the heavy burden of the platform dominates the card. There is a sense that the man is out of his depth and that his attempt to balance everything within his remit is more difficult.

Overall theme

The overall theme of a card is the generalized message that may apply to a single card spread. The overall theme of Two of Pentacles is as follows:

Not everything is controllable, but if it is within your power, then do what you can to reach a harmonious balance of the things you can control.

CHAPTER 78

THREE OF PENTACLES

Three of Pentacles relates to a joint enterprise. Three of Pentacles is an experience of recognizing that teamwork does not mean equal, better, or worse, and sometimes the motives for the team

to work together are unclear or even manufactured. However, humans live in societies that require us to work together, finding ways to fit our personal inspirations into outcomes that will coincide with the personal inspirations of others, thereby contributing to a broader societal outcome.

First impression

Three figures convene at the entrance of a cathedral. One is a stonemason, demonstrating his craftsmanship. The other two figures are a woman of nobility, holding the cathedral's architectural plans, and a monk, who is looking on with interest.

Basic definitions

In the upright position, Three of Pentacles represents collaboration, teamwork, and pooling resources and ideas together to achieve a mutually beneficial outcome.

In the reverse position, Three of Pentacles represents problems at work, disputes with coworkers, taking shortcuts, and poor-quality workmanship.

Interpretation of symbols

Three of Pentacles is a far more complex, and potentially controversial card than most people recognize. In fact, some are misled by the cleverness of the imagery. The three figures represent the diverse nature of humanity and how working together, despite our differences, can achieve positive results. However, there are also subtle messages in the imagery that are reminders of the perceived hierarchy of humans. Each of the figures is recognized for the contribution they uniquely provide in the construction of this sacred building.

The woman is likely to be the financier of the cathedral project. She wears a striking cloak of orange and red to demonstrate her energy and active participation in, or contribution to the project (red), and her creativity and the ideas she has put forward for the creation of this cathedral (orange).

The monk looks on in interest, but his attire is secondary to that of the woman. He is partly obscured by her presence. This represents the fact that the woman is bestowing the creation of the cathedral unto the monk, and the monk is a passive or grateful recipient.

The stonemason is standing elevated on a wooden bench. This is the same bench that appears in Eight of Pentacles, and its significance in Three of Pentacles is twofold. Firstly, it represents the grounded nature of working with natural wood and the value of hard work and practical skills. Secondly, it elevates the stonemason and demonstrates that without his craftsmanship there would be no cathedral. The stonemason is elevated higher than the other two figures, demonstrating that he is the most important figure in the scene. This is further supported by his clothing. The violet tunic represents closeness to heaven and spiritual virtue. The blue tights relate to truth, and the yellow apron expresses the stonemason's conscious knowledge of a practical skills.

It may therefore appear that the image is one of three figures, working together as equals, even with the stonemason in charge of the cathedral's construction. However, the bench that elevates the mason is made of wood. It is a temporary fixture. Once the job is complete the mason will return to his former position in the hierarchy of humans.

Three of Pentacles is the only card in the Pentacles suite that displays coins in black and grey, rather than gold. The purpose is to show that the value of the creation, achieved in collaboration, results in a satisfactory outcome that transcends monetary value. However, the blackened aspects of the coins are hollow and take on the darkness of the interior of the cathedral. This can also relate to the incompleteness of the coins, or their failure to fully develop the plan. In reverse, the coins may be a message of cutting corners, or inferior workmanship. The blackness of the cathedral's interior relates to mystery, danger, and potential difficulties down the line.

In summary, Three of Pentacles can easily be the depiction of a convenient and positive partnership between people. The convenience is one in which shared goals are realized. Everyone chips in what they are uniquely able to contribute so that all may achieve a positive collective outcome. However, Three of Pentacles may also be a warning of the motives of man when working together. We can never know what motivates another. Conspiracies of darkness, the power of money to influence the Church, the illusion of equality, and of stature or virtue, are all aspects of this card.

Overall theme

The overall theme of a card is the generalized message that may apply to a single card spread. The overall theme of Three of Pentacles is as follows:

Participate in the development of life, and value your own contribution and the contribution of others. It does not matter who or why, it only matters that the work achieves a mutual satisfaction.

CHAPTER 79

FOUR OF PENTACLES

Four of Pentacles relates to material security. It depicts the introversion of a person, away from the security of shared reward, love, and trust. There is a focus, to some degree, on material

acquisition and pursuit of physical security. Depending on the direction and positioning of the card, and the context of the reading, Four of Pentacles may relate to a healthy mindset or an attempt to restore a healthy perspective by establishing a practical approach to saving money and maintaining prosperity. However, Four of Wands also has a hint of unhealthy attraction to possessions, which may include hoarding, obsession, and jealousy, such as that of a troubled mind.

First impression

A man sits upon a stone bench. He has two coins beneath his feet, one tightly pressed to his chest, and another balanced onto his crown. Behind him is a city landscape with many dwellings and towers.

Basic definitions

In the upright position, Four of Pentacles represents stability, material security, isolation, hoarding, or attempting to hold onto what you have.

In the reverse position, Four of Pentacles represents stinginess, payment delays, material possession, severe hoarding, and being afraid to leave your comfort zone.

Interpretation of symbols

The coins in the Four of Pentacles represent the man's sense of material wealth, prosperity, security, and satisfaction. His proportions and posture demonstrate this in a few ways.

Firstly, the man has two of his pentacles below his feet. This represents the importance of having a foundation for material security. The man also has a pentacle pressed to his chest, in a manner that appears awkward, but also shelters his heart. Despite being awkward, the man's hands infer a circular motion, linking the man's wealth to his sense of wellbeing, and prevents anyone else from snatching his coin away from him. This suggests that he is jealously guarding of his wealth and may have a defensive approach to security and wellbeing. The positioning of the coin at his heart relates to an emotional connection to money, physical comforts, and his sense of material adequacy.

The coin that sits atop the man's crown is a demonstration of how materialism governs his thinking. This is not necessarily a negative aspect of the card, because having a sensible and practical approach to money, wealth and comfort helps to provide a stable and satisfactory life. However, the man's crown is an indication of his disproportionate attraction to material wealth. This man is not a king, and yet he has fashioned a stone bench that is like a small throne and wears a crown.

These symbols reflect his mindset. To be wealthy is to be adequate, equal to, or better than, others.

The man is the central figure, and his proportions are large in comparison to the background, which seems quite a distance away. He is sitting on an elevated platform, quite high above the landscape features. The coins beneath his feet are bigger than the other two, and this indicates that without a firm material foundation the man would feel unsupported, insecure. This indicates that he is less than comfortable in his faux-throne, or the construct of his royalty.

We know that the man's faux-royal presentation of himself is a construct, rather than a reality. The reason for this is that his crown, whilst appearing to be made of gold, consists of a less valuable substance such as bronze or painted tin. When compared to any of the court cards in the Rider Waite deck, and other figures denoting heavenly wisdom[ix], this man's crown is a closer color match to the painted towers in the distance behind him.

In fact, the buildings in the background support the idea that his man feels a sense of uncertainty about his continued prosperity. Some of the buildings represent dwellings and the comfort and security of housing and material achievement. These buildings have red roofs. The other buildings, whether grey or yellow, are likely to represent the 'ivory towers' of self-importance and elitism. The grey towers denote natural acquisition and inheritance[x]. The yellow towers denote earned wealth and artificial elevation of stature. Regardless of who resides in which tower behind him, the man may compare his own achievements against the achievements of others.

The man's red clothing represents his passion for material possessions and the degree of importance they represent for him. The black cloak, which he has wrapped around him, is a sign that he wants to conceal his possessions, to avoid losing his wealth.

Whether in the upright or reverse, Four of Pentacles includes an aspect of hoarding or jealous guarding of one's material wealth. However, what appears as an enthusiastic and practical approach to money and possessions becomes obsessive or fearful when the card is in reverse.

Overall theme

The overall theme of a card is the generalized message that may apply to a single card spread. The overall theme of Four of Pentacles is as follows:

Establishing a firm foundation will help to resolve struggles of the past, will protect against troubles of the present, and will pave the path for your stable and successful future.

CHAPTER 80

FIVE OF PENTACLES

Five of Pentacles signifies a sense of abandonment or isolation. It relates to the hardship that arises from inequality and the failure to live by one's own stated principles. The card is a reminder of our interconnectedness and demonstrates that adherence to one's faith is a practical matter that must be acted upon to be real.

First impression

Two impoverished figures walk past a church window. One of the figures is old, barefoot, and hunched forward. The other figure is young, but injured or disabled by a physical impediment, and may also be blind. There is a harsh winter storm, and the figures are alone in the snow.

Basic definitions

In the upright position, Five of Pentacles represents material loss, destitution, poverty, physical frailty, illness, and financial or material challenges.

In the reverse position, Five of Pentacles represents gaining access to support, gambling, a turning point, loss of everything, or going from bad to worse.

Interpretation of symbols

Five of Pentacles demonstrates the stark comparisons between those who 'have' and those who 'have not.' It is also a representation of selfishness and insincere faith.

The two figures present the same message. Both are hard on their luck. However, as with all the Rider Waite illustrations, there are subtle distinctions that help to broaden the representations of the human condition.

The taller, female figure is older as demonstrated by the whisps of grey in her hair. She is barefoot and her clothes are torn and worn. Nonetheless, she leans forward into the wind and snow. The orange hue of her garments demonstrate that she is not broken. She is a character that signifies the perseverance of the human spirit, even during difficult and challenging times.

The small, male figure is young as demonstrated by his size, and the pinkish hues to his hair. He wears a bell around his neck, has a bandaged foot and walks with the aid of crutches. He represents the medieval person with leprosy. A person considered forgotten, excluded from society, and unworthy of being touched. In fact, touching him may result in his disease spreading to others. He wears his bell as a warning to stay far away. His crutches serve two purposes, in the upright they remind us that this boy-man must learn to support himself, because no other assistance is forthcoming for him. In the reverse, support from an outside source may be available.

The snow carries an obvious meaning and relates to hardship, coldness, and discomfort. The cold may be weather-related, or it may relate to the coldness of being alone and unaided by others. The snow also carries a subtle meaning and reminds us that a new beginning is possible when the card is reversed. The snow dominates the scene and relates to a change in circumstances, but the outcome is not yet known.

For this reason, the turning point might be a risk for all involved.

The black walls of the church contrast with the white snow and highlight the contrast between wealth and poverty, warmth and coldness, abundance, and starkness. Black also relates to mystery, and the risks involved when one does ask for, or receive help, from others. Issues of motive and sincerity are relevant when the card is in reverse, primarily because of the aspects of the card relating to the stain glass window.

The window sits in colorful contrast to the scene below it, and its height is no accident. There is an air of privilege behind the window, which further supported by the window features.

The colors of the window align with the abundance of a prosperous life. The five pentacles are arranged into the five branches of a money tree. This is a reference to the 'money tree' or Chinese Jade Plant, which is thought to bring luck, prosperity, wealth, and success to those who care for it. The Jade Plant has been blended with the Kabbalistic Tree of Life[xi]. This implies that in the material world, life and prosperity can be perceived as interchangeable. By blending the two features, the window symbolizes insincerity of faith, or a failure of man to adhere to his own spiritual principles.

At the very top of the window, is a glimpse of an ivory tower, depicting elitism, disconnectedness, and privilege. It hints at the idea that there are wealthy people inside this church, and they have conveniently chosen to ignore whatever is happening outside their own safe and comfortable lives. This is in direct contrast to their location. The purpose of attending church is to gain closeness to the Creator of all existence.

There is also a subtle but hugely powerful message present in the card. Despite being a five-pentacle card, the imagery includes a partly obscured sixth pentacle at the top of the money tree. No other card in the Rider-Waite deck includes a superfluous elemental symbol, which reinforces the significance of this extra pentacle. Do you notice anything peculiar about this pentacle? The pentagram is inverted, depicting blasphemy, corruption and evil.

With all the virtues that religion claims to bring to the faithful, this symbol is a reference to a message in the Bible, conveniently overlooked by performative Christians[xii].

The message in this card boils down to this smallest of details. To deny one's brother or sister and to continue to claim Godliness is false faith, and a closer resemblance to the forces of darkness than to good.

Overall theme

The overall theme of a card is the generalized message that may apply to a single card spread. The overall theme of Five of Pentacles is as follows:

Your loss feels like the biting cold of a winter storm. The warmth of a life connected to others is just around the corner. Find the door and the warmth is yours.

CHAPTER 81

SIX OF PENTACLES

Six of Pentacles reflects the one holding the scales of justice, highlighting acts of giving and receiving, though not always fair or balanced. It relates to the sharing of earthly abundance and can

also pertain to gifts of wealth, success in business, lucky wins, welfare protection, and generosity. It may be a reminder of how some people regard status, or inherited wealth, to be evidence of virtue. The fact is that neither, in isolation of other factors, bears any resemblance to virtue.

When the card is in reverse, Six of Pentacles can represent a lack of material harmony and cooperation, and even fraud or misrepresentation of wealth and money matters.

First impression

A wealthy man of nobility stands before two beggars. In his left hand he holds counting scales. With his right hand he offers coins to one of the beggars.

Basic definitions

In the upright position, Six of Pentacles represents generosity, charity, and giving or receiving support.

In the reverse position, Six of Pentacles represents greed, jealousy, fraud, money disputes, and unpaid debts.

Interpretation of symbols

As with other cards in the Pentacles Suite, Six of Pentacles demonstrates the idolization of wealth in the material world. There is an immediate recognition of the coolness towards concepts of inequality or fairness, which may alternatively represent a lack of judgement. The grey-white sky, and pale grey platform indicate that whether lucky or not, people tend to get what they deserve. The colors of the platform and sky indicate that there is no sense of emotion towards any of the figures. The platform might even represent the idea that the standing figure, assumed to be of wealth and nobility, earned his riches simply by existing.

The nobleman's clothing, both colors and style, demonstrates his wealth. The red robes denote his energy and passion, and the deepness of the color has aspects of purple, which adds a hint of royalty to his persona. Consider that purple, a darker shade of violet, is a combination of blue and red, indicating that the nobleman is bestowed with good passion by virtue of his wealth. There is no other way to interpret the goodness of royalty, other than having been born of privilege that allows an assumption of goodness.

The nobleman's blue and white striped tunic can have a range of meanings. Firstly, the blue represents truth, the white relates to beginnings or virtue. The stripe travels up and down, demonstrating reciprocity, the giving and receiving of wealth. However, the stripes also create a divide between light and dark.

The nobleman's holds counting scales in his left hand. The left hand represents receiving, and therefore the scales remind us that with possession of wealth comes the power to decide what to do with it, or who to share it with. The position of the scales, sitting above the beggar who is not receiving coins, may be a message. A reminder that neediness does not guarantee receipt, and that sometimes reality is unfair.

With his right hand, the hand of giving, the nobleman drops gold coins into the hands of the other beggar. Note that his fingers form the sign of a blessing, as depicted in The Hierophant.

The two beggars are deliberately colored differently, which would be peculiar in life, as both would ordinarily be wearing similarly worn out mismatched or greyish clothing. Consider, for example, the previous card, Five of Pentacles, in which two desperately poor figures are dressed very differently to the beggars in Six of Pentacles. This would indicate there is a reason for the distinction. As mentioned throughout this book, nothing is by chance when it comes to the Rider-Waite illustrations.

Firstly, consider the figure on the right. He wears a blue cloak and his hair looks thinned. Is this a sign of stress? His blue robes denote truth, indicating that he is in genuine need. The small rip in his clothing shows a section of red, demonstrating that he has a passion, for survival. It is an exact color match to the nobleman's clothing, evidencing their similarities, rather than their differences. However, the nobleman ignores this beggar, as he dangles his gold coin counter directly above the beggar's head, but beyond his reach.

The figure on the left appears to have a head injury, depicted by a stained bandage. However, it is curious that his robe is the same color as the coins. Is he really a poor and destitute man? Or is he a fraud? He also looks the nobleman directly in the eyes, which demonstrates an element of pride, unlike that of someone who has spent their life in poverty or disadvantage. A yellow robe may even be a sign of envy or contempt.

Pamela Coleman-Smith demonstrated exceptionality in her ability to express the insincerities and inequalities of life, through deceptively simple illustrations. Was she secretly expressing her own firsthand experiences, as the artist who brought life to the Rider-Waite deck, without credit until more than a century later?

Overall theme

The overall theme of a card is the generalized message that may apply to a single card spread. The overall theme of Six of Pentacles is as follows:

If you are in need, your call for more has been heard by another.

CHAPTER 82

SEVEN OF PENTACLES

Seven of Pentacles relates to matters of discontent. It provides a recognition that life is not always going to be the fairytale we hoped for. There will be times of disappointment, and if we keep our eyes open to the realities of life, and proceed with caution, we are more likely to save something of ourselves to redirect into a more prosperous outcome.

When Seven of Pentacles appears in a tarot card reading, it can be a prompt to do what you can, to avoid disappointment later.

First impression

A man stands, leaning on his hoe, having just finished working on his bounty.

Basic definitions

In the upright position, Seven of Pentacles represents disappointment, missed opportunities, errors in calculation or prioritization, and falling short of expectations.

In the reverse position, Seven of Pentacles represents unemployment, lack of skills, feeling let down, being lazy or tardy.

Interpretation of symbols

In life, even with the best of intentions, sometimes things do not adequately go well. Effort does not always pay off. Seven of Pentacles indicates that in its current manifestation, a situation is unlikely to end in success. This is not to say, however, that success is unachievable, and the presence of the card in a reading may be a prompt to change something, to improve the chance of boosting the outcome. Nonetheless, things do not always go to plan, end fairly, or produce the result that we have worked hard to achieve. In this instance, Seven of Pentacles can be a helpful reminder of what might come, or it may be a proclamation of what has already transpired.

The man is standing but weary, and so he leans against the hoe that has served him as a tool. If there was to be a positive outcome, there would be a representative symbol in the imagery. This is a crucial lesson regarding the illustrative language within the Rider-Waite deck. If it does not appear somewhere in the card, and if there is no hint of it in the card's features, then it does not help to assume its existence. So, let us take a closer look at the signs that a positive outcome is unlikely.

Firstly, the man is weary, rather than physically exhausted. Proof of the alternative may be a smile, elevation to a higher level, or wearing colors that denote happiness and promise of something new. There might be lush green grass at his feet, or blossoming flowers in his harvest. Instead, he is weary in a way that appears almost defeated. His face expresses disappointment, with downturned mouth and a heavy bowed head. He has put his genuine effort into his work, this is clear from the blue aspects of his clothing. But the orange-brown tones of clothing also demonstrate that he is a realist. The pile of pentacles he has prepared sit upon a vine that produces no fruit. Further, this is not a young vine that is soon to blossom. It is old, with withering brown leaves mixed among the faded green of the vine.

The six pentacles in a pile are the efforts he has genuinely made to do well. The genuine effort is depicted in his clothing and the spiritual virtues, heavenly aspirations, honesty, and innocent passion that appear in the pinks, blues and violets of the landscape, and the white collar of his attire. However, the landscape is barren. The only thing left to work with is the final seventh pentacle at the man's feet.

This man knows he has missed opportunities in the past. The work already undertaken made him weary but produced no harvest. The seventh pentacle is the decision he must now make. Invest the last pentacle like the previous six? Cut his losses and move forward onto something new? His opportunities are slim. They are possible but to succeed he must do something differently than before.

In the far left, atop the wilting vine, a small white bird is watching. This symbolizes the broader perspective and patience required to overcome disappointment. We are reminded that growth and success take time. All is not lost, but decision-making can be challenging part of life. It is important to remain hopeful, and to consider more than just the here and now. In the long term, benefits are waiting, even if arduous labor has not yet produced visible results.

When Seven of Pentacles is in reverse, the withering old harvest becomes dominant in the card. It becomes more likely that the man went ahead and invested his seventh pentacles, just like the previous six, and the result has let him down entirely.

Overall theme

The overall theme of a card is the generalized message that may apply to a single card spread. The overall theme of Seven of Pentacles is as follows:

There is always time to turn back. Unless your first step was to jump off a cliff.

CHAPTER 83

EIGHT OF PENTACLES

E ight of Pentacles relates to the potential for growth. It is a reminder that recognizing and utilizing skill, capability, and perseverance helps to achieve a positive or prosperous outcome.

First impression

A young craftsman sits on a bench, carving the pentagram design into each of his coins.

Basic definitions

In the upright position, Eight of Pentacles represents education, change of career, training or skills development, and an increased focus on work-life.

In the reverse position, Eight of Pentacles represents boredom with work or life, feeling undervalued or underappreciated, being stuck in a rut, and having a dead-end job.

Interpretation of symbols

The craftsman in Eight of Pentacles has a youthful appearance. He may be an apprentice, and this would assist in understanding the card, although it is not necessarily the case. The man is simply hard at work, building his pentacles, or carving the pentagram design into each existing pentacle in his possession. Either way, the purpose of his craft is to build from what he already has available to him.

There are clues that the man is taking a sensible and grounded approach to his future. His clothing consists of a blue tunic, denoting truth, and honest hard work. A glimpse of his white belt demonstrates the innocence or virtue with which he approaches his work. He is a simple and honest man who is ready to invest in the benefits of honest hard work to achieve his success. There is no desire to cut corners or cheat his way to the top.

Another aspect of the man's clothing that reinforces the message of the man's diligence is the blackness of his coverall tunic. Black is the color of mystery and unknown outcomes. The man's tights and shoes are shades of red, demonstrating the passion with which he attends to his craft. This is a man who has no idea what his hard work will achieve. But he enjoys and takes pride in his craft and works hard to provide a prosperous future for himself, in an honorable manner.

Most of the man's pentacles appear to be hanging from the trunk of a large tree. This represents the growth of the man's career and prospects for the future. The tree trunk extends far beyond the parameters of the card, which is a sign that anything is possible. Success may be significant, beyond the man's wildest dreams. The opportunities and outcomes are not yet measurable. The distant dwellings range between humble homes and a tall tower. The man is working towards what lies in the distance, and the dwelling that will be his, is determined by the investment he makes in himself.

As with Three of Pentacles, there is a wooden bench appearing in Eight of Pentacles. It represents the temporary nature of the man's early career sacrifices, or his apprenticeship status. The temporary nature of a wooden bench implies that it may be replaced with stone as the man begins to prosper from his hard work. For now, however, it is time for the man to work towards his success, with genuine heartfelt effort, developing skills, and passion for his craft.

Overall theme

The overall theme of a card is the generalized message that may apply to a single card spread. The overall theme of Eight of Pentacles is as follows:

Invest in yourself and the dividends will pay well.

CHAPTER 84

NINE OF PENTACLES

Nine of Pentacles relates to achievement and self-attainment. It acts as a reminder that each of us lives in a world of natural abundance. We can harness the abundance with the power we possess, in such a way as to not only achieve personal prosperity, but also respect the lives of others, our environment, and ourselves. When reversed, Nine of Pentacles relates to the loss of one or more of the attributes that provide us with a sense of self-sufficiency. There may be a loss of freedom, exploitation, or simply a lack of satisfaction.

First impression

A woman stands in a vineyard, gazing at a small bird that has come to rest on her arm. She is surrounded by lush farmland.

Basic definitions

In the upright position, Nine of Pentacles represents independence, sovereignty, self-sufficiency, appreciation, and being happy in one's own company.

In the reverse position, Nine of Pentacles represents lack of satisfaction, freedom, or sovereignty, looking for a way out, and being stuck in a gilded cage.

Interpretation of symbols

Despite the gender differences depicted in the cards, Nine of Pentacles could be considered a step forward into the future of Eight of Pentacles. In Nine of Pentacles, the scene is one of having invested in oneself, worked hard, and then looking back and seeing all that you have achieved because of your dedicated investment.

Each of the Nines in the Minor Arcana Suite relates to the near end of a cycle. The central figure in the Cups, Swords and Wands suites is decidedly male. Nine of Pentacles is illustrated with a female as its central figure. This reminds us of the feminist equality ideal, despite feminism not yet being a recognizable word at the time of the cards' creation. The equality ideal, even if unnamed, was still present in the minds of those who valued it.

Keeping in mind that absolutely nothing that we see in the illustrations of the Rider-Waite deck is by chance, the message is clear. The power of the feminine is present, most obviously represented by the flower motif on the woman's gown, similarly styled to that of the symbol of Venus[xiii]. Although sometimes overlooked by patriarchal societies, feminine power can provide the same outcome as the power of the masculine, when recognized and valued.

Two aspects of Nine of Pentacles tend to stand out. Firstly, the overall scene of the card is one of abundance and success. The central figure wears a gown of flowers, with plenteous fabric that drapes generously about her body, and across the ground. The vineyard is thriving, with bountiful, healthy-looking bunches of grapes scattered throughout the crop. We know it is a crop, rather than a wild vine, due to the wooden structure on the right-hand side of the card, over which vine is looped. The structure symbolizes a human factor in the vine's cultivation. This aspect of the imagery implies that the woman is fully capable of cultivating the land herself. Her dwelling appears far in the distance, but she is not there, tending to the needs of men and children. She is feminine, beautiful, and wealthy, but she is also self-sufficient. She has acted on her own needs, perhaps in addition to the needs of others. Nonetheless, she has never neglected her own. The statement is a powerful one related to gender.

The second standout feature of Nine of Pentacles is the predominance of yellow, red, and green. The red relates to fertility, passion, wealth, and abundance. However, the greens and yellows often blend in the imagery to provide a sense of conscious connection to nature. The message of the colors is a reminder that free will has no limits on what it can achieve, and combining one's will with the offerings of an abundant Earth can bring great prosperity.

The red-brown hills in the distance are topped with a thin line of violet. This indicates that the woman could take her achievements further, as far as the heavens. It is a testament to just how prosperous a life of conscious and deliberate action can be.

The bird which rests on the hand of the woman has its head covered in a red hood. There is also a snail slithering across the ground. Both symbols relate to the need to control one's spirit and mind, to gain the best from one's passion.

The woman has six of her coins piled up beside her, and her hand rests protectively on those coins to demonstrate her sovereignty. These coins belong to her, she owes no one and relied upon no one to achieve her wealth. The remaining three coins sit in a smaller pile, behind her. She seems disinterested in these coins, and they may represent her sense of generosity towards others. She may regard these coins as the necessary wage paid to farmhands and other workers, or they may represent a reinvestment into her vineyard, or her community. The general message is that the woman is not motivated by greed. Her motivation comes from a sense of personal achievement and the freedom to pursue an abundant life.

Finally, many of the messages in Nine of Pentacles are reinforced by the single glove that the woman wears on her left hand. The glove represents practicality, refinement and elegance, wealth, and self-control. The addition of the glove gives us confidence that this woman is to be admired for her temperate management of her own prosperity. There is no need for her to pretend to be a man, or to act like a man. She has sovereignty to harness all that she is, in the manner that works best for her.

Overall theme

The overall theme of a card is the generalized message that may apply to a single card spread. The overall theme of Nine of Pentacles is as follows:

You are everything you need to be, and you have everything you need to have, to follow your path toward attainment of anything you desire.

CHAPTER 85

TEN OF PENTACLES

Ten of Pentacles relaters to the material kingdom. It represents material wealth that has an intergenerational dimension. The completion of pursued wealth by one generation, and the beginning of a new journey of wealth to a future generation.

First impression

A group of people gather at the entrance of a grand dwelling. An old man sits petting his dogs, while a young child peeks out from behind the protection of a woman's gowns. The woman converses with another, younger man.

Basic definitions

In the upright position, Ten of Pentacles represents family structure, wealth, business planning or succession, and intergenerational cooperation.

In the reverse position, Ten of Pentacles represents family quarrels, rejecting group ideals, disputes over inheritance or wealth distribution, and the degeneration of a large, prosperous entity.

Interpretation of symbols

The first thing to note in Ten of Pentacles is the blue sky. Even though it can seem overshadowed by the busy nature of the rest of the imagery, the sky provides us with the context by which everything else appears. Blue relates to clarity and truth. The percentage of sky in the card has been minimized by the walled nature of the setting. This is a closed community, so the truth is only available to those who live within the boundaries set by the walls. Everything else in the card is potentially a construct, for the purposes of servicing the outward-facing reality of the walled community.

In each of the Rider Waite cards, the positioning of the elements is likely to carry significance of some kind. However, the need to understand the position of every wand, cup, sword, or pentacle is not necessarily going to enhance a reader's understanding of the card. Ten of Pentacles is an important exception. The position of each pentacle is crucial to the understanding of the card. The ten pentacles are placed in accordance with the Sefirot[xiv] in the Kabbalistic Tree of Life. The Tree of Life, however, connects each Sefirot to another with the use of twenty-two pathways, which are not necessary to understand in detail, but provide a methodical construct of how the attributes are able to exist.

In Ten of Pentacles, the coins representing the Sefirot have no pathways. This immediately brings up the question of what is real, and what is illusion, further supporting the concept of the walled, private, or mystical, nature of the prosperous entity. It also means that everyone inside the entity must work together unwaveringly to keep the secrets safely out of view, and to maintain the collective wealth. When one person falters, the risk of collapse of the entire entity is possible.

Each of the figures in Ten of Pentacles has a unique part to play in helping to interpret the card's meaning. The old man sits on what may be a throne, his cloak of grapes, like that of King of Pentacles, indicating that he may be the patriarch. He may even be the older version of King of Pentacles, the man who has earned the family fortune in the first instance. He is connected to the child in the picture, by the dogs that

283

come to greet him.

This connection is a subtle reference to the poem by the ancient Greek poet, Homer, entitled, Odyssey. In the poem, Odysseus, King of Ithaca, was left wandering the Earth for 10 years. Upon return to his kingdom, he appeared as though he was a beggar. His dog was the only one who recognized him and came to greet him. The relevance in King of Pentacles is that the young child is born into wealth, without the appreciation of how wealth is achieved. The child may grow to adulthood, without ever having known, and being entirely unprepared for how to survive the unexpected loss of wealth.

The two adults who converse with one another are likely to be mother and father of the child. One of them may also be child of the patriarch. The woman represents the fertility of the entity, as depicted by her red clothing, and acts as a connection between the generations.

The man has his back turned. He is looking towards the dwellings that make up the community. He holds a tall staff, which provides us with a clue as to what the man is likely to be focusing his attention on. We would otherwise be unable to see the truth, perhaps because the man's back is turned, and due to the private inner world of this entity to which we are not entitled. To the left of the staff, a tiny, often missed figure in black is present. This figure represents the family's potentially ominous secrets. The realities that no one must know for the wealth of the entity to prevail. The man has his back to us because he is guarding the family secrets, as he cloaks himself in blue to distract us and make us believe he only sees truth.

The various emblems and symbols that appear on the stone structures that surround the walled community include coats of arms, castle-like imagery, a tower, lines, and waves. These collectively refer to structure, emotions, privilege, and public recognition or esteem. Nonetheless, all these symbols are the outward-facing things that people tend to focus on. Outward appearances may or may not bear a resemblance to the inner truth.

To really understand Ten of Pentacles is to recognize that a large entity of wealth and prosperity requires the cooperation and cohesion of a multigenerational or diverse group of people. For as long as everyone is loyal and dedicated to the central cause (a matter also relevant to the presence of dogs), then the entity is destined to thrive.

Finally, Ten of Pentacles may have complex issues associated with the walled community it represents. However, it is also a card of legacy, ancestry and sharing or contributing with others who are part of the recognized collective. Those who live inside the confines of the stone walls will see things very differently to someone looking in from the outside world. Protecting shared family interest, group loyalty, financial security and enduring success are also aspects of this card.

When Ten of Pentacles appears in reverse, it means that the complex requirements needed to hold everything together, are unravelling. Alternatively, someone inside the walled community is no longer acting on behalf of the collective.

Overall theme

The overall theme of a card is the generalized message that may apply to a single card spread. The overall theme of Ten of Pentacles is as follows:

You are the sum total of every desire, thought, act and outcome of everything and everyone that has come before you.

CHAPTER 86

PAGE OF PENTACLES

Page of Pentacles relates to the prospect of plenty. There are two shared features of all four Page cards in the Rider Waite deck. The imagery of each depicts a young man, and each carries a message.

The message portrayed by Page of Pentacles relates to something new, and which is likely to be tangible or material in nature.

First impression

A young man stands poised to move forward in a grassy field. He holds a gold coin up towards the sky and gazes at it, intently.

Basic definitions

In the upright position, Page of Pentacles represents curiosity, studentship, and learning, focusing on something new, and a message.

In the reverse position, Page of Pentacles represents preoccupation with material possessions, wanting things easy, sense of entitlement, and lack of curiosity.

Interpretation of symbols

The young man in Page of Pentacles, stands in a field of grass and flowers. This represents the newness or freshness of his circumstance. He is also dressed in green, reinforcing the new matter that has his attention. Just like Page of Wands, this young man is fully attentive to what he can see in the coin that he holds up to the sky. Note the man's posture, and how he is holding the coin. There is a precious and valuable message soon to be revealed and the Page does not want to miss a thing.

The coin is a representation of the young man's own prosperity, and the message he is seeking is likely to relate to the way he should invest his skills and abilities, so that he can cultivate a prosperous future. The nearby cultivated crop is a sign of this. However, because the man is young and likely to be immature, Page of Pentacles allows for a selfishness to appear in its definitions when the card appears in reverse. A sense of unearned privilege or entitlement, a self-obsession and material greed, a lack of curiosity about how to better oneself, and preoccupation with material attainment are all features of the card when reversed.

The gentle landscape that appears in the card provides a natural, gradual growth. Starting small, learning along the way, building credibility, skills, and valuable knowledge, and subsequently using those new attributes in ways that provide a practical path towards a prosperous life. The practicality appears in the gentle browns of the young man's clothing. Practicality and a desire to evolve in positive ways is a surefire way to success.

The man wears a simple band or bracelet around his right wrist. The band is not of gold and is consequently not a sign of wealth or materialism. Instead, it is a sign of ambition, and the commitment to achieve an ambitious outcome. This young man is beginning his material venture and has ample motivation. The card is a reminder to approach the pursuit of material things in a practical way, and that dreams can become reality.

Overall theme

The overall theme of a card is the generalized message that may apply to a single card spread. The overall theme of Page of Pentacles is as follows:

You will begin a new venture that includes the prospect of a rewarding future. To ensure success, stay grounded, learn from any mistakes made along the way, and meet challenges head on.

CHAPTER 87

KNIGHT OF PENTACLES

K night of Pentacles relates to loyalty and steadfast commitment. Each of the four Knights in the Rider Waite deck relates to a distinct influence that helps to shape one's personality and manner of response to a variety of situations. Knight of Pentacles is influenced by a methodical and deliberate approach towards manifesting material security or wealth.

First impression
An armored knight on stationary horseback, rests adjacent to a freshly ploughed field.

Basic definitions
In the upright position, Knight of Pentacles represents a diligent worker, loyalty, reliability, and hidden depths.

In the reverse position, Knight of Pentacles represents social ineptitude, obsessive work practices, or being work-shy and lazy.

Interpretation of symbols

Each of the Knights sits atop a different colored horse, and this is relevant to the general theme of the card. The horse in Knight of Pentacles is black, denoting mystery and unknown forces. In this respect, Knight of Pentacles, known for his loyalty and steadfastness, may have his own motives for being so loyal. There is a clue, in that he is gazing into the pentacles that he holds with his right hand. Is he offering the pentacle to his King? Or is he considering his own prosperity and the right course of action to attain his own material wealth?

There is an unknown reason this knight is not moving. The purpose of being a knight is to activate, protect the kingdom, fight for freedom and ideological principles, defend against the enemy, or at the very least, run an errand for the King. This knight does not appear to be in a hurry to go anywhere, do anything. He sits on a resting horse, which is wearing harnesses for both riding and pulling a plough. And when the implications of the horse are fully acknowledged, we begin to understand that the knight is weighing up what the best course of action, if any, might be to ensure his own prosperity.

Loyalty serves a purpose for all parties involved. It provides protection and security for those who possess the loyalty of another. There is also a value associated with those who are loyal. Some people recognize the importance of perception, and so calculate their every move and how it may appear to others. This knight is methodical and calculates every step before he acts. In the upright position, this serves him well. But in reverse, while he is waiting for the perfect calculation, another knight, one with an ideological case to prove like the Knight of Swords, could easily overcome this slow-moving knight. For this reason, a sense of ineptitude or laziness can apply when the card is in reverse.

Both the Knight and his horse have matching green plumes, worn as headdress. This represents growth and manifestation, an investment in the future. The horse's bridle wear is a deep dark red, almost purple in color. The passion to charge ahead is present, but heavily tempered by methodical approach. The ploughed field supports this further.

Overall theme

The overall theme of a card is the generalized message that may apply to a single card spread. The overall theme of Knight of Pentacles is as follows:

There are times when a person should slow down and consider why and how to best approach the next requirement. Now is your time.

CHAPTER 88

QUEEN OF PENTACLES

Queen of Pentacles relates to the effective management of prosperity. Each of the four Queens in the Rider Waite deck is an aspect of The Empress and provides insight into an influence affecting personality. Queen of Pentacles represents the body aspect of the Empress, the connection with Earth and nature, and feminine qualities related to warmth, practicality, and nurturing. The appearance of a Queen in the tarot reading relates to a person in the querant's life, or a person of influence that may not be immediately apparent but is somehow relevant to the circumstances.

Queen of Pentacles relates to a person or influence who values, respects, and effectively deals with material concerns, and who can directly influence outcomes related to wealth, health, and wellbeing.

QUEEN of PENTACLES

First impression

A majestic woman sits atop her throne under an archway of flowering vines. She gazes at a gold coin that she holds in her lap. Around the woman is a lush landscape of flowers, fields, and cultivated crops.

Basic definitions

In the upright position, Queen of Pentacles represents efficiency, practicality, material comforts, and wealth or career management.

In the reverse position, Queen of Pentacles represents hoarding, doubts, mistrust, unrealistic expectations, putting possessions ahead of people, and fixation on luxury goods.

Interpretation of symbols

The Queen sits in a tilted half profile position. This reflects her self-awareness and confidence. She is a level-headed woman who can effectively manage her own affairs. The half-profile posture is a way to demonstrate that the figure need not be unduly alert. She already has command of her environment. The Pentacles Suite relates to the earth element and material comforts, and as such, this is the Queen of material concerns and physicality. She sits in a relaxed pose, gently holding her coin so that it rests on her lap. The nurturing posture of the Queen, particularly towards her coin, demonstrates that she would value the wealth of the coin, but also put it to effective use so that it serves her well in return.

The Queen's throne, made of stone, symbolizes security and stability. Its ornate carvings include images of fruit, in particular pears. Pears are a sign of fertility and longevity. This is a Queen who manages prosperity so that it continues to pay in the long term. The carvings of the throne also include goat images. Goats represent sensuality and excess, but also relate to the card's association with Capricorn, a relevant sign in the zodiac. The winged goat that appears on the Queen's crown provides a link between the practicalities of earthly matters, and spiritual ascendence.

The side of the throne includes a carved image of a nymph. Nymphs represent sensuality, harmony, and transformation. This is likely to be a wood nymph, which helps us to understand that the flowered vines that crown the Queen of Pentacles card are likely to be part of a larger forest environment not visible from our vantage point. Forests are dense with vegetation and provide shelter from harsh climate conditions and are therefore particularly fertile. This, the rabbit, and the body of water in the landscape, are all symbols of fertility. They add weight to the material outcomes made possible by the Queen's transformative powers when it comes to matters of money. It is also a testament to her nurturing or parental qualities.

Nature surrounds the Queen, highlighting her deep connection to an abundant earth. Whilst the landscape is mostly natural, a small, cultivated area is also visible. This is a recognition of the Queen's ability to nurture and cultivate wealth and wellbeing and manage it in ways that will allow it to grow and further prosper.

Queen of Pentacles represents the feminine element of nurturing and practicality. The card relates to a person who may naturally gravitate towards healthy eating, cleanliness, nurturing, caretaking, or monetary management and independence. There is also an inner strength and endurance to this Queen, which is symbolized by the deep blue mountains that appear in the scene.

Overall theme

The overall theme of a card is the generalized message that may apply to a single card spread. The overall theme of Queen of Pentacles is as follows:

To derive success from your surroundings, recognize the value in everything and everyone you have in your life, and consider the long term as you manage the present.

CHAPTER 89

KING OF PENTACLES

King of Pentacles relates to the mastering of Acquisition. Each of the four Kings in the Rider Waite deck is an aspect of The Emperor and provides insight into an influence affecting

personality. King of Pentacles relates to the body aspect of The Emperor, his practicality, power, and business acumen. The appearance of a King in the tarot reading relates to a person in the querant's life, or a person of influence that may not be immediately apparent but is somehow relevant to the circumstances.

King of Pentacles relates to a person or influence that represents power, grounded stability and safety, and protectiveness. When in reverse, this King may relate to an exploitative nature.

First impression

A regal man sits on a throne adorned with bullheads, surrounded by a garden of flowers, grapes, and vines.

Basic definitions

In the upright position, King of Pentacles represents wealth by honorable means, pride, nobility, and a prosperous businessperson who is self-educated, or self-made.

In the reverse position, King of Pentacles represents exploitation, self-gratification, corruption, abusive behavior, and an unloved character.

Interpretation of symbols

The fact that King of Pentacles has his eyes closed, seems like a minor aspect of the card's imagery. However, this is yet another testament to the subtle brilliance of Pamela Coleman Smith's artistry. The act of closing the figure's eyes provides a complex understanding of the King's unique qualities. His steady confidence and inner focus, plus the confidence he has in himself, allows him to feel perfectly comfortable without sight. He also has a complete sense of trust or confidence in the physical realm, and a deep connection to Earth, money, and possessions. This King does not need the approval of those around him. Instead, he looks within for guidance. He appears in what may be a meditative state, with the safety and security of his wealth of acquisition all around him.

In the first instance, it may seem that the King's crown and his throne are one in the same. This is a deliberate reference to the importance of possession and wealth. The King is his fortune, and the two are indivisible. He is also adorned from head to toe with grapes and vines denoting wealth and abundance. In his right hand, the King holds a scepter, which relates to his power. In his left hand, the coin he balances on his knee relates to his material wealth and influence. The coin implies that this King is generous towards others. All in his kingdom will prosper with him on the throne.

Four bull carvings adorn the King's throne. The bulls associate the King with Taurus, which is the zodiac sign related to the card. The bulls also represent power, and were used to pull ploughs, which connect the carvings to the bountiful grapevines that adorn the King and his surroundings.

The King's right foot appears in armor. He rests it on the head of a boar. This signifies the King's mastery over his own base instincts, and the battles he has endured to achieve his great wealth and material success. Further, the sight of the King's castle in the background highlights his achievements and is a symbol of everything he has built with determination and physical effort.

King of Pentacles represents a man who has conquered his environment. He has mastered business matters, is self-disciplined, grounded to the earth, and highly prosperous. There is a practicality, and leadership acumen, associated with the card, and it is implied that the King has earned his wealth and success, rather than inherited it. Everything this King touches transforms into a form of abundance.

The King's throne is not much taller than his head, and plenty of sky appears above the throne. When the card appears in reverse, there is a clear disconnect between the King's craving for wealth, and any concept of spiritual enlightenment. The throne acts as a barrier that prevents the King from accessing a higher perspective. He only thinks about what he wants, and what will enrich him further.

Overall theme

The overall theme of a card is the generalized message that may apply to a single card spread. The overall theme of King of Pentacles is as follows:

You could turn your vision into a tangible, achievable reality.

CHAPTER 90

WELCOME TO GRADUATION!

At the earliest point in my journey of learning to read tarot, I practiced at home alone. I found value in this method, but only to a point. I was self-conscious and did not trust my interpretations, so I was reluctant to attempt a reading for someone else.

During the time when I sat alone and began reading for myself, I often drew a single card for the day. Shuffling the cards, I would try to focus on the question, what should I know about today? At some point I would feel a subtle urge to stop shuffling, and so I did. Sometimes the urge to stop might come quickly, after just a few shuffles. At other times, it felt as though I should shuffle longer. I simply trusted the urge.

Laying the cards, face down, onto a table, I would spread them out so that the back of each card was visible, perhaps not entirely, but enough for me to see it was there. Then, I would glance over the entire sweep of cards, until one card called to me. That would be my card of the day.

As I went about my day, I would allow myself to think about my card of the day. Keeping an eye out for signs that were relevant to the card's definitions.

Learning to recognize signs

The following is a true account of an experience I had in my early days of learning tarot, and one card in particular – The Chariot.

I was still quite new to the world of tarot in late 1986. I worked in the city, about an hour commute from home. I was in learning mode and had drawn a single card for myself for the day as I was having breakfast. The card was The Chariot, representing negotiation, tolerance of others, and overcoming differences to reach a win-win solution.

It was summertime, and a beautiful, sunny day. With the card's definitions in my mind, I went to work as I always had. I walked from my apartment in the Southeastern suburb of Melbourne, to the nearby train station and took a train to the city, and then transferred to a connecting train which circled the city area, until I had reached the closest stop to my job. It was just a short walk of two or three blocks to the office. I had done this commute a hundred times before, and on this morning, it was a predictable door-to-door commute of one hour.

As the day progressed, the weather began to change. It started raining at some point, which was not unusual for the time of the year. What was unusual, however, was that the weather continued to get worse and worse. Until the entire city and surrounding areas were engulfed in an unanticipated angry storm.

At around 5:30pm, the shops and offices all began closing, and workers from the concentrated business and retail centers began piling into the street. On a normal afternoon, the trains, trams, and buses would start filling up with people, standing room only, and within an hour or so, the streets of the city would depopulate. In those days, Melbourne was not a city with a lot of nightlife. The restaurants and bars were mostly outside of the business district, and by 7:00pm, the city streets would be empty and quiet, until the new day of commuters began to arrive.

This day, however, was different. Most city workers had spent the day unaware of how severe a storm was building throughout the day. As I joined my hundreds of thousands of fellow shop and office workers on the streets of Melbourne, we were all about to discover that battling our way through gale force winds and blinding rain, to get to our usual transport terminal, was a wasted effort. Every train, bus, and tram out of the city, cancelled. And those of us who turned back to return to our workplaces, mostly discovered that the building was empty and locked. Senior staff and business owners were the small percentage of commuters with cars parked in the city. They had locked up and left for the day and were now stuck in traffic as they too tried to flee the city storm.

Weather updates began to spread throughout the crowds of stranded commuters. Mobile phones were rare at the time and were the size and weight of a small suitcase, filled with bricks. People who had managed to call friends and family had used the city's payphones.

They were told that an even worse, freakish weather front was coming our way and expected to last the night. By this point, the rain was already so heavy that I could not see more than six feet ahead, and walking or cycling, or even motorbiking, was completely out of the question. There was no internet, no Uber service to call upon. Demand for taxis was so high that drivers had begun giving preference to passengers who looked as though they could afford a taxi. I looked like the young, broke, dripping wet junior office worker that I was, so no taxi stopped for me. The taxicabs that picked up passengers, travelled out of the city once, and did not return for another fare.

As I stood in line for a public phone the rain began turning to hail. After trying a variety of friend and family phone numbers, I finally got through to a relative who explained that the weather was too bad to pick me up. They suggested I stay in a hotel overnight. I said, "okay, thanks," and hung up. I did not have money for a hotel. I dialed more phone numbers. Each attempt rang through to an answering machine.

I stood under the eaves of a shopfront, watching the hailstones fall at my feet. They were growing, from half-carat diamonds, to glistening golf balls. I had a typical twenty-year-old's bank balance of near-zero, no credit card, and typically around twenty dollars in my purse. It may have been sufficient for a taxi at that time, but the taxis were not stopping. And it certainly was not enough for a hotel.

Just as I was about to embark on a trek to the basement McDonalds a few blocks away, to see if it was open late, and might have room for one more person, a big black SUV-like vehicle pulled up, its headlights beaming, and wipers running at full speed. A man with brown hair and a thick beard, rolled down the passenger window and yelled out to anyone and no one in the small group of people around me, 'Does anyone know how to get to St Kilda from here?'

For a moment I was tempted to let someone else respond to the man's question, and as I looked around, it was as though no one else had even heard him. They may not have heard him, because the rain was loudly pounding all around us. I had heard him, and in that instance, I remembered The Chariot card I had drawn the morning. Negotiation, win-wins, and tolerance of others.

I shouted through the rain, 'I live near St Kilda. I can show you if you agree to drive me home!'

'No worries!' replied the man, with a smile. He pushed open the passenger door and I got in, soaked to the core. His car looked expensive and had an immaculate interior. This was the kind of car that parked underground somewhere in the city during the day. I decided straight away that this guy was wealthy, or he had a very prestigious job, somewhere like the Stock Exchange.

I felt guilty because I knew I was dripping all over his pristine prized possession.

'I'm really sorry about all the water,' I said sheepishly.

'Don't even worry about it, mate,' the man replied. It is only water and water will be wet.' He laughed, which made me laugh, and although it took over three hours to get home, he did as he promised and dropped me directly at the front door of my apartment building. I had, in turn, provided illustrated directions on how to continue to his destination, on a piece of paper he had handed me out of his suitcase. The paper was a sheet of printed letterhead, with something typed at the front. I wrote on the back, but the name on the letterhead did not escape my notice. It said, Australian Equal Opportunity Commission (AEOC). In the 1980s, the AEOC was the national governmental policy group for equal opportunity, tolerance, and inclusivity of minority residents of Australia. I never did find out who the man was. But, for obvious reasons, I certainly remember the story. And it was the perfect way to learn about The Chariot card, and the unexpected ways that tarot messages may coincide with any given day.

There have been countless examples of how a single card of the day helped me to understand how to navigate my day. But this day was an example to share that I hope will help you to see how subtle, yet meaningful, the cards can be.

How to begin learning.

Think about how the Rider Waite tarot deck has been developed, combining imagery, elements, colors, numbers and positioning to speak a language. Breaking each of these components into single focus tools can help a new reader begin to automatically recall the significance of a card, without having to memorize everything.

If you are a person who identifies with numbers, then begin with numbers. Each of the numbered cards aligns to a numerological description. This will tell you an aspect of what the card is communicating. Ones are new beginnings. Twos are partnerships. Fours relate to structure. Tens are completions.

If you are a person drawn to colors, then begin with colors. If a certain color, or color mood, dominates the card's imagery, this imparts an aspect of the card's message. Cards filled with reds and oranges speak of energy and passion. Greyish cards relate to lack of judgement or indifference. A card filled with black or darkened features are likely to include a warning or mystery.

Travel with The Fool and familiarize yourself with his journey. Stories are far easier to remember than bullet points. The Fool's journey takes him through a natural and logical path of spiritual growth and maturity. Yes, The Magician is powerful, but lives in the world all alone. It is not until he meets The High Priestess that he begins to consider the possibility of more than just himself. The Emperor is powerful, more powerful than any other. But only as far as the material world exists. He has no power beyond that which is earth-bound. The World is the final card in the Major Arcana Suite, and so it is the end, but also the moment immediately preceding the beginning.

If you want to keep it as simple as possible in the beginning, you can also reduce your learning to four different elemental rules. Pentacles relate to earth, which is tangible and provides material security. Cups relate to water, which speaks of emotions, relationships, and sense of identity. Wands relate to fire, in which inspired actions lead to creativity. Swords relate to air, which provides the breathing space for mental clarity, and communication.

Regardless of how you choose to springboard your learning, the language of tarot will develop and grow. The key is to persevere, and to trust that the language is there.

Choosing the right spread for a reading

Something I have always found peculiar is that most tarot card readers stick to the well-known traditional spreads. I have even received criticism over the years by people proclaiming that I am *doing it wrong!*

There is no right and there is no wrong. There is the language expressed between two entities, which relies on consistency to develop a conversive relationship.

For example, one of the most used layouts for tarot is the Three Card Spread representing past, present and future. In this instance, an optional Signifier card is placed at the top of the reading, with three additional cards placed below.

From left to right, the bottom cards read as past influence, present situation, and future outcome. Indeed, if you are comfortable reading a three-card spread in this manner, then it is a perfect and simple method of tarot. However, it is not the only way in which to read three cards, and if you stick to only one way of reading three cards in a row, then you may miss other interpretations.

Tarot is a language between the tarot card reader and the spiritual force that the reader is communicating with. It is therefore reasonable to expect that if a person is communicating with a spiritual force of supernatural origin, that force will have observed the reader's language of communication, be of intelligence advanced enough to adopt the language, and will reciprocate the communication appropriately.

If this is not happening, then the tarot card reading is not likely to be the result of a spiritual connection, regardless of the spread.

And so, in short, there is no wrong way to read tarot cards. However, to read the cards the way that I read the cards, it is crucial to commit to a language that serves its purpose. This book is an offering of the language that I use to communicate messages consistently, with the spiritual force that I have relied upon for decades. I have been playfully teased, sometimes reprimanded, but never failed by this method.

The following are example tarot card spreads that I have favored over the years.

Single Card for the Day

Reading with a single card for the day is a wonderful way for a beginner to become acquainted with the relevance, definitions, and symbolism of each card in the Rider Waite deck. Shuffle the cards whilst asking a question, such as, what should I know about today? Then, either cut the deck in half, as it feels appropriate, or alternatively, fan the cards facing down across the table. Choose the card that you are drawn to and place it face up so that you can examine its features. The card may appear upright or in reverse, depending on how you have shuffled. Either way, there will be positive, negative, and neutral relevance, and depending on the circumstances, there may be cautionary considerations. Take the entire card into account and consider its meaning throughout your day. A single card spread may also inform you of your week, your month, or even a significant event (e.g., job interview, wedding).

Three Key Aspects of Life

This is a common three-card spread that may include an additional Signifier card. The three aspects may comprise of:
- past, present, and future;
- home, relationships, and career;
- health, prosperity, and love;
- influences, identity, and considerations moving forward;
- mother, father, and siblings;
- anchored theme, flanked by competing forces; or
- three life aspects of your choosing.

Shuffle while asking for life guidance. Decide whether you will include a Signifier card before you finish shuffling. Choose your cards and lay them into a face up row of three, plus the optional Signifier card placed above the row. Cards can read from left to right, right to left, or with the central card acting as the foundation or anchor for the other two cards.

Full spread

Over the years I have developed what I consider to be the most effective tarot card spread, for clarity and accurate outcomes. Those who have seen me read tarot cards will recognize this spread as the one I use in every circumstance in which I want to achieve a clear and concise, and complex answer to what may be a complex question.

My full spread is an adaptation of the traditional Celtic Cross. However, it does differ in ways that I feel make it easier to learn, and easier to interpret.

Shuffle the cards as you normally would. You may feel you also want to cut the cards. You will be building two rows of five cards each, facing upward[xv], as below.

Top line (*left to right*): Signifier, conscious thoughts, subconscious thoughts, the past, the short-term future.

Bottom line (*left to right*): Challenge card, self-perception, external factors, hopes and fears, the final outcome.

Signifier

The Signifier provides an anchor for the tarot card reading. It may represent the Querent, a person central to the reading, or the subject of the reading. The purpose of the Signifier is to provide focus, and a layer of personal connection.

The Signifier also acts as a starting point for the reading and will influence how other cards in the reading are interpreted. When two or more competing factors are present in a reading, the Signifier may represent the higher principle. If this is the case, other cards in the reading may be split between one or all of the competing factors.

Challenge card

The Challenge card indicates relevant obstacles or difficulties that surround the Signifier. It may relate to matters that require extra attention, or which need to be overcome.

Challenges in a tarot card reading may link directly to matters from the past, a person's self-identification, their hopes and fears, or something that is about to become relevant in the short term.

Whether it appears upright or in reverse, the full range of definitions of a challenge card may be equally relevant to the reading.

Conscious thoughts

The Conscious Thoughts card relates to the matters that the signifier is actively thinking about, or is consciously aware of, related to the circumstances. It may relate to ongoing considerations, motivations, daily activities, routine responses, or externalized desires. Conscious thoughts tend to be the product of past experiences, self-perceptions, environmental factors, or anxieties.

Subconscious thoughts

The Subconscious Thoughts card relates to the deeper, often hidden aspect of the Signifier. This may include underlying feelings, beliefs, and motivations, including secret desires, strategic intentions, and even unexplored patterns of behavior. In circumstances where two or more competing factors are present in a reading, the Subconscious Thoughts card may compete against the Conscious Thoughts card.

The past

The Past card represents events, experiences, or influences from the Signifier's past that have shaped the current situation. It provides context and background, and links past actions, decisions, and circumstances to the present moment.

The past may include repeated patterns of behavior, lessons, or unresolved issues that are continuing to impact the present time and may provide a clue on how to move forward with greater awareness.

The past can relate to a long time ago, recently, or even the immediate passing moments.

Short term future

The Short-Term Future card provides a glimpse ahead. Generally, the timescale will be days, weeks, or just a few months. The purpose of the glimpse forward is to identify trajectories, and opportunities to navigate, avoid, or intercept. As energy is always in motion, the short-term aspects of a reading can change quickly, having a knock-on effect on the rest of the reading.

Self-perception card

This card reflects the perception of a single factor of the tarot card reading. It is often the way the Signifier sees themself, however, when competing factors are present, other cards in the reading will provide clues as to which factor is reflected in this card. There is a strong connection between the Conscious Thoughts and Self-Perception cards.

External factors card

This card relates to how others perceive the Signifier, and the related circumstances. This may be a direct perception of a key person, or the subject in general. Alternatively, this card may reflect the wider environment in which the circumstances are taking place. For example, societal, cultural, economic, or other environmental influences may be relevant. It is important to remember that perceptions can also be influenced by environmental factors.

There is a strong connection between the Subconscious Thoughts and External Factors cards.

Hopes and fears

The Hopes and Fears card relates to any conflicts relevant to the reading. This may include conflicting interests, inner conflicts, or a personal dilemma. The hopes of one person relevant to the reading may appear as a fear for another. There is a strong connection between The Past and Hopes and Fears cards. Hopes and fears can also be closely linked to self-perception, and the perception of others.

Final outcome

The Final Outcome card reflects the likely result if the current trajectory continues uninterrupted. The purpose of this card is to help the Querent to see how the situation will evolve, based on the energies and influences that are currently at play. It provides an opportunity to make changes where there is a power to do so.

My full tarot card spread incorporates complex relationships between each card, for consideration alongside apparent color moods, numbers, symbols, and other card representations. It may take repeated effort and consistent practice to proficiently learn to read my full spread. However, it is my favorite because it has proven to be remarkably accurate over the years. Once mastered, it is a tarot spread that, I believe, demonstrates the real possibility of communicating beyond the parameters of the material world, without having to be a "psychic."

Taking it to the streets

As much as I enthusiastically studied the cards, it was only when I began to attempt to read for other people that my skill dramatically improved. I was still too self-conscious to tell anyone that I was learning to read tarot cards, and I never wanted to try to explain whether I was psychic, and I felt that describing myself as someone who had a supernatural ability was a self-aggrandizement, setting me up for failure, or at the very least arrogant.

Instead, I spent time in coffee shops, or quiet bars, sitting with a cappuccino or a glass of wine, and studying the cards. Every time I did, without fail, someone would approach me and ask if I was a tarot card reader. My response was always the same, I am learning, would you like me to see if I can read your cards? Invariably, the person was thrilled to get a free tarot reading, and so I would invite them to sit with me, and I would do my best.

Because I had immediately described myself as being a learner of tarot, rather than an experienced reader or psychic, there was no real pressure for me to find exactly the right answers. The other person was having fun just sitting alongside me, looking to see what the messages may be, and trying to link those messages to their life. I admit, it was helpful to have the wine at hand. A little liquid courage for the inexperienced tarot card reader.

The more I offered myself as a student who wanted to learn, the easier it became to recognize where I was going wrong, what I was doing right, and my proficiency grew surprisingly quickly. My self-confidence as a reader also strengthened, which meant that less and less did I doubt what I was seeing in the cards. It was not my imagination, nor wishful thinking, nor ego. If I kept to the range of definitions and symbolism I was coming to know, and examined the cards individually, in groups, and as an entire reading, the messages were always there.

If, on occasion, I was unable to decipher a message from the spread, I would simply put the cards away and try again later. It was always most helpful if I did not put too much pressure on myself to know everything, all at once.

In the early days, I used a single card of the day for myself, and sometimes for others. I also learned the traditional Celtic Cross and three-card spreads. I later developed my own spreads, based on how I read the language of tarot and what I felt aided my overall interpretation of the cards.

I no longer read tarot for myself. I only read for others, and I never charge for readings. In fact, I have never charged anyone for a tarot card reading, and I doubt that I ever will. It just feels right for me to practice tarot the way that I do. My method of tarot card reading only fails if I allow ego, materialism, or wishful thinking to get mixed into my interpretations. And so, I do what I can to avoid that happening.

The responsible tarot card reader

Tarot card readers, psychics, mediums, and all other types of spiritualists get badgered with the label of con artist or other similarly unflattering marker at some point in their life. There is good reason for this. Some who purport to communicate with the spirit world are disingenuous. Not all, of course. However, the history of spiritualism dates to a time when women were excluded from fully participating in a patriarchal structure of authority. To compensate, some of these women proclaimed to have the gift as a means of elevating their status in a world ruled by men. Some of these women were genuinely gifted, but for others it was an act of survival. It worked, and for some it continues to work today.

It is far too easy to claim to receive messages, and spirits are conveniently invisible and unprovable. So, whilst I will not linger in this section of the book for long, my hopes are that anyone who benefits from this book will do so with honest intention, and ethical behavior moving forward. The most powerful person in someone's life is the person from whom they seek counsel. That person has the power to uplift and heal. They are bestowed with this power, because that is their purpose.

Just as there are doctors, lawyers, politicians and performers, who become prone to arrogance and an inflated sense of their own importance, so is the risk for spiritualists. It can be quite a challenge to refrain from claiming that you are more than you are. Particularly when people come to you in search of crucial answers in their life. To the spiritualist it may seem harmless. But if that is the case, then the spiritualist has forgotten the fundamental concept of connecting to spirit is to acknowledge the interdependence between all that exists.

A woman once emailed me to say that a well-known psychic had vaguely stated in a public address, that a cure for her malignant cancer was coming soon. She wanted me to double-check the psychic's information, to see if it was accurate. She wanted to avoid chemotherapy and the discomfort this and other invasive treatments would inevitably bring to her life. She could not afford to contact the psychic for a private reading. It may also be true that a part of her was doubtful about what the psychic had said.

I wasn't sure how to reply at first, so I looked up the psychic she referred to by name and discovered that they charged $500 an hour for a reading, refused to accept direct correspondence without prior payment, had a lengthy *Terms and Conditions* statement on their website, and forbade customers from tape recording sessions, or bringing a potential witness with them into a reading. Unless, of course, they paid double.

To me, this psychic looked like a scammer. To the woman who needed hope, they looked like hope.

I replied to the woman's email. I wrote a heartbreaking explanation of why I would not, and could not, help her. And I suggested, with sadness that consumed me for days thereafter, that she compares the advice of a variety of medical professionals.

It has been years, but I still get angry when I think about this story, and others like it.

Spirituality is entwined with the concepts of human ascension and enlightenment. The number one rule is to recognize we each are connected, blended, and interdependent. A good spiritualist experiences a continuously expanded awareness of their impact on others. A bad spiritualist, simply put, is a materialist, pretending to be a spiritualist.

If you are still not sure how to proceed ethically and morally as a tarot card reader, revisit the Fool's Journey, paying close attention to the four essential virtues.

Not quite the final word

I am confident that by the time you have reached this chapter, the mysterious world of tarot cards will have become less of a mystery.

Of course, there are readers who will skip to this chapter, to see how it ends. There will be other readers who dip into the book for the various nuggets of information they feel they need as refresher. The wonderful thing about having a clear and concise instruction on how to do anything is that it does not require cover to cover reading to gain a degree of learning. However, it is wise to remember that everything about the Rider Waite tarot deck starts with a basic understanding of certain principles:

Gaining a clear understanding of the Fool's Journey will provide a tarot reader with invaluable sense of how the language of tarot links to the human experience.

Recognizing that learning to read tarot proficiently is like learning to speak any other language. A basic understanding of the syntax will provide a solid root system from which practice and improvement can grow and flourish.

Nothing that you see in the Rider Waite tarot deck is by chance. Every color, every symbol, every aspect of the landscape, the directional pose of a character, the number or lack of human characters, size, proportions, and numbers. Each serves a purpose.

The better a tarot card reader learns to read the language of tarot, the less they will need to rely on psychic ability. Without the pressure of trying to distinguish between ego, imagination, wishful thinking, eagerness to please, and genuine intuition, it immediately becomes easier to just read the messages, as though you are reading a book.

Tarot is not a science. It is not empirical. If you get things wrong, just remember that being human means not being perfect. Next time is another opportunity.

How to know when you are connecting

My response to the question of when you will know that you are conversing with the cards is to ask that you recall when you realized you were connecting with other aspects of learning.

When did you finally figure out algebra at school? When did you first realize you were floating in the water? Or balancing on a two-wheeled bicycle? Or that you had finally baked a lasagna as delicious as your mother's?

It is with tarot as it has been with every other new skill you have learned. When you begin to connect with the cards, you will know.

ABOUT THE AUTHOR

Elena Olympia Collins has dedicated nearly four decades to studying tarot and its intricate connections. Passionately committed to her life's purpose, she shares her extensive knowledge with the world. Residing in the picturesque Mornington Peninsula of Australia, Elena is proud to present her debut book, with her second one already in the works.

Endnotes:

ⁱ Defined in Greek to mean 'herald's wand'.

ⁱⁱ A form of disinformation designed to manipulate opinion and shape perception.

ⁱⁱⁱ In Greek mythology Hermes was a messenger, able to fly between the world of mortals, the underworld, and the spiritual world of the divine.

ⁱᵛ A symbol of fertility and creation.

ᵛ The most sacred religious relic of the Israelites; a wooden box, covered in gold, which housed the Tablets of the Law, onto which God delivered the Ten Commandments to Moses.

ᵛⁱ Located at the base of the spine, near the perineum.

ᵛⁱⁱ Aligning with yin and yang, rather than any predetermination of what is appropriate for gender; balance and harmony between opposing elements.

ᵛⁱⁱⁱ A shorthanded farming tool with a semicircular blade, used for cutting corn and other tall crops.

ⁱˣ The Empress, The Hierophant and Justice.

ˣ In a materialistic society inherited wealth is a sign of superiority.

ˣⁱ A fundamental mystical symbol of Kabbalah, which signifies the sequence of creation, the flow of divine energy and the interconnectedness of everything in existence.

ˣⁱⁱ James 2, 14-17.

ˣⁱⁱⁱ As found in The Empress card.

ˣⁱᵛ Emanations, relating to the attributes of the physical and metaphysical realms.

ˣᵛ Face down image is for illustrative purposes only.

Made in United States
Troutdale, OR
12/15/2024

26293348R00182